Men of
GOD,
Men of
WAR

Men of GOD, Men of WAR

*Military Chaplains as
Ministers, Warriors, and Prisoners*

ROBERT C. DOYLE

Naval Institute Press
Annapolis, Maryland

Naval Institute Press
291 Wood Road
Annapolis, MD 21402

Library of Congress Cataloging-in-Publication Data

Names: Doyle, Robert C., author.
Title: Men of God, men of war : military chaplains as ministers, warriors, and prisoners / Robert C. Doyle.
Other titles: Military chaplains as ministers, warriors, and prisoners
Description: Annapolis, Maryland : Naval Institute Press, [2024] | Includes bibliographical references and index.
Identifiers: LCCN 2023046746 (print) | LCCN 2023046747 (ebook) | ISBN 9781682474181 (hardback) | ISBN 9781682479292 (ebook)
Subjects: LCSH: Military chaplains—United States—History. | Church work with prisoners of war—United States—History. | Prisoners of war—United States—History.
Classification: LCC UH23 .D68 2024 (print) | LCC UH23 (ebook) | DDC 355.3/470973—dc23/ eng/20231107
LC record available at https://lccn.loc.gov/2023046746
LC ebook record available at https://lccn.loc.gov/2023046747

♾ Print editions meet the requirements of ANSI/NISO z39.48–1992 (Permanence of Paper).

Printed in the United States of America.
32 31 30 29 28 27 26 25 24   9 8 7 6 5 4 3 2 1

First printing

To my loving wife, Beate Engel-Doyle,
who passed away on October 19, 2021,
whose love and devotion
for thirty-five years
cannot be duplicated.

Her faith in God
and faithfulness to his will
caught fire and brought me back
to a faith I nearly abandoned.

I dedicate this work to her memory.

❧ CONTENTS ❧

❧ PREFACE ❧

AMERICAN SOLDIERS, sailors, airmen, and Marines love their chaplains. Sometimes they serve as vital links to home, family, and faith; other times, the chaplain buries them after death in battle, at sea, or in a prison camp. Chaplains serve as sounding boards when life goes sour and join celebrations when life goes well. In short, the chaplain, or padre (father), is present for them at all times, in all places, in all circumstances. This is the chaplain's mission and the tradition in the American armed services, at least in principle.

I was raised a Roman Catholic in southwest Philadelphia, complete with Catholic grade and high schools, and as a young Boy Scout, my father took me to a communion breakfast sponsored by our Troop and the parish Holy Name Society. One Sunday morning, a very tall Jesuit priest spoke to us, including our fathers who were World War II veterans, about his experience in Nagasaki during the dropping of the atomic bomb in August 1945. He was a German Jesuit and noted that the Japanese permitted German Jesuits to practice and administer the Catholic faith in Japan during World War II. As far as the Japanese were concerned, the German Jesuits in Nagasaki were allies, not enemies. He said he was saying morning Mass when the atomic blast blew out the windows of the Catholic cathedral, and he showed us the scars on his neck from the glass. My father winced. Years later, I found an American chaplain's reminiscence of Nagasaki after the bomb attack: "In the heart of atomic bombed Nagasaki we saw a beautiful Christian Church located in central Nagasaki. In the midst of devastation, the frame of this church was still standing. The tower stood erect, carrying on its peak a cross, the church tower and cross dominated the mass of ruins and stood as a silent but unfailing testimony to a way of life where love and brotherhood rule supreme instead of hate and destruction."[1] As children of the early Cold War, we confronted the myth of survival of atomic bombs daily, but when we heard what that Jesuit priest experienced, not a word was said by anyone, although some of the fathers commented that the atomic bomb had saved them. At that young age, few of us really understood what these men were talking about. That came later.

After four years at Penn State University in its Naval Reserve Officers Training Corps, between 1963 and 1967, I served nearly five years on active duty in the U.S. Navy. During that time, I encountered and required the service of a Navy chaplain only once, on board the USS *Steinaker* (DD 863), on one fateful weekend in 1969. This experience ultimately generated the desire to tell the story of chaplains from all of America's wars.

In 1969 the USS *Steinaker* was in the Norfolk Naval Shipyard at Portsmouth, Virginia, for a year's overhaul. The captain, Cdr. Harold Sacks, USN, appointed me command duty officer (CDO), and I was in charge of the ship for my first weekend's duty. For me, it was stunning. On a Saturday, my first day as CDO, one of our young new sailors screamed out loud, "I can't take this shit anymore!" Then he attempted to jump over the side. Trouble was, we were in dry dock, and his intention was suicide. In a flash of fury and resentment, I thought, "How dare you kill yourself on *my* watch?" So, in a millisecond, I tackled him as hard as I could, knocked him down, and ordered the ship's master at arms to "take this man below and wrap him around a stanchion." What to do now? Knowing that this sailor was a Catholic, I called the quarterdeck of the USS *America*, a huge aircraft carrier also in the Portsmouth Naval Shipyard for repairs, and asked for Chaplain Patrick A. Dowd, USN. I briefly told him what had happened and asked him to come to the ship. He was there very quickly, and along with the Shore Patrol (Navy Military Police), they took the young, very confused, and angry sailor off the ship. I then called the captain at home and told him what had happened. In my mind I thought I might be charged and possibly receive a court-martial for attacking an enlisted man. The captain calmed me down. Everyone, including the captain, the chaplain, and the Shore Patrol, realized that I had saved this young man's life. The young sailor, part of Project 100,000, initiated by Secretary of Defense Robert McNamara, allowed nonqualified men into the military services during the Vietnam War years.

My young sailor was fortunate: he lived, and I hope he has had a long, happy, and fruitful life.

I met Chaplain Patrick A. Dowd, USN, at the base officers' bar on many Fridays in 1969, and we became friends. In his raspy yet beautiful voice, he always called me "Bobby," and although I found it not a little embarrassing, I liked it. Unknown to me at the time, Father Dowd had served as a chaplain in 1968 with the Marines in Vietnam and had seen far more combat than I would ever see. Chaplain Herbert L. Bergsma, USN, recorded a letter that Chaplain Dowd had written about his Marines in Vietnam:

> Upon reporting to the 2d Battalion, 9th Marines, I was in for a new experience! I had a pretty good idea what to expect in a line unit, but within the first two weeks I was out on Operation Double Eagle. I learned first how to pack a pack and carry one. It was at this time that I really got a good look at the life of the "grunt." I had always had great respect for these men, but this put all the finishing touches on it. The greatest and bravest men I know are the men in the line companies. They don't live; they exist. All they want is for someone to at least recognize the fact that they exist, asking for little more. Every day they wake from too little sleep, faced with another day which might just be their last. They eat C-rations three times a day; body odor doesn't bother them any longer. There are only two luxuries that interest them, mail and warm beer. I marvel at these men. I wish there was a special medal just for them. These are the MEN.[2]

After the encounter with the distressed sailor, I never saw Father Dowd again, sad to say, but I never forgot him or the service he rendered to the Marines in Vietnam, to that unfortunate seaman on board the *Steinaker*, and to me. Thank you, Father Dowd.

In December 1969, I received orders for a tour in Vietnam. While there I never saw a Catholic chaplain in the field. Our Advisory Team 88 hosted a visit by a Protestant chaplain once. He was very cordial and wanted to know if the Catholic men were okay. Well, we were not okay, so a small group of us decided to attend Mass from time to time at the local Vietnamese church. My first visit became a cultural catastrophe. I entered the church alone, not wanting anyone to take notice of me, and then I slid into the first available pew. Trouble was that it was on the left side of the church. In my haste, I never noticed that only women and children sat there. A cultural faux pas of major proportion, I thought at that time. Moments later, a very old man came over to me, gently took me by the arm, and led me to a seat next to him. I saw that he was one of the elders of the congregation; he saw that I was embarrassed. He honored me by seating me next to him. I believe that Father Dowd's spirit introduced itself again, this time in 1970 as an elder in a Vietnamese Catholic church in Ben Tre City, Kien Hoa Province, Republic of Vietnam. His kindness was extreme; I will never forget that moment or him. Thank you, sir.

This brings me to explain what this book is all about: from the Revolution to the Vietnam War, American chaplains of all denominations came into harm's way for the most part unarmed, except for Bibles, hymnals, rosaries, and Mass Kits. They kept their faith in God, their men, and their respective churches while serving their soldiers and sailors, always as volunteers, and, as a result, they were killed in action, wounded in action, and taken prisoner. This work attempts to tell the story about those chaplains who served the United States with honor in wartime, especially those who were taken and kept as prisoners of war: who they were, what they did, and where they lived and sometimes died in service to their flocks. Are they heroes? Some were, no doubt, but truthfully, none of them would ever claim hero status for themselves. On the other hand, I think it is fair to say that only readers and, ultimately, God can decide that.

Robert C. Doyle
Steubenville, Ohio
2023

❊ ACKNOWLEDGMENTS ❊

I WISH TO ACKNOWLEDGE the late Dr. Stanley Weintraub, Evan Pugh Professor Emeritus at Penn State University, for planting the idea of researching the issues of prisoner of war (POW) chaplains in my mind years ago and encouraging me from the beginning to the end. I once asked him what he wanted from me. "Words," he replied. The same can be said of the late Dr. Arnold Krammer, emeritus professor of history at Texas A&M University, the dean of POW studies in the United States, especially from World War II. His loss in 2018 cannot be replaced.

No one writes books alone. I could not have completed this work without the librarians who cared about the project, namely, Kathleen Donohue and Zachariah Zdinak at the John Paul II Library at the Franciscan University of Steubenville, as well as James Brockman, curator of the American Defenders of Bataan and Corregidor Museum and Education and Research Center in Wellsburg, West Virginia. I wish to acknowledge and thank history majors Jacob Condi and Johannes Bergsma, who constantly found sources in obscure places, and, most important, William Henri of Houston, Texas, friend and former member of Advisory Team 88 in Ben Tre. A friendship of more than fifty years has been most fruitful. Without Bill Henri, nothing.

I wish to thank the numerous Franciscan friars I have gotten to know at the Franciscan University of Steubenville. Fr. Stanley Holland, TOR, is a Vietnam veteran like me, and we have spoken often about our experiences in that war and the chaplains we met along the way. One of our former university presidents, Fr. Terry Henry, TOR, had a father who was shot down during the U.S. Army Air Forces (USAAF) raid on the Ploesti oil fields in Romania and taken as a POW during World War II. His encouragement is noted with pleasure; likewise, the father of my department chair in history, Dr. Kimberly Georgedes, became a POW during the Battle of the Bulge as a prisoner of the Germans at Stalag IX-B, Bad Orb, one of the most horrid POW camps in Germany, in December 1944. Her encouragement, along with my other colleagues and friends, is deeply appreciated. I also wish to thank my dean, Dr. Regina Boreo, and the vice president for academic affairs, Daniel Kempton, for granting me a sabbatical in 2020 to concentrate on writing this book.

Without these folks' extraordinary efforts, no data could or would have come my way, and I would have had no precious time to write. I am humbled and blessed by their friendship and thankful for their individual and collective efforts.

—·》《·—

Introduction

HISTORIANS FEEL COMFORTABLE DEALING with chronological time where events take place and then are followed by other related events. It is not possible to approach this standard in the introduction; rather, I use a kind of thematic approach more common in cultural history where historians tend to jump from issue to issue in spite of the thematic timeline. Perhaps in this case, it is best to suggest that readers go with the flow rather than demand a strict adherence to chronological time.

All three of my books on American POWs were based on a commitment to two ideas: victory and survival. All three show how these ideas came to life and generated American wartime experiences from the Revolution to Vietnam and beyond. The first book, *Voices from Captivity: Interpreting the American POW Narrative* (1994), showed that individual experience contributed to the structure of the American captivity narrative. It also showed the determination of American POWs to tell the truth about their individual experience behind the wire. The second book, *A Prisoner's Duty: Great Escapes in U.S. Military History* (1997), showed how and why American POWs activated the Principle of

Intolerable Cruelty—the understanding that the captor was going to execute the POWs—and attempted to escape even when chances were less than remote. *The Enemy in Our Hands: American Treatment of Enemy POWs from the Revolution to the War on Terror* (2010), the third book, examined how Americans treated enemy POWs in American hands. What is left to consider?

I never considered chaplains per se, some of whom found themselves POWs. It was time to get to work and dive into what for me was the relatively unknown universe of Catholic priests, Protestant ministers, and Jewish rabbis who served in war zones, came under fire, and went behind barbed wire from the Revolution to the Vietnam War and beyond. Who were they, why did they do their duty, and how did they live, die, and serve their flocks in very difficult circumstances? What were the variables in all this? How did the spirit of the times affect how these men behaved under fire, as captives, or both? Did faith really provide bedrock ideas that conquered human fear and made men's feet boulders in the face of oppression? Perhaps these are simple questions to ask, but they are not easy to answer.

The term "chaplain" dates from antiquity, at least in Christian times, from the era of Saint Martin of Tours who fought against paganism during the Merovingian era in France around 356 CE. The story goes that on a freezing day, Martin, a Roman cavalryman, gave half of his winter cloak away to a beggar who turned out to be a vision of Christ. Hence, the pagan soldier Martin eventually became a Christian and then Saint Martin, bishop of Tours. Saint Martin left the Roman army, became the first Christian military chaplain, and is both remembered and venerated as such. Thus, the term "chaplain" was born and evolved into the institution of the military chaplaincy, one that grew into a nearly universal corps of clergy who tend to the spiritual needs of soldiers.[1]

The reliquary in which the *cappa*, or cloak, was kept was known as the *Chappellanus*, which became the *chappellan* in French, or "chaplain" or "keeper of the cloak" in English.[2] To dive into religious military advisers of antiquity or even the Christian military orders of the Crusades is beyond the mission of this study; rather, it is my intention to examine the issues of the eighteenth, nineteenth, and twentieth centuries, specifically the status of chaplains in the military services of the United States, as the focus in this book. True, the American Revolution is a historical problem, not because there is little data about those men who served God and their cause equally, but because many of those men were not simply men in service of God; many carried weapons and served as officers in their respective units against the British and Loyalist forces.

Finding biographical materials on chaplains, especially those taken prisoner, was much more difficult than other POW materials with which one becomes familiar over time. Aside from a small handful of autobiographies, the search became difficult nearly beyond imagination. Each state that supported a line unit in the Continental army and militia units kept records and recognized chaplains for heroism under fire and service to their respective states. The Civil War also had good records, and many chaplains wrote narratives of their respective wartime experiences and captivities. For more modern experiences of chaplains, I contacted the Chaplain School at Fort Jackson, South Carolina. The archivist there told me that they had nothing on chaplains who were taken prisoner. I received a similar response when I contacted the Catholic military bishop's office: nothing specific on chaplain POWs. I did have one personal reflection to consider, a Korean War POW's response to my question posed during a 1999 POW reunion, "Did you know Fr. Emil Kapaun?" "A wonderful man," he responded, with a tear in his eye. Thus, normal institutional research was not possible in this project.

World War II was very different, however. Chaplains who survived the war and captivity did publish autobiographies, and several authors completed good historical studies. Most chaplains gave reports to their superiors or bishops after repatriation. Many others gave evidence about the deaths of fellow chaplains at the hands of the enemy. Some memoirs were published by recognized university and commercial presses; others were self-published. All had marvelous tales of courage, fear, sacrifice, and life and death, some on board Japanese hell ships en route to Japan from the Philippines in 1944, others behind barbed wire. Like most captivity narratives, chaplain stories follow the usual sequence: precapture freedom, deployment, battle and capture, long death marches, everyday life behind the wire, escape or rescue, liberation, and a final reflection, what I have called the lament for lost time, friends, and opportunities. With this in mind, what differentiates their stories from secular ones is how their dedication to the service of God, both in and out of captivity, played a vital role in either their survival or, in some cases, their deaths.

Also important for this study is their orientation to their jobs as chaplains in the armed forces. In short, although they were indeed Catholic priests, Protestant ministers, or Jewish rabbis first, they were also officers in the American Army, Navy, and Army Air Force who swore to uphold and defend the Constitution of the United States. Rarely did chaplains have any problem with the oath of office, and rarely was there any significant competition or poaching on other faith communities' communicants. Yes, it did happen, but it was a rare occurrence, and it is fair to point out that for the chaplain communities, the Civil War and World War II were most certainly the beginning of Christian ecumenism.

There is another issue that will be addressed: the rules that evolved in dealing with chaplains who fell into the hands of the enemy. We will see how a war without real rules began in 1775, how Gen. George Washington imposed rules on the chaplains under his command, and how civilians became chaplains during the Revolution and what happened to a few of them imprisoned by the British. Because the American Revolution and the War of 1812 were wars fought by state militia units for the most part, those chaplains who served the soldiers were also soldiers mostly from their own ranks who volunteered for chaplain service in addition to their martial duties. The idea of an unarmed chaplain was unthinkable at that time.

Looking back to the Mexican-American War, 1846–48, the chaplain situation began to focus on the thousands of American Catholic soldiers, mostly Irishmen, who had no chaplains when the war began. At the time, the U.S. Army was full of nativist "Know-Nothing" officers, mostly southerners who found their Irish soldiers both Catholic and barbaric, strangely different in the way they saw the world, the United States, patriotism, and, of course, religion. President James K. Polk, a Protestant and southern Democrat, realized that without chaplains, the U.S. Army had a real problem with its Catholic soldiers. After consultation with John Hughes, the bishop of New York, he appointed two priests as chaplains. Their stories and the subsequent story of the Saint Patrick's Battalion make for eye-opening reading about religion, war, chaplains, and the Army before the Civil War.

The religious fervor during the Civil War was remarkable on both sides, and there were several chaplains taken prisoner, though not many. The Federal Army did appoint chaplains to regiments, as did the Confederates. Normally, one thinks of the Union army as an admixture of ethnicities from northern Europe, immigrants and sons of immigrants, meaning that Catholics, Protestants, and Jews were all there. They were indeed, and they brought their chaplains or clergy with them or had volunteer chaplains from their ranks. Both sides feared their enemy's chaplains. Why? According to Warren B. Armstrong, both Union and Confederates observed that chaplains were political as well as religious influencers in their respective armies. In captivity especially, chaplains often molded and influenced opinion among the men they served, just as they had as clergy in the communities in which they served as priests, pastors, rabbis, and rectors before their military service.[3]

At the beginning of the conflict, both sides used the Articles of War as a guideline for action, but more specific rules were set in place in 1863, with the Rules of Land Warfare, General Order 100, known as Lieber's Laws, which codified for the first time who could or could not be a prisoner of war. Chaplains were considered "protected personnel" and by law could not be put into a POW camp. Despite the rule book, some practiced their faith in captivity, namely, Fr. Peter Whelan in Georgia and Fr. James Sheeran from Louisiana, imprisoned in Maryland, both Irish Confederates but with very different stories. The changes in the law and the unique nature of their lives will function as some of the focus of the Civil War discussions.

The Frontier Wars from 1865 to 1890 continued the tradition of assigning chaplains to service behind the lines in educational capacities in the western forts. The War of 1898, the Philippine Insurrection, and World War I found no American chaplains taken prisoner of war, but the nature of the chaplaincy changed significantly. It is vital to show how the institution changed as the nation's priorities evolved and how the military services decided to update their chaplaincies to better service their soldiers and sailors in the field and on board ship.

World War II brought a large number of chaplains into enemy captivity, despite the 1929 Geneva Convention's prohibition against taking protected personnel into custody against their will. By far, the greatest number of American clergy POWs were taken by the Japanese in the Philippine campaign in 1942. Their fates, both positive and negative, lie at the heart of this work, both in substance and in passion. They set the example for what the chaplain corps evolved into in our own time. They demonstrated what it meant to be men of God not only in terms of the practice of faith but also during the overt and covert activities in which they played a part in places such as Camp O'Donnell, Cabanatuan, and other Japanese POW and internment camps. Refusing to be intimidated by the Japanese, they tried their best to keep men alive in heart, soul, and body. Their stalwart behavior on the hell ships in 1943 and 1944 calmed men going insane from the searing heat, dangerous overcrowding, and utter hopelessness, while they brought prayer to their soldiers as a weapon against those who wished to kill them outright. It should be noted that most of the chaplains who died in the Pacific area of operations perished in these filthy, overcrowded Japanese merchant ships torpedoed by American submarines or bombed by American aircraft.

When the Americans invaded North Africa, their chaplains came with them. Most people of that generation remember the story of the four chaplains of the USAT *Dorchester* who, after the ship's torpedoing in 1942 en route to North Africa, suffered as martyrs and gave away their life jackets to the men they served. These gallant men of God met their maker when they went down with their ship, and, like their brothers in the Pacific, they became beacons of hope and prayer to those around them. Like the other Americans who went to war in 1942, the Army chaplains scratched their way through the hills and wadis of North Africa in search of the Afrika Korps, and then finally in May 1943, after the battles in North Africa were over, the battles of Sicily and Italy began.

On June 6, 1944, the world changed again; the challenge to Nazism in Europe began when the Allies invaded Normandy, France, before the sun came up that day. As in all the other fields of battle, the chaplains accompanied their men into the jaws of death. Most came ashore with the infantry; others jumped from the hundreds of C-47 aircraft that carried the paratroopers of the 87th and 101st Airborne Divisions behind the lines of invasion into the German positions. Chaplain Fr. Francis L. Sampson, also known as the "Paratrooper Padre," leaped into the night air. There were others too, and we will get to know some of them and their remarkable exploits. The same is true for the Korean War, 1950–53, where we will meet Fr. Emil Kapaun, a veteran of World War II who pestered his bishop for reassignment to the U.S. Army's Chaplain Corps for duty in Korea when the enemy guns fired from North to South in

1950. Chaplain Kapaun died in enemy captivity on May 23, 1951, at the age of thirty-five. He received the Medal of Honor posthumously from President Barack Obama, and the Vatican is considering him for sainthood.

No chaplains were taken POW during the Vietnam War, 1959–73; instead, the American POWs in Hanoi tended to their religious needs themselves. In a real way, these men reinvented the American chaplaincy to meet the needs that they had behind the wire. Prisoners such as Guy Gruters, Jeremiah Denton, Charles Plumb, Gerald Coffee, Robinson Reisner, and others took their faith seriously and discovered that it not only created a kind of philosophical bedrock for them to resist their captors but also gave them the strength to reach out to many of their comrades who teetered on and perhaps searched for a base to build the kind of solidarity necessary to return home with honor.

This is what this book is all about: the stories of chaplains who did their duty selflessly to God and to their country. Sometimes because of and sometimes despite the issues they faced intellectually, religiously, and even practically in service to their soldiers, sailors, Marines, and airmen, they found themselves in some very dire circumstances over the stretch of three hundred years. I have often asked myself: Where do we get men like these? The simple answer is this: I believe in miracles.

One

—•⟩⟩ ⟨⟨•—

Chaplains of Muskets and Sail
The Revolution

*Let vice and immorality of every kind be discouraged as much
as possible . . . and as a chaplain is allowed to each regiment, see
that the men regularly attend during worship.*

—Lt. Gen. George Washington, instructions to
the brigadier generals, May 26, 1777

THE AMERICAN REVOLUTION was a not a simple affair fought by
large standing armies organized perfectly around the Continental Congress
by men who knew exactly what they were doing at all times. Nor was the
Army a perfectly put together, finely tuned fighting machine ready to take
on all comers in a way that perhaps it is today. It was at best a very loose,
amateur organization consisting of state and local militias usually organized
by prominent local well-to-do persons who could afford to arm, feed, clothe,
and transport a military militia unit for a relatively short period of time. At
best, such units could conduct operations against local or regional tribal forces,
especially in the eastern colonies during the seventeenth-century Forest Wars,
but never could such an army face a major European force in the field as the
Americans did in 1775.

The notion of a military chaplaincy came from England along with the
earliest militias in the new settlements. The first recorded instance of a chaplain
pastor assisting a militia took place in 1637 when Rev. Samuel Stone of Hartford,
Connecticut, served as chaplain and adviser to Capt. John Mason, who managed

8

to all but wipe out the Pequot Tribe in the present state of Connecticut at the Mystic River fort. Between Mason and Stone, after prayer they came to the conclusion that their victory was in the hand of Providence, that is, God's will. Of course, Stone received a land grant for his advice during the campaign, and the bloodletting of and in the Forest Wars continued until 1763 when Britain and France made peace, with Britain taking possession of Canada and all the people in it, tribes included.

Names like Hope Atherton appear as chaplains during King Philip's War in 1677 and others in subsequent campaigns large and small. One chaplain, John Norton, minister of the church at Bernardson, Massachusetts, served on the province's frontier in 1745 and was taken prisoner, held for a year, and later released through a prisoner exchange.[1] Norton left his experiences in his personal narrative, *The Redeemed Captive*.[2] He noted that his French captors treated him very well and permitted him and his Protestant comrades to practice their religion freely: "Here we had the free liberty of the exercise of our religion together, which was a matter of comfort to us in our affliction." In all these cases, the chaplains ensured that regular religious services took place and that some semblance of order was kept in camp or in captivity by the officers and men of the militias. Like most captives in this era, they were returned home, usually in an exchange of some sort. Although Norton does not note the details, he does express his joy of repatriation: "We arrived in Boston. The sick and infirm were taken to the hospital. Colonel [John] Winslow desired me to come to him while I continued in Boston. May I never forget the many great and repeated mercies of God towards me."[3]

Arising out of the French and Indian War (1754–63) was George Washington of the Virginia Militia who insisted that his soldiers attend religious services even in his earliest days of service. According to Eugene Franklin Williams, "Washington's concern for the moral and spiritual welfare of the men in the armed services grew out of his leaning toward religion." Like many Virginians, he was born into the Anglican Church and practiced his faith to the degree that he could under the circumstances that presented themselves. In the field, Washington consistently asked for a chaplain to be sent by the governor of Virginia, Robert Dinwiddie, to his troops. Dinwiddie was unable to find a suitable chaplain for Washington and his men, so Washington attempted to foster a spirit of religion by himself by issuing orders against swearing, the use of foul language, and excess drinking.[4] From these days to the end of the American Revolution, Washington never changed one bit in his relationship with religion or chaplains for his men. It mattered not that George Washington was a religious man or not; he cared for the welfare of his soldiers.

During the colonial period governors often appointed chaplains to military units; in some colonies the legislature did it for the established church in that colony. At other times and places, brigade officers appointed them, as did ships' captains. Ultimately, in the words of historian Charles H. Metzger, "Moral worth, coupled with enthusiastic patriotism, must mark the chaplain."[5] For sure, American chaplains served in both American and British units, and it is curious to note that of the chaplains who served in the French and Indian War, nearly half came from New England.[6] These men evolved into important opinion makers before the Revolutionary War. They were, after all, the best-educated men in the colonies, and people took them seriously when they preached not only the Gospel but also a righteous dose of politics within the four corners of a sermon. For the British, as time showed, and in future wars driven by ideologies, they were indeed dangerous elements to their enemies.

The fights at Lexington and Concord, Massachusetts, between the American militia units and regulars of the British Army were predicated by very deep religious feelings throughout the colonies. The Revolutionary War began at Lexington Green and Concord Bridge on April 19, 1775. Present were four chaplains: William Emerson, later killed on active duty; Joseph Thaxter, later wounded at Bunker (Breed's) Hill; Philip Payson; and a Reverend Foster. Of these four chaplains, all but Chaplain Emerson carried arms against the British.[7] Approximately 174 chaplains served in the Continental army, while 93 served in the various state militias during the American Revolution.[8] Three chaplains were killed in action, 2 were wounded in action, more than 10 were captured, and 8 died natural deaths while serving.[9]

By 1775 there were approximately 3,105 religious organizations in the American colonies. According to Eugene Franklin Williams, New England, the Middle Colonies, and the South accounted for about a thousand each. The dominant faith in New England was the former Puritan or Congregationalist Church in the 1770s, and all the groups were staunchly in support of the American

Revolution. Closely related to the Congregationalists were the Presbyterians, often consisting of newly arrived Scots strongly supportive of the British Crown, and like the Congregationalists they had a highly educated clergy. Yet despite the newly arrived Scots, the vast majority of American colonial Presbyterians supported the Revolution more than the British Crown in this contest from 1775 to 1783. One question is this: Did the officers of the Continental army agree about their chaplains? Of course not; Americans rarely agree about anything if they do not have to. There were disagreements about theology, ideology, politics, and who got whom or how many chaplains in their units; however, to worry about these kinds of issues lies well beyond the scope and intent of this work.[10]

The Baptists also wholeheartedly supported the Revolution, in part because they often opposed the Anglicans, who held them in contempt. It took a while to calm both the Baptists and the Anglicans enough to accept one another in the Revolutionary fold, but they reconciled not by words but by actions. The Anglicans, also known in the United States as Episcopalians, were most numerous in Virginia and Maryland.[11] Men such as George Washington, James Madison, Patrick Henry, John Marshall, John Morris, John Jay, and Alexander Hamilton all belonged to this denomination. However, like the newly arrived Scots, newly arrived Anglicans (Church of England) were often loyal to the Crown.

Opposing the Revolution was another set of Englishmen, the Society of Friends, or Quakers, mostly in Pennsylvania, who opposed all armed conflict, regardless of what may have been its root cause. By 1777 the local revolutionaries in Philadelphia feared that the local pacifist Quakers intended to do business with the British who were about to occupy the city. They appealed to the Pennsylvania state authorities, claiming that the Quakers were loyalists at heart, and insisted that they should be incarcerated. The wives of these innocent Quakers appealed to General Washington himself, then at the Valley Forge winter encampment, but Washington demurred to state authorities, and the Quakers came home considerably harmed and demoralized by their political imprisonment.

There were a small number of Quakers, the "Free Quakers," who believed that they were indeed justified in opposing the Crown. Names such as Gen. Nathaniel Greene from Rhode Island along with Thomas Mifflin and Betsy Ross from Pennsylvania dominate this group. Unfortunately for General Greene, after the war's end and his petition for readmission to his Quaker community, the Quakers refused his plea, and he died of heatstroke in South Carolina, excommunicated from his home meetinghouse in Rhode Island.

Aside from the Quakers, Germans dominated the religious congregations in the Middle Colonies, especially Pennsylvania. The German Reformed and Lutheran congregations both supported the Revolution, and after Henry Melchior Muhlenberg formed the first Lutheran Synod in 1748, his son Peter became a general in the Continental army and represented his Lutherans in Congress from 1779 to 1780. Unlike the German Lutherans, the German Mennonites, pacifists like the Quakers, refused to join the Lutheran and Reformed soldiers. The state authorities did little against them for this and basically ignored them.

Where were the Catholics? There were not great numbers of Roman Catholics in the American colonies at this time. Most resided in Maryland, but there were parishes in Philadelphia where there were no restrictions against the practice of their faith. The Quebec Act, passed in Parliament in 1774, which permitted Roman Catholics to hold office in French Canada, caused New England's Puritans, radical anti-Catholics, to erupt against those few Catholics who lived near them. There were restrictions everywhere, and Catholics were often prohibited from bearing arms. All that changed overnight after the Declaration of Independence in 1776; all were welcome. Thus, the Catholics of Maryland under John Carroll and Pennsylvania joined the Army and fought the British like their Protestant neighbors. From time to time, the Americans also witnessed the presence of French or French Canadian soldiers who joined the Revolution. As a result, some, not all, Americans learned that Catholic neighbors and Frenchmen could be both good Catholics and good patriots at the same time.

There were Jews on both sides of the American Revolution, too. Like the Catholics, Jews suffered social and religious discrimination in the colonies. Approximately twenty-four Jews served as officers in the Continental army, and many served the Revolution faithfully as civilians. Mordecai Sheftall of Georgia, for example, was only fifteen or sixteen years old when he was appointed assistant deputy commissary general of issues to the Georgia troops. He was captured by the British in 1778; the British kept him until 1780, when he was put in charge of a mercy ship that delivered provisions to American POWs held in Charleston, South Carolina.[12]

The emergence of the military chaplaincy came after Congress appointed its own chaplain in 1775. In July 1775, the Second Continental Congress voted to pay military chaplains twenty dollars a month, just above lieutenants. At that time there was no authorized uniform and no particular or required doctrine. The ministers simply showed up at an encampment of the Continental army or a state militia unit and volunteered for duty as a chaplain.[13] On Tuesday, July 9, 1776, Congress appointed Rev. Jacob Duche to pray daily before a session opened in the morning.[14] Congress never stopped the practice, and it continues to this day. When the New England militias became the Continental army in 1775, several chaplains began serving under General Washington. On July 29, 1775, the Continental Congress gave the chaplains its official authorization, and nearly a year later General Washington issued the following general order:

> The honorable Continental Congress having been pleased to allow a chaplain to each regiment, with the pay of thirty-three and one-third dollars per month, the colonels or commanding officers of each regiment are directed to procure chaplains—accordingly persons of good character to see that all inferior officers and soldiers pay them a suitable respect, and attend carefully upon religious exercises. The blessing and protection of heaven are at all times necessary but especially it is in times of public distress and danger. The General hopes and trusts that every officer and man will endeavor as to live and act as becomes a Christian soldier, defending the dearest rights and liberties of his country.[15]

By 1776 Washington was able to recruit more soldiers and chaplains for his new Continental regiments. But it was Connecticut that first showed an interest in providing a chaplaincy and has bragging rights that it supplied the second-highest number of chaplains to the Continental army during the American Revolution. Radically religious Massachusetts, of course, provided the most.

During the American Revolution, each new state drafted and passed its own Articles of War. Some states provided for chaplains; others did not. In short, no centralized system existed as there is today, and attempting to make any sense of its frustratingly complex nonsystem would be fruitless at this point. Congress was not helpful either; however, it did establish a chaplaincy for the Continental army on July 29, 1775, but the pay was too low to attract anyone competent to do the job with any consistency. By February 1777, Congress understood that it had a responsibility to supply its soldiers a dedicated chaplaincy. In April 1777, Congress increased chaplains' pay to forty dollars per month, not very much at all, especially when one considers what a chaplain's duties and expenses were at this time.

During the Revolutionary War, the chaplain was all things to all people. Thus, some served for the duration of the war, while others managed for a few days or weeks until they wore out or could not take the stress anymore. Eugene Franklin Williams writes that chaplains during the Revolutionary War were responsible for three things in particular: they were to conduct divine services, obey their superior officers, and act as representatives of God.[16] What they did, in reality, was set the tone of service for those who came after them for three hundred years, that is, until our own time. Aside from divine services, visiting the sick, burying the dead, and writing letters home for those men who for various reasons, including illiteracy or wounds, could not, they visited the imprisoned, read the Bible, and conducted hymn sings when and where possible. Commanding officers wanted their chaplains to help build unit morale. Divine services among Protestant soldiers consisted of the chaplain's sermon, prayers, hymns, and communion, depending on the denomination. Often the gravity of soldiering during the Revolutionary War generated intense sermons about integrity and truths that often stayed with the soldiers well into later life. And, of course, the chaplain always conducted the funeral for the unit's dead regardless of the cause. Thus, beginning with the chaplains of the American Revolution, the position of chaplain gathered ever more importance in the American Army, then and now.

Who got caught? Who were they? What happened to them? There were not many, but there were some who became POWs during the American Revolution. Charles H. Metzger notes that chaplains who were made POWs elicited General Washington's special interest. He advocated their exchange or release as soon as possible and believed that they should not be taken POW at all under any circumstances.[17]

Moses Allen became a chaplain of a Georgia brigade in 1778. He was a native New Englander who trained as a Presbyterian minister at Prince College in 1772 and migrated to the South by 1775.[18] In 1777 he moved to Midway, Georgia, where he preached against the Crown in the open. During the spring of 1778, the Loyalists, known then as "Tories," grew so strong in Georgia that Governor Houston launched an expedition against them. Reverend Allen then joined the Georgia brigade as a chaplain, despite his youth. When the Tories approached his small town—he was pretty well known as a hotheaded proindependence preacher—the British burned down not only his church but his house as well. Allen and the brigade then left for Savannah, where they were taken as POWs when the city fell to the British. Immediately, Allen and some of his comrades were put in the prison ship *Nancy* at Cock Spur (Savannah) and tried as traitors.[19] Allen had the distinction of being charged as the "head rebel" of the entire region and received the usual horrific treatment accorded rebels by the British.

In the midst of the filth, disease, and ill treatment by the British, Chaplain Allen attempted an escape, most probably because he recognized the high probability of his own death under the conditions in which he was placed. He believed that he had no choice at this point and managed to slip over the side of the prison hulk and swim for shore. His strength was sapped by this time, and neither his courage nor his determination overwhelmed his fatigue. When his body washed ashore on Tybee Island, his fellow prisoners, some of whom were his former parishioners, asked to bury Allen properly. The British, however, simply pushed his body unceremoniously into the mud to share the kind of burial given by the British to all who died on the prison hulks, north in New York Harbor or south in Savannah and Charleston.

Some chaplains became "fighting parsons" during the Revolution, and as a result some were killed in action. Today, of course, rules forbid chaplains from carrying weapons or being counted as combatants. But times and rules—what there were of them—were different back then. James Caldwell, the minister of the First Presbyterian Church of Elizabethtown, New Jersey, became chaplain of the 3rd New Jersey Brigade from February to November 1776. Well known for his fiery sermons against the British occupation, his reputation guaranteed his popularity with the patriots and hatred among the loyalists. He had his own spy ring and knew where the British and loyalists were most of the time. If there was trouble, Chaplain Caldwell was close by. His church was regularly used as a hospital for wounded Americans, but loyalists burned it down in January 1780. According to Joel Tyler Heady, "The villain, in confession of the deed afterwards, said he was sorry that the 'black-coated' rebel was not burned in his own pulpit." Mrs. Caldwell was shot and killed in 1780 by Hessian soldiers led by General Knyphausen while she was tending her servants and children in her own home. In 1781 Chaplain James Caldwell was shot and killed by a sentry at Elizabethtown Point, New Jersey. The American loyalist sentry James Morgan was subsequently tried and convicted of murder and hanged in 1782. Heady writes, "Caldwell was as earnest in the pulpit as he was out of it. He seldom preached without weeping himself, and often would melt his audience to tears. He was a man of unwearied activity, and of wonderful powers, both of body and mental endurance. Feelings of the most glowing piety, and the most fervent patriotism occupied his bossum [sic], at the same time without at all interfering with each other. He was one day preaching to the battalion—the next providing ways and means for their support, and the next marching with them to battle." The loyalists referred to Caldwell as "the Rebel High Priest"; the Americans simply called him Chaplain.[20]

Known as the "Martyr of the Revolution," John Rosebrugh (Rossburgh) died at the hands of Hessian troops on January 2, 1777, after their defeat by General Washington at Trenton. Rosebrugh was the pastor of the Presbyterian Church of Allen Township, Pennsylvania, when war was proclaimed. He read General Washington's appeal to his congregation, and they consented to enlist if Washington commanded them. Rosebrugh was commissioned chaplain at age sixty-two in the Pennsylvania Militia on December 24, 1776. He stepped toward the bank of the Delaware River at Trenton at the battle of Assunpink (second Battle of Trenton) and lost his horse in the confusion of the moment. Chaplain Rosebrugh suddenly came upon a unit of Hessians under the command of a British officer and was subsequently taken prisoner and stripped of his possessions. The Hessians, still furious at the Americans about their loss, bayoneted Rosebrugh to death while he implored mercy and begged for his life.[21]

John Cordell served as chaplain with the 11th Virginia Regiment and was taken prisoner at Fort Mercer on October 22, 1777. By this time in Virginia, arrangements were made with the British to free any chaplain taken prisoner and held as a POW. After being freed by the British in 1777, the Virginia militia reorganized, and Chaplain Cordell was released from active service. Andrew Hunter served as chaplain to several New Jersey units: Col. Stephen Van Courtlandt's Battalion, Heard's Brigade of the New Jersey Militia, 3rd Battalion Second Establishment, Continental army, New Jersey Line, General Maxwell's Brigade, and the 3rd Regiment and Brigade from 1780 to the end of the war. While serving as chaplain to Maxwell's Brigade in 1779, Chaplain Hunter marched through north New Jersey to Easton and farther into the Wyoming Valley in northeastern Pennsylvania to help stop cruelties perpetrated by the British and their Indian allies in the region. While near Elizabethtown, he was taken prisoner by the British but managed to escape.[22]

There were very few Catholics serving in American armies during the Revolutionary War, either in Continental or state militias, but there were a few, namely, a French Canadian unit, Livingston's Regiment, recruited in Canada during the ill-fated attack by Gen. Benedict Arnold and Gen. Richard Montgomery in 1775. This regiment recruited sixty-year-old Recollect Father Louis Lotbiniere of the Diocese of Quebec as chaplain, and he served for the entire length of the war. Gen. Benedict Arnold offered him rations, firewood, candles, and a monthly salary of $41.30. Along with every member of the regiment, he was ex-communicated by Bishop Jean-Olivier Briand of the Roman Catholic Diocese of Quebec from 1766 to 1784; Briand forbade any of his parishioners or clergy to join the American side of the fight. As a result, Father Lotbiniere lived on his small pension from the government and died penniless in Philadelphia on October 11, 1786.[23]

Daniel McCalla served as Protestant chaplain to the 2nd Pennsylvania Battalion and was taken prisoner at Three Rivers (Pittsburgh) on June 8, 1776; he was paroled in August 1776 and never returned to the Army. His story was not quite that simple, though. Early in the war McCalla became chaplain to General Thompson, who had been ordered to attack Three Rivers by surprise; however, the unit had been discovered by the British who then attacked Thompson's force. The Americans attempted to escape by fleeing into a swamp, but the British caught up to them quickly and took General Thompson, McCalla, and two hundred troops prisoner. McCalla and many others were transferred to a prison ship where they suffered the filth and vermin of the British prison ships. According to Headley, Chaplain McCalla was

> Crowded into the hold with the sick and dying, breathing the foulest air—made the companion of vermin, and compelled to perform the most menial of offices, and assailed with jibes and insults, he lay for months on board this filthy floating lazar-house. At length apparently tired of the attempt to wear out the life of this brave young chaplain, not yet thirty years of age, they released him on parole, and he returned to his congregation.

After his release on parole in August 1776, Chaplain McCalla continued to support the American cause for the rest of the war. He migrated to South Carolina in 1788 and remained there until the end of his life in 1809.[24]

Naphtali Dagget was acting as president of Yale College in 1777, a devout Presbyterian minister, and at fifty-three years of age, he volunteered as a private in the defense of New Haven, Connecticut, in 1779. He made himself so obnoxious to the British after his capture that they forced him to act as a guide in front of bayonets. Joel Tyler Headley tells Chaplain Dagget's story in the flowery style of the 1860s, beginning with his capture:

> If I let you go this time, you old rascal, will you ever fire again on the troops of His Majesty?" "Nothing more likely," was the imperturbable reply. This was too much for the good temper of the old Briton, and he ordered his man to seize him. They did so; and dragged him roughly down the hill to the head of the column. Dr. Dagget as he lay covered with blood and dust, requested the officer to release him. He did so, and their wounded patriot was carried into a home nearby, more dead than alive. His utter exhaustion and brutal wounds combined brought him to the very gates of death. He, however, rallied and was able a part of the next year to preach in the chapel, but his constitution had received a shock, and in sixteen months he was borne to the grave, one more added to the list of noble souls who felt that the offer of their lives to their country was a small sacrifice.

Chaplain Dagget is remembered as a hero of the Revolution.[25]

Without a doubt, one of the foremost chaplains of the Revolutionary War in General Washington's army was Alexander McWhorter. Chaplain McWhorter was a Presbyterian minister, trained at Princeton in 1757, and he earned his doctorate of divinity at Yale around 1760. His service as a chaplain began in 1778 with Gen. Henry Knox's Artillery Brigade. He was actually sent by Congress in 1775 to convert the Loyalists of North Carolina; however, he was not successful. His library and furniture were destroyed by the British. On October 12, 1778, General Washington asked him to visit two condemned spies and counterfeiters from whom the Americans had been unable to extract any information. General Washington suggested to the good chaplain that he might obtain important military intelligence if he made it known he was preparing them for their entry into the next world. Chaplain McWhorter cooperated fully.[26]

The small Continental navy commissioned only five chaplains. Chaplain Benjamin Balch served on board the frigates *Boston* under the command of Capt. Samuel Tucker and *Alliance* under Capt. John Barry. Chaplain Thomas Birch, an Episcopal minister, served under Capt. John Paul Jones on board the *Bonhomme Richard* and was wounded in the engagement against the HMS *Serapis* in 1778. Chaplain Edward Brooks served as chaplain on board the frigate *Hancock* under the command of Capt. John Manley. In 1777 he was taken POW by the British and confined at Halifax, Nova Scotia, where he died in prison. Chaplain John Reed served on board the *Warren* in 1777, and John Watkins served as a chaplain on board the *Alliance* under Capt. Peter Landis in John Paul Jones' squadron.[27]

The French sent a host of chaplains, more than one hundred priests, along with army and naval units to America after Benjamin Franklin negotiated the deal with the French that called for French help in money, arms, and men in 1777 after the British catastrophic surrender at Saratoga. Although it cost the French dearly during the war, approximately $40 million, American successes during the War of Independence did give King Louis XVI and his nobles the revenge they sought after they lost New France to the British in 1763. The French and Indian War, fought by the British and Americans against the French from 1754 to 1763, settled claims for dominance in the New World. After the Revolutionary War, however, the French suffered severe financial difficulties by the 1790s, and in response the French Revolution caused most of the French nobility and churchmen to be murdered in public on the guillotine.

One positive effect of French assistance was the end of New England anti-Catholicism that raised its head after the British enabled the Quebec Act in 1774. This act allowed Catholic French Canadians to take part in government, something anathema to New Englanders. In their eyes, they perceived this move as the devil himself coming to North America. It also mandated French Canada to extend down the Mississippi River, expanding Canadian holdings considerably. It also gave cause to the American Revolution. After 1777, however, it made no sense to hate one's ally.

One of the most unusual chaplains of the Revolution was James Johnson, a British officer captured at Saratoga in 1777, who, after investigating the grievances of the colonies, resigned his commission in the British Army and joined the Americans. He was with the Virginia troops as chaplain at Yorktown in 1781.[28]

There were also several Loyalist chaplains taken prisoner by the Americans during the Revolutionary War. Daniel Batwell was chaplain of the New Jersey Volunteers. He was captured shortly after hostilities began and put in a jail in York, Pennsylvania. Congress gave him leave to remove his family to the center of loyalism, New York City. After the end of the war in 1783, Chaplain Batwell went to England and died there.[29] Other Loyalist chaplains suffered similar fates: they lost their property, wealth, comforts, and status in the United States. As a group, the Loyalists relocated to Canada or England, always as outsiders and foreigners in their own land, never able to return home to an America that had changed completely. The British did keep their promise to runaway slaves who sided and fought with them, however, evacuating them from the slaveholding United States to freedom in Canada, England, and Sierra Leone.

Although none of the Pennsylvania Lutheran men of the Muhlenberg family were ever taken prisoner of war, each one of them served the religious and political cause of liberty at the time. Conrad Augustus Frederick Muhlenberg served as an assistant at Christ Church in New York when war broke out, and he immediately laid aside his religious duties to represent his German brethren in the Continental Congress for the duration of the war. Pastor Ernestus Henry Muhlenberg was driven from Philadelphia by the British General Howe in 1777; he devoted his entire life to writing and laboring for the American cause. Henry Melchior Muhlenberg founded the Lutheran Church in America. True, he was too old for service in the Revolutionary War, but he suffered just the same. Last, John Peter Gabriel Muhlenberg served not as a chaplain but as a brigadier general in the Continental army and fought at the battles of Charleston, Brandywine, Germantown, and at Monmouth. He froze with his men at Valley Forge and always served close to the battlefronts. After the war, General Muhlenberg was elected U.S. senator and served as honorably as he did in the field.[30]

It is fair to argue that the chaplains of the Revolution were patriots first, soldiers second, and men of God third. Unlike their German Mennonite and Quaker neighbors in Pennsylvania, they were not pacifists. In fact, many carried their muskets into battle with one hand and their Bibles with the other. As patriots they were determined to stand up for the cause of liberty from the Crown and Parliament in England. Most certainly, as men of God, they preached the Gospel, but as soldiers they also felt the right of citizens to defend their home and families. And the price? As we have seen clearly, it was extremely high indeed. Of the 218 chaplains who served in the Continental army, about 25 were killed or died in the war, which constituted 11 percent, the highest casualty rate for chaplains the U.S. Army ever experienced in a war.[31] To the British, they were dangerous adversaries, even more so as men of religion.

Two

—·⟫⟪·—

1812 to 1848

Mexico, Catholicism, and the San Patricio Problem

Mexico has invaded our territory and shed American blood upon American soil. She has proclaimed that hostilities have commenced, and that the two nations are now at war.

—James K. Polk, war message to Congress, May 11, 1846

THE WAR OF 1812 found chaplains serving with regular troops and state militias, much as they did in the Revolutionary War. Only ten names survive of the chaplains of this period, and of that group only James J. Wilmer is known to have died on active duty. Undoubtedly, many more served and suffered, but when the British burned Washington, the records burned too, and thus a huge gap was left in the history of the American chaplaincy.[1] With that said, historian Kenneth E. Lawson, a major historical force at the U.S. Army's Chaplain School at Fort Jackson, South Carolina, tells us that it was not until after the end of the Revolution that Gen. George Washington made Rev. John Hurt the first officially appointed chaplain in the brand-new U.S. Army. By 1798 provision was made for four chaplains for the whole Army. From Congress the American chaplaincy merited hardly any priority at all, and those military districts that did warrant a chaplain had little or no interest in being associated with a chaplaincy directed by the new federal government. Thus, the U.S. Army chaplaincy at the beginning of the War of 1812 was a disorganized mess and terribly inadequate.[2]

Regular army units that deployed against the British or the Indians in the Northwest did so without chaplains. The same can be said of some state militia units—no chaplains—while others, like New York's militia units, had many chaplains. Ohio was full of Presbyterians who served as chaplains; Joseph Hughes was one of them. According to Kenneth Lawson, Chaplain Hughes was commissioned chaplain in May 1813 and was assigned to the Army near Detroit just in time for Maj. Gen. William Hull's unnecessary surrender to the British. Most historians agree that this event represented the lowest point for the Americans in the entire war. The British literally walked into Detroit and took over the fort without a fight; Hughes was part of the 2,500-member American force that Hull surrendered. In 1813 the British were more interested in booty than POWs, and they managed to parole the prisoners, while they busied themselves in seizing tons of supplies, equipment, cannons, horses, a sailing ship, and, of course, the dominance of the land in such a strategic position as Detroit, Michigan.[3] After the war Chaplain Hughes returned home to Ohio and lived to 1823, when he died of a fever.

Also serving General Hull in Detroit was a French Catholic priest, Fr. Gabriel Richard, a thoroughly fascinating individual who served unofficially. Born in France in 1767, he immigrated to the United States in 1792. After teaching in Maryland, he was assigned as a missionary to the Indians in what would later be called the states of Illinois and Michigan. He established himself in Detroit at St. Anne's Church, surrendered to the British in 1812, and became a POW. He was released only when the renowned Native leader Tecumseh, despite hating all immigrants and native-born Americans, insisted that this priest be released in recognition of Father Richard's work with the Indians.[4]

Tending to the needs of enemy POWs was an important aspect of the work of military chaplains, especially when the War of 1812 was coming to an end. The largest capture of enemy POWs took place after the Battle of New Orleans in January 1815. Chaplain Samuel J. Mills of Connecticut found himself tending British and American wounded in February 1815. Kenneth Lawson tells the story using Chaplain Mills' personal diary:

Feb. 10: I called in company with Mr. H[ennern] at the public prison; there are three hundred English soldiers in the prison. A number of Bibles had sometimes since been distributed among them. We found many of them reading with great attention [and] we gave them some additional supply. They received the Bibles with evident expressions of joy and gratitude [and] returned many thanks for them. In the course of the same day, we called upon Dr. Dow who informed us that he had furnished some of the prisoners with a number of *Watt's Psalms* and some other religious books.[5]

Thus, one can see that the treatment accorded prisoners on both sides improved considerably from the time and circumstances that existed during the Revolution. Prisoners were indeed POWs with rights and enjoyed the protections traditionally given to uniformed surrendered enemies. That the chaplains attempted to ameliorate their sufferings is indeed an act that would be repeated in the nineteenth and twentieth centuries in different wars and circumstances.

Chaplains served in the U.S. Navy regardless of how small it was at the time. Not only did chaplains serve the spiritual needs of the officers and crew members, but they also served as schoolmasters. In the larger ships of the line, chaplains were excused from teaching duties and tended only to spiritual ones. The story of Chaplain Samuel Livermore on board *Chesapeake* under the command of Capt. James Lawrence that sailed from Boston in 1813 and encountered HMS *Shannon* in a deadly fight illustrates the kind of chaplains and captains who served in the American fleet at the time. Lawrence was quickly wounded mortally, and British captain Philip P. V. Broke boarded the *Chesapeake* victoriously. According to legend, Lawrence seized a pistol and shot at Captain Broke. Livermore, according to legend, grabbed a cutlass and attacked the British captain. Broke fought back vigorously and attacked Chaplain Livermore, the first naval chaplain to be wounded and captured at sea after combat. *Essex* was also captured at sea, as was its chaplain. No one was harmed, and everyone was properly exchanged.[6]

Leaving the War of 1812 without telling the story of Reverend Joshua Thomas of Tangier Island, Maryland, is impossible. Generally, the British were respectful of civilians and their property, and Reverend Thomas believed that Adm. Alexander Cochrane and Maj. Gen. John Ross, the officers who ordered the assault on and burning of Washington, D.C., and planned the assault on Baltimore and Fort McHenry, would respect his and his parishioners' property. By the summer of 1814, Cochrane had returned his Royal Navy command to the waters of the United States, overseeing the raids of the Chesapeake region. Cochrane landed the ground troops to invade Washington and presided over the bombardment of Fort McHenry and the Battle of Baltimore.[7] Kenneth E. Lawson unearthed Reverend Thomas' unique tale. "During the operations of the British squadron in the Chesapeake, in the years 1813–1814, a permanent encampment was made on Tangier Island, which became the base of operations for their marauding expeditions." Rev. Joshua Thomas, a rather illiterate Methodist preacher, left some interesting notes on the British occupation of that place.[8] Interactions between the British and the Tangier Islanders were rather cozy, at least not hostile in any real way, until the summer of 1814, when something important stirred both sides. Thomas called for a religious service for all the British soldiers with the fleet, and they came, about 12,000 men in boats, and landed on Tangier Island, with hats off, ready for prayer. Reverend Thomas recalled,

> I warned them of the danger and distress they would bring upon them-selves and others by going to Baltimore with the object they had in view. I told them of the great wickedness of war and that God said, "Thou shalt not kill." If you do, he will judge you at the last day; or before then, he will cause you to "perish by the sword." I told them it was given me by the Almighty, that they could not take Baltimore, and would not succeed. I exhorted them to prepare for death, for many of them would die soon, and I should see them no more until we meet at the sound of the great trumpet before our final judge.[9]

The British, of course, did not listen to their prisoner Reverend Thomas. They attacked as Admiral Cochrane ordered, lost the battles, and finally withdrew to England, never to return armed or in anger to America's shores again.

The story of the War of 1812 remains a complicated and difficult one to tell in detail. The country was experiencing federal growing pains in that citizens remained loyal to states instead of the country as a whole. Although the Constitution was in force, it is easy to see that many people did not understand its federal implications, especially pertaining to the military, very well. States fielded militias much as they did during the Revolution, while the Federal Army remained small and ineffective for the most part.

Also in the vein of the Revolutionary War, there were no Catholic chaplains appointed to the U.S. Army during the War of 1812. There were some Catholic clergy, however, who did serve in unofficial ministries. In Louisiana Fr. Abbe DeBourg of the Cathedral of New Orleans said Mass for American troops and was a strong public supporter of Gen. Andrew Jackson during the 1815 Battle of New Orleans. Fr. Gabriel Richard served as a Catholic chaplain to Major General Hull and was made a POW along with Hull's entire command in 1812. Last, Fr. Joseph Flaget prayed for the Indiana militiamen and regulars before they went out on patrol in the forests. Although they were not appointed by Congress or their respective states, resident French Catholic priests served as volunteer chaplains to the American Army in the War of 1812.

❰ The Mexican-American War, 1846–1848 ❱

The Mexican-American War may well have been a questionable war of conquest, or an aggressive war, but at the time no one, or, perhaps very few people outside the transcendentalists in New York and New England, thought much about its legality, morality, or potential religious problems and issues that changed the heart and soul of the United States in the nineteenth century. Without a doubt, it was the nation's Manifest Destiny war, a war that completed the American mythic vision of a divinely mandated continental nation from the Atlantic to the Pacific shores. At the end of the war, after the signing of the Treaty of Guadalupe-Hidalgo (1848), the United States acquired the present-day states of California, Nevada, Arizona, Utah, and New Mexico, as well as parts of Wyoming, Kansas, and Colorado.[10]

The war against Mexico brought new lands to the United States and confounded all previous accommodations with the slave states. In 1820, thanks to the Missouri Compromise, which stipulated that slavery would not be allowed above the southern border of Missouri, the Mason-Dixon line, Whigs and Democrats achieved an equilibrium of twelve slave states and twelve free states. The acquisition of Texas, south of Missouri's border, tipped the scale in favor of the slave-owning states. However, the Missouri Compromise was not equipped to explain what to do with the newly acquired lands to the west, leading to the Compromise of 1850 and the Kansas-Nebraska Act of 1854, both of which negotiated the future expansion of slavery.[11]

The Mexican-American War also brought out the great fears of a religious invasion from Catholic Ireland, the likes of which had not yet been seen on America's shores. The situation for newly arrived Irish immigrants from 1845 onward who left a starving Ireland and found themselves in the U.S. Army, most probably due to promises of thirteen dollars per month and three meals a day, had two serious problems: lack of patriotism toward the United States and a very hard-shell kind of religious practice in a nearly all Protestant Army with a Protestant officer corps and a body of chaplains who were universally hostile to the Catholic religion that bound the Irish people together for centuries.

Midwestern cities such as Chicago, Mississippi basin towns such as New Orleans, and eastern cities such as New York, Philadelphia, Baltimore, and Charleston all had relatively large and growing Catholic immigrant populations from Ireland mostly after 1845 and Germany before and after 1848. The Irish came as refugees from a starving land ravaged by a potato blight that seemed to know no end. The Germans came as war refugees, losers in a vicious fight against Prussia to gain their freedom and independence. German Catholics and Lutherans migrated to Illinois, Missouri, Wisconsin, and Minnesota, whereas the Irish remained in the cities, some never going farther than a few city blocks from where they landed. The Irish created ghettos in cities such as New York, Philadelphia, St. Louis, and Chicago, but many Irish bachelors joined the U.S. Army instead. Unknown to them at the time was that they faced cultural and religious opposition in addition to the weapons of the Mexican Army.

Everything about them was attacked: the way they talked, dressed, smoked, drank, ate, behaved, and especially worshipped. As Catholics they kept an ancient faith that meant a great deal to them. It was something many had died for in Ireland's many uprisings against the English, especially since the Reformation brought an intense Protestant faith to the British people. Memories of radicals such as Oliver Cromwell, the killer of priests, nuns, and religious people in general during the English Civil War in the 1600s, were never far from their consciousness. Why should that be important? Too many people died during the invasion and murderous escapades by Cromwell and his Roundheads to be forgotten anytime soon. They also knew of *Foxe's Book of Martyrs*, first published in 1563, a scurrilous set of phony indictments of false Catholic misdeeds in the

Old and New Worlds. The Irish of 1836–46 knew all of this, but they came to America anyway.

To the nativists who made life miserable for them, Catholic immigrants were a dangerous mass of men and women completely controlled by their priests of the Church of Rome. The fact that most Irish and German Catholics supported the Democratic Party did little to endear them to the Whigs.[12] Immigration was for them not only an act of defiance in order to survive; they were starving people who would do nearly anything to live. Coming to America was just that, an act of total defiance in the face of death in order to survive another day, week, month, or year, and maybe a lifetime.

The Catholic Irish and Germans faced nativist opposition that reached to the core of their existence. Lyman Beecher in his book *A Plea for the West* (1835) attacked not only their physical being but also their moral and spiritual base. John C. Pinheiro explains this phenomenon very well: "Their religion was inimical to republicanism. Led by foreign priests, this ignorant rabble would 'throw down our free institutions.'" To make matters worse, Protestant parents passively assented to this future by placing their children in Jesuit schools, where they sat side by side with immigrants. These Jesuits, claimed Beecher, "had been trained in Europe to undermine the American republic by indoctrinating the young. Bishops and priests, who refused to assimilate and held complete sway over their pliant flock, now sought to extend Catholic schools and churches."[13]

The hostile anti-Irish, anti-Catholic soldiers in the American Army called these immigrants "mics," "paddies," "papes," and "potato heads." They often disrupted religious services in Mexico or forced the Catholic soldiers to attend Protestant services in camp. There is little wonder that the Mexican generals understood the value of proselytizing these vulnerable and valuable Catholic immigrants, not yet Americans in the American Army, to switch sides. One of General Santa Ana's leaflets said,

> Irishmen! Listen to the words of your brothers, hear the accents of a Catholic people. Is religion no longer the strongest of human bonds? Can you fight by the side of those who put fire to your temples in Boston and Philadelphia? Did you witness such dreadful crimes and sacrilege without making a solemn vow to Our Lord? If you are Catholic, the same as we

are, if you follow the doctrines of Our Savior, why are you seen sword in hand murdering your brethren? Why are you antagonistic to those who defend their own country and your own God?

Come over to us; you will be received under the laws of that truly Christian hospitality and good faith which Irish guests are entitled to expect and obtain from a Catholic nation. May Mexicans and Irishmen, united by the sacred tie of religion and benevolence, form only one people.[14]

On July 1, 1847, General Santa Anna issued an order that read, "Two infantry companies of territorial militia are to be formed from the unit known as the Foreign Legion. They are to be named the First and Second Territorial Militia Companies of San Patricio."[15]

Between 1815 and the war in Mexico in 1846–48, chaplaincy in the U.S. Army was at its lowest ebb. Most Army service took place in the West, often at isolated outposts. If any chaplains were assigned at all, they became post schoolteachers, or, in the parlance of the time, nonessential personnel. There was an argument in Congress that the role of chaplain interfered with the idea of the separation of church and state in the Constitution itself. Yet it was the future Union political general Benjamin F. Butler of New York who convinced Congress that although the Constitution did indeed prohibit the government from establishing a religion in the United States, it did not prohibit providing soldiers the opportunity to worship God wherever they were stationed.[16]

President James K. Polk of Tennessee, a Jacksonian Democrat, understood well that he had thousands of Irish Catholic soldiers in his army fighting in Mexico. He also understood that the Mexican authorities, all Catholics, were proselytizing the Irish soldiers in the American Army with a brutal intensity; once combined with the hostile and badly prejudiced behavior of the anti-Catholic Americans, it would all make sense to the Irish. The Mexican government promised the Irish Catholics several important things: they could worship in the Catholic tradition, they would be welcomed into the Mexican Army, and at the conclusion of the war they would be given land and citizenship and could marry and settle in Mexico.[17] In short, the Mexican government developed propaganda that made Protestant Americans look like barbarians and themselves the Catholic promised land. For penniless and religiously oppressed

Irishmen who perceived truth in these promises, the future looked good, and more than 175 soldiers deserted the U.S. Army. Not all but many of these Irish deserters joined the Mexican Army and formed the St. Patrick's Battalion under the leadership of the former British sergeant John Riley, now a deserter from the Americans and an expert in artillery. The issue in 1846–48 was how to deal with this seeming catastrophe in the ranks in addition to winning a war that had become unpopular in the United States.

On May 20, 1846, President Polk realized that he had to confer with a select group of Roman Catholic bishops at the White House, specifically Bishop John Hughes of New York. On July 5, 1846, they met to discuss introducing Catholic chaplains into the U.S. Army.[18] Within six weeks two Jesuit priests, John McElroy, S.J., sixty-four, of Washington, D.C., and Anthony Rey, S.J., thirty-nine, of Georgetown College, joined Gen. Zachary Taylor's American Army, which had only one chaplain assigned, an Episcopal minister, John McCarty. Chaplain Rey, former vice president of Georgetown College, bravely entered into battle at Monterrey, Mexico, on September 20–23, 1846.

Under General Taylor, the commander of the Army of Occupation, a force of U.S. Regulars, Volunteers, and Texas Rangers laid siege to the city of Monterrey, in northeastern Mexico. Despite having no prior or preparatory military training, Chaplain Rey was there on the battlefield to care for the more than 368 wounded U.S. soldiers and deliver last rites to the dying during the bloody battle that saw mounting American losses. Four months after the battle, in January 1947, Father Rey went outside of the U.S. garrison in northeastern Mexico to minister to locals, despite warnings of danger, and was killed by Mexican guerrillas. Fr. Anthony Rey, a Jesuit of "old school" aggressive practice of the Catholic faith, is remembered as the first Roman Catholic chaplain to die in service of the U.S. Army.[19]

Father John McElroy, a much older man, did not like Mexico, Mexican clergy, or the lower-class Mexicans he found living around him. As a result, he served in garrison, ministering to hospitalized Americans, until his health began to fail, and he left for the United States. At the request of the bishops in Boston, Fr. McElroy founded Boston College in 1858, with classes beginning in 1864. Fr. John McElroy died in 1877, the oldest priest in the United States and the oldest Jesuit in the world.[20]

After the Mexican surrender and terms after the Battle of Monterrey, the Americans took note of the Irish members of the Mexican Army who marched out of the city under arms, flags waving along with the Mexicans. Something must be wrong! Many of the American Irish soldiers recognized the Mexican Irish as deserters from their own American Army. Was the proselytizing so successful that the Americans had something to worry about? According to Robert Ryan Miller, some Mexican parish priests were intent upon proselytizing Irish and German Catholic soldiers into the Mexican Army. Stories abound of soldiers who testified that Mexican priests attempted to convince them to defect. Perhaps the most important of this group was Fr. Eugene McNamara, an Irish priest named as a principal conspirator to take soldiers from Scott's army to the Mexican Army. An Irishman, McNamara felt a strong loyalty to the Mexican side in the war and counseled with high Mexican officials on ways to entice Irish in the American Army to switch sides. The Americans wanted to prosecute this priest, but he eluded capture and returned to Britain in 1848.[21] Another priest was captured and charged by the Americans, Fr. Pasqual Postrato. Supposedly, he attempted to remove several Irish deserters to the interior of Mexico; however, the name he used on his passport was different, and the case was probably dropped.[22]

The St. Patrick's Battalion served the Mexicans very well. As an artillery unit, they stood their ground and forced the Americans to give up many lives to take their positions. This was especially true in the Battle of Churubusco at the convent of San Angel. The Mexicans put more than 1,400 defenders into the convent; of the more than two hundred San Patricios, some served as infantrymen and held their position until overrun, while others serviced three of the garrison's seven cannons. After the cannons were taken by the Americans, they turned them on the convent. In all, the San Patricios lost nearly two companies of officers and men. Eighty-five were taken prisoner; seventy-two were accused of desertion from the U.S. Army.[23] Gen. William Worth reported, "Of prisoners we paused to make but few; although receiving the surrender of many, to disarm and pass them was deemed sufficient. Among whom, however, are secured twenty-seven deserters from our own army, arrayed in the most tawdry Mexican uniforms. Here wretches served the guns—the use of which they had been taught in our own service—and with fatal effect, upon the persons of their former comrades."[24] After Churubusco, peace efforts began, but to little or no avail. The war was not won yet, and the Mexicans believed there was still hope. There was no hope, however, for the captured San Patricio soldiers, deserters all.

Robert Ryan Miller explains that each San Patricio soldier had the chance to present his defense at his court-martial, and he names several, such as Pvt. John McDonald, who claimed he was dragooned by the Mexicans. Pvt. Martin Landon's story was much the same, as was Patrick Dalton's. Few of these tales were accepted by the American court's members, intent in their minds to enforce military law: soldiers will not desert, especially after war has been declared, when it becomes a capital offense. Of course, the most interesting trial was that of John Riley, the supposed leader of the San Patricio Battalion. The question was what to do with Reilly. Execute him along with his comrades, all guilty of desertion? Or punish him severely but less than death? Gen. Winfield Scott, himself a lawyer and a long-serving officer, came up with the compromise solution: he confirmed capital punishment for fifty San Patricios, pardoned five men, and reduced the sentences of fifteen others.[25] These reduced sentences seem completely outrageous to us today, but they were not in 1847: fifty lashes "well laid on the bare back" and a hot iron branded with a *D* for deserter, some on the right cheek, others on the hip; then at war's end, just prior to release, the Army shaved their heads and took all their money. The whippings were administered in the San Angel cathedral plaza. Reilly spent the rest of the war, nine months, at hard labor. According to Thomas J. Craughwell, "The day he was released, several Mexican generals came to the prison to meet him. They brought him a horse and a gift. Surrounded by his prison guards, Reilly opened it. He pulled off his filthy prison shirt and put on the tunic of a colonel in the Mexican army. Then he mounted the horse and rode off with the generals."[26]

After the whippings and brandings, the Army executed sixteen condemned San Patricios by hanging.[27] There were thirty condemned San Patricios remaining to be dealt with. Two days after the executions at San Angel, Col. William Selby Harney made the last batch of deserters meet their fate. Looking back at his obituary, it is fair to say that Harney was a cruel man, malevolent in his nature, especially toward those who received punishment. He also had a flare for the theatrical in that he coordinated the executions with the lowering of the Mexican and the raising of the American flag over the Chapultepec Castle. When Lt. George Pickett raised the American flag, the hangman dropped the San Patricios to their deaths.[28]

Without a doubt, the Mexican-American War was a triumph for the United States and a series of tragedies for Mexico. Thousands of deaths took away nearly an entire generation of young Mexican and American men who could not be replaced, as all wars do, and left even more widows and orphans. Yet most historians agree that Mexico played a role in the tensions that erupted into a bloody war, too. Political and financial chaos did not help matters. Yet many people in Mexico were sympathetic to the foreigners in their army and believed that the American invaders were nothing short of barbarians; some remember this war as if it were fought yesterday. Amazingly, to Americans the San Patricio Battalion remains an honored unit.[29]

Jesuit fathers Rey and McElroy, the two chaplains called to mind here, are all but forgotten. Also, it is fair to remind readers that the numbers of Irish deserters were minuscule compared to the thousands of Irishmen serving honorably in the United States Army at the time. Thus, it is easy to overstate the significance of the San Patricio Battalion in the Mexican-American War, but it would be completely unfair to deal with its issues without them or the two Catholic chaplains. Charles W. Hedrick summarizes the issues and problems that the U.S. Army and its chaplains faced: "It would be too much to expect that chaplains of the mid-nineteenth century would have been as effective as chaplains in the modern Army. Indeed the Chaplaincy as a professional Army Branch does not emerge until 1920. But then during the Mexican-American War neither did the U.S. have a truly professional army. But the tragedy is that there were virtually no chaplains, even though there were numerous volunteers to serve! The civilian ministers who did serve, served with distinction and their ministry was appreciated by the soldier."[30] The Mexican-American War was indeed a historical, if not a social, anomaly in American history. There were ten battles all told, and the Americans won all ten. The American Army fought well, and it gave birth to a tradition of northern and southern passion for victory in the field. It is also the second and last war in which the Army went into combat without chaplains.

Three

─·≫≪·─

Civil War

A War against God

*The President, Commander-in-Chief of the Army and Navy,
desires and enjoins the orderly observation of the Sabbath by the
officers and men in the military service.*
—Abraham Lincoln, Executive Order, November 27, 1861

THE MIDDLE OF THE NINETEENTH CENTURY had remnants of 1840s' Know-Nothings, especially among the evangelical chaplains in both armies, North and South, but the immigrants, especially the Irish and Germans, made their own presence and cultural influence felt as well. One result is that the chaplaincy of the Civil War era resembled what it evolved into in our own time, the beginning of the twenty-first century. However, during the Civil War, the term "Chaplain" did not represent an established military rank; rather, it represented a title, not yet a corps in the military services, as it is today. A chaplain's rank was relative, a kind of brevet or temporary rank that fixed precedent at official and social functions; however, the mandate to perform spiritual and humanitarian service for soldiers or sailors never changed.

Although a chaplain may have worn the insignia, for example, of a major, and exercised prerogatives pertaining to the rank, it did not necessarily command the pay of a major.[1] Both the Union and the Confederate governments paid their military chaplains: The Federal government paid them a captain of cavalry's month's wage plus a food and forage allowance. The Confederates were more reserved. They paid their chaplains eighty-five dollars at first then reduced it to fifty dollars, which lasted only a short time until they raised it to eighty dollars per month, the same as a second lieutenant in the Confederate army.

Most certainly, there were cultural leftovers from previous wars: for example, some chaplains continued to bear arms and led troops in battle. Chaplain J. P. McMullen, CSA, was killed at the Battle of Resaca, Georgia, not far from Chaplain Milton L. Haney, USA, 55th Illinois Volunteer Infantry, whose lifeless hand gripped his musket. However, according to the U.S. Army's history of its chaplain corps, the first and second winners of the Medal of Honor, were Chaplains John M. Whitehead of the 15th Indiana Volunteer Infantry and Francis B. Hall of the 16th New York Volunteer Infantry.[2] This kind of action in battle came to an end in 1863 with the introduction of the Law of Land Warfare to the Union army that made clear that chaplains were "protected personnel" and took their guns away.

The American Civil War is awash in heroic chaplains, North and South, as both armies expanded the fight: Confederate chaplain William Hoge ran the Union blockade to bring English Bibles to Southern soldiers; Chaplain Fr. William Corby gave the first general absolution to Irish soldiers before Pickett's Charge on Gettysburg's third day.[3] Chaplain Charles C. McCabe of the 122nd Ohio Volunteer Infantry refused to leave his wounded at Winchester and became one of the "Winchester Eight" chaplains who were captured on June 15, 1863. He was among the small number of chaplain POWs who worked hard to lift and maintain the morale of the officers in Libby Prison in Richmond, Virginia.[4] McCabe and some other POWs created the "University of Libby Prison" where the POWs taught other prisoners French, Spanish, Latin, Greek, rhetoric, English grammar, arithmetic, geometry, and other studies. Chaplain McCabe became fluent in French in Libby.[5]

Only two of the Winchester Eight chaplains ever returned to their units after their captivity: Edward C. Ambler, 67th Pennsylvania Volunteers, and Ebenezer Walker Brady, 116th Ohio Volunteers. The rest of the chaplains entered hospitals and were discharged medically before the end of the war. Chaplain McCabe returned to duty briefly, but he resigned on January 8, 1864, due to his inability to recover his health. He did not leave war service, however; rather, he became a delegate of the U.S. Christian Commission that served the Union army in the field religiously by providing Bibles and religious tracts to the troops.[6] Chaplain Charles A. Humphreys remained behind in Virginia to bury a trooper of the 2nd Massachusetts Cavalry killed by a Confederate sharpshooter when John Singleton Mosby's Partisan Rangers arrived on the scene. Taken POW and not permitted to bury his man, the chaplain was forced by the Rangers to walk thirty miles next to his mount. He was then sent to the officers' prison in Charleston, Castle Pinckney, for three months before he was exchanged. Chaplain Humphreys despised the politics of the South and believed that the enemies of the federal government at home and in the field were equally guilty of treason. He remained angry, and like many others he rejoined his unit after release.[7]

Jewish chaplains, African American chaplains, and American Indian chaplains stepped forward to serve their men in the Army, too. The Civil War found its chaplains improving in quality and sense of mission as the war progressed. Great revivals swept the armies, and the role of chaplains increased and intensified as the war progressed from 1861 to 1865. Behind the wire, they functioned as morale builders, teachers, and curricula builders. On the battlefield, sixty-six Union chaplains perished; twenty-five Confederates met the same fate.[8]

The Navy's chaplain situation was different from the Army's. On November 14–15, 1861, at a national convention of the YMCA, the Christian Common was formed with the purpose of assisting chaplains in ministering to the spiritual and temporal welfare of both Army and Navy men. On March 8, 1862, Chaplain John L. Lenhart became the first Navy chaplain to be killed in action on board the USS *Cumberland* when the ship was rammed and sunk by the CSS *Virginia* at Hampton Roads, Virginia. On April 26, 1862, Admiral Farragut issued the earliest known order regarding the display of the church pennant on board a warship. On July 14, 1862, Congress forbade the use of alcohol on board Navy ships, something advocated by the Navy's chaplains for a long time. On July 17, 1862, the Navy changed the rules regarding church attendance. No longer was there any mention of mandatory attendance of daily morning or evening prayer services on board ship. On November 15, 1862, President Abraham Lincoln issued a general order encouraging the observance of the Sabbath by the officers and men of the Army and Navy. In 1863 former U.S. Navy chaplain Joseph Perl Bell Wilmer was arrested for attempting to bring medical supplies and Bibles back to the Confederacy from England. Confined briefly in Old Capitol Prison in Washington, D.C., he was released quickly because his claim that he was on a mission of mercy was accepted by Union authorities. In 1865 *Navy Regulations* outlined the duties of the chaplain: hold divine services, visit the sick, instruct the men in the principles of Christian education, arrange for the secular education of the young men on board ship, and report quarterly his activities to the commanding officer with a condensed report at the end of the year.[9]

During the Civil War, Union men had to apply for the position of chaplain to the regiment in which they wanted to serve. The regiment's colonel then had to approve, and the appointment was then approved or not by the War Department in Washington, D.C. The chaplain then received a direct commission at the captain-of-cavalry level, which included base pay plus food and a forage allowance for his horse(s). The chaplain was expected to wear a modified uniform devoid of any rank insignia, and his orders remained vague.[10] For this, each chaplain had to report the moral and religious condition of his regiment and conduct religious services in accordance with his denomination.[11]

Some denominations like the Baptists and Jews do not require clergy to conduct religious services because they do not have a sacramental system that requires clergy to conduct services exclusively. Catholic soldiers and sailors understood this and demanded that their chaplains say Mass, hear confessions and grant absolution, give last rites, and bury the dead when and where necessary. Senior American Catholic bishops were reluctant to release their diocesan priests for military duty, in part because it took a certain kind of manliness to handle these sorts of human challenges, to say nothing of the real possibility of being shot dead or wounded in battle. More important, the bishops believed that they needed the available priests to serve their growing flocks at home and not be wasted, so they thought, in the military services. Thus, it is fair to say that the Roman Catholic hierarchy in the North was not especially helpful in supplying dependable clergy for the military services' chaplaincies during the Civil War. They were always happy to rid themselves of any "problem" priests, but they were determined to keep whom they considered the good ones close to home. There were exceptions, however. One was Father Paul Gillen, who served early in the war as an unofficial chaplain in the Army of the Potomac. He got on well with Gen. George McClellan, who gave him a horse and permission to serve his Catholic troops. Gen. Ulysses Grant would have none of McClellan's odd behaviors and first arrested and then kicked Fr. Gillen—still serving as a civilian—out of camp. Finally, Gillen accepted a military commission and served as chaplain to the 170th New York Infantry and served until the end of the war.[12]

Politicians and military leaders took more important roles in recruiting Catholic clergy by often turning away diocesan clergy and recruiting members of religious orders for the Chaplain Corps. Fortunately for the Union army, these orders were based at universities, not in dioceses that coveted the number of priests they had at their command. The Order of the Holy Cross, a French order at the College of Notre Dame, provided seven priests as chaplains in the Union army; the Jesuits at Georgetown College also provided a good number of chaplains. But, of the 2,300 regimental chaplains who served in the Union army, only forty were Catholic priests, not a good number for the growing number of its Catholic soldiers.[13]

The question here is not the numbers: forty is significantly more than one during the Revolutionary War and two who served as roving Catholic chaplains for thousands of Catholic soldiers in the Mexican-American War; rather, it is the fundamental religious relationship between the Catholic chaplains and their soldiers, both officers and enlisted men, that takes precedence. Of all the issues, nothing is more important for Catholic soldiers awaiting battle than the Sacrament of Reconciliation, called confession by practicing Catholics. Normally, it takes place one-on-one, confessor (priest) and penitent. In the field, hundreds, if not thousands, of men waited for battle, and often the clergy had no time for one-on-one confessions. The Catholic chaplains devised a solution by necessity: general absolution, the forgiveness of sin with the promise of normal confession at a later time. In other words, Catholic soldiers could go into battle completely at peace with God and themselves, what they called the State of Grace. The list of priests who gave general absolution during the Civil War is impressive.[14] Catholic chaplains also tended to their men during battle, regardless of what was needed at the time: absolution for the living and dying, burying the dead later, and making sure the wounded got to a hospital.

Yet religious competition, say nothing of outright bigotry, got in the way of religious harmony. On the one hand, there was a considerable amount of competition for parishioners among chaplains in the Civil War. The majority of military clergy were recruited from Protestant denominations, and there were just not enough Catholic clergy serving as chaplains in the Union army to make a huge difference. Prejudice remained strong in American society, as did the effects of the Civil War on some soldiers.[15] Catholic chaplains had to battle with Protestant commanding officers often to permit them to say Mass or to gain the resources to procure and use religious reading or religious materials, including rosaries, medals, and prayer books. Reading Protestant anti-Catholic religious materials for these men was simply unacceptable. On the other hand, interactions between chaplains of opposing Christian denominations often caused a personal mutual respect among chaplains that can only take place through shared dangers and shared hardships. For example, one can picture two chaplains warming themselves on a cold, wet December night under a wet blanket, one a Jesuit, the other a Congregationalist from New England. Mutual suffering generated mutual respect such as praise of a priest's bravery under fire from a Know-Nothing commanding officer after he observed what the Catholic chaplain did for the wounded and dying. In short, such interactions often reduced the hostility between religious rivals; hence, this sort of ecumenism might well have begun the spirit of reconciliation that most folks wanted after the war concluded.

The ministers and priests in the Confederate chaplain service faced a totally different set of difficulties than their Union counterparts. At the war's beginning in 1861, Jefferson Davis and other Confederate authorities negated any sort of government-sponsored chaplaincy. Instead, the Confederates expected the major denominations to select their own clergy and send them as volunteer military chaplains. Little attention was paid to qualifications, education, affiliation, or standing. Whereas Union pay was the same as a captain of cavalry, the Confederates paid their chaplains only as second lieutenants, the lowest-ranked officers in the army. Thus, it is reasonable to believe that the position of chaplain was not held in high regard or esteem. Gardner H. Shattuck Jr. states that this sort of treatment rankled the chaplains, and "many were tempted to quit the army altogether, and by midpoint of the war only about half the Confederate regiments had any chaplains."[16] Yet the major Protestant denominations in the South stepped forward, including the Southern Baptist Convention, the Presbyterians, the Methodists, the Lutherans, and the Episcopalians, and thus there was a high degree of participation of churches. Many sent "missionary chaplains" to Confederate units in the South, civilian volunteer ministers rather than army clergy who were actual members of the military units. Herman Norton in *Rebel Religion* (1961) gives us some fascinating numbers to consider: Southern Protestants from 16,000 churches outnumbered Roman Catholics from 2,543 churches about 5,160,000 to 124,000. Among Protestants, Methodist membership stood highest at about 2,000,000 with the Baptists not far behind. Presbyterians were next with over 700,000, while Episcopalians trailed with approximately 193,000. There were about 113,000 Disciples of Christ in the South during the Civil War, and 10,000 members of the German Reformed Church.

Herman Norton notes too that there were more than thirty Catholic chaplains in the Confederate army compared to more than five hundred Protestants. The Presbyterians, a smaller denomination, furnished as many chaplains as did the Baptists. The Episcopalians furnished sixty-five, and about twenty-five came from Protestant groups other than these four.[17]

We must never forget, however, that religion, much like nearly every cultural aspect of life, was fundamentally different in the North and South in 1861–65. The United States was truly two different countries at this time, yet both sides practiced religion intensely. Revivalism was perhaps one of the most powerful tools that evangelicalism had, then and now.[18] It is an act of renewal of mind and spirit, rebirth in the form of rebaptism, and the bestowal of grace directly from God Almighty. In the words of William Bennett to a minister who headed the Soldiers Tract Association of the Methodist Episcopal Church, revivals were "blessed works of grace" that not only transformed the army into a "school of Christ" in wartime, but also helped ease the pain of military defeat for Southern whites during the Reconstruction period.[19] "The Fighting Parson," Southern Baptist J. William Jones, served in the Confederate army from 1861 to 1865 and became a missionary chaplain in A. P. Hill's Corps, Army of Northern Virginia. After the war, he became chaplain general to the United Confederate Veterans and the secretary of the Southern Historical Association. As the founder of the "Lost Cause" myth, his book *Christ in the Camp* (1904) made the point that robust religion creates a robust soldier. Although Jones' Lost Cause belief remains a hotly debated issue among Civil War scholars today, his belief in the relationship between religion and soldiering demands consideration.

The laws of war changed radically during the Civil War, and some of the changed rules addressed the chaplain issue. Traditionally, any soldier, chaplains included, bearing arms and taken prisoner during or after a battle was considered a prisoner of war. As a POW, the soldier is protected from arbitrary punishment, execution, and ill treatment. Prior to the Union's issuance of General Order 100, the Laws of Land Warfare, the U.S. Army depended on the Articles of War to which both sides, Union and Confederate, agreed. In 1863, however, the world turned upside down. The new rules became more than a tradition; they became law. As far as chaplains were concerned, General Order 100 stated in Article 53: "The enemy's chaplains, officers of the medical staff, apothecaries, hospital nurses and servants, if they fall into the hands of the American Army, are not prisoners of war, unless the commander has reasons to retain them. In this latter case; or if, at their own desire, they are allowed to remain with their captured companions, they are treated as prisoners of war, and may be exchanged if the commander sees fit."[20] What is important to notice here is that a chaplain must indicate to the enemy force, that is, his potential captors, that he desires to remain with his troops. He is not a POW by nature of his uniform or anything else. On June 16, 1862, Gen. Braxton Bragg, commander of the Confederate Western Department, wrote to Union major general Henry H. Halleck, USA, commander of U.S. Forces at Corinth, Mississippi, and indicated that he believed the release of chaplains to be a routine event: "I have also to suggest that chaplains should be released if captured with the least delay practicable."[21] Unfortunately, both sides were suspicious of captured chaplains and kept them as POWs for a while, not terribly long, though. Scholars of the Confederacy often note that although Northern officials wanted their chaplains freed as soon as possible, others feared that their individual and collective influence among the prisoners became problematic. Col. William Hoffman, the Union commissary of prisoners, believed that chaplains were the most dangerous officers he held.[22] Thus, holding chaplains was more a matter of fear rather than military law.

Although much has changed in international law from 1863 to the present era, this provision has not. A chaplain is a noncombatant and cannot be made into a POW unless he requests that status in order to remain with his men. In subsequent wars, especially in World War II and Korea, chaplains often requested an enemy force to grant them the status of POW in order to remain with their men. Granting that request and honoring it are different and dangerous matters entirely.

Aside from the laws of war, we need to ascertain whether we are dealing with saints or sinners in the Civil War chaplain corps. For this we turn to the writing of Bell Irwin Wiley, perhaps the most honestly critical historian of the chaplain issue. He reminds his readers that his research revealed that civil warriors were not as religious or as deferential as some historians would make us believe. "Holy Joe" was the term used most commonly for chaplains of all religious denominations, and it was not all that respectful. America's civil warriors did make serious demands on their chaplains. First, the chaplain had to be where the soldiers were; second, they had to be brave but not necessarily heroic in battle. Physical courage was required, and good chaplains were those clergy who shared the hardships and dangers of the battlefield. Any sort of feelings of superiority that a chaplain might show was rejected immediately.[23]

Who could be a chaplain? The federal government required a chaplain to be a graduate of a seminary of some kind and enforced by the religious denomination he belonged to. According to Wiley, these requirements came from the Union's indiscriminate commissioning of chaplains early in the war. In order to identify chaplains, Union regulations allowed them to embellish their uniforms with a "US" in silver inside a wreath on their hats and some herringbone braid around their buttonholes. The Confederate government was not so precise or demanding but not more respectful to ministers in general, either. The chaplains wore a gray suit with a Maltese cross on their collars, nothing more to identify them as chaplains.[24] Whether they were considered as officers depended, really, on when they entered chaplain service. Early in the war, the Union army considered them as merely a kind of auxiliary officer. It is fair to say that they were considered neither fish nor fowl officially but were considered officers in practice. The Confederates, especially Jefferson Davis, had little respect for chaplains in general and made no provision for them in the Confederate army at first.

Wiley does state his position regarding the quality of Civil War chaplains in general, and it was not good: "The quality of Civil War chaplains was poor, though many notable exceptions were to be found on both sides. The most accomplished and experienced ministers were reluctant to abandon the security and congeniality of their civilian positions for the hardships of chaplaincies." He went on to state, "If the more outstanding clerics ministered to soldiers, they preferred to serve as occasional evangelists or short-term missionaries representing benevolent or ecclesiastical organizations. In these capacities they could satisfy the urge to do something for God and country in a time of crisis without abandoning responsibilities and comforts of home. Scores of eminent divines both North and South availed themselves of the opportunity to visit the armies and returned to regale their parishioners with. accounts of their glorious participation in the triumph of righteousness over the enormous sins of camp." Complaints abound about the sins and misdeeds of chaplains in both armies early in the war, but as the war dragged on battle after battle, the religious aspect of war, battles, men's lives, and eternity took on a quite different hue.

The quality of chaplains improved, too. Wiley points out, "Many chaplaincies throughout the war were held by good men, impelled by lofty motives and thoroughly devoted to the cause of righteousness. The devoted chaplains shared fully the hardships and dangers of field service, were tactical and discreet in their utterances, set good examples in conduct, and in general sought to promote the physical and spiritual well-being of the organizations to which they were assigned." Wiley gets even more specific: "The devoted chaplains, far from seeking shelter when battle was imminent, went forward with their units, blessed the men as they prepared for the assault, performed the last rites over the dead, wrote messages of condolence to the home folks, and forwarded personal effects."[25] From the era of the Civil War to today's Army, this is what chaplains do, nothing more, nothing less. Complete devotion to duty, integrity, goodness, and a sincere interest in spiritual matters are all qualities that are highly appreciated by American soldiers, sailors, Marines, and airmen, then and now. As historian Warren B. Armstrong stated, "It is true that individual chaplains were the subject of sharp criticism from time to time during the war, but a more balanced view of their work reveals that they actually helped to establish the chaplaincy as a permanent and continuing institution in the American military tradition."[26]

There were indeed some chaplains whose service distinguished them from the many who served honorably on both sides. Fr. John Bannon, an Irish immigrant, belonged to a parish in Missouri at the war's onset, and he immediately volunteered as a civilian chaplain for the Irish volunteers in the Missouri Confederate militia that established Camp Jackson near St. Louis. On July 4, 1861, a battery of Union artillery and infantry surrounded the camp, and the Union commander demanded an unconditional surrender. Thus ended Missouri's only formal Confederate force, and Fr. Bannon was made a POW with the rest of the militia soldiers. But the victors dallied quite a bit, and many of the local civilians, armed of course, gathered and hovered on the outskirts of Camp Jackson. A shot rang out from somewhere, no one knew from where or whom, but most probably it came from one of the armed Confederate sympathizers, and all hell broke loose. Hundreds of civilians were hit by the Federal bullets, and Fr. Bannon watched in helpless rage while his people were shot down. About six hundred pro-Confederate militiamen were then marched to a large warehouse where paroles were prepared, and Fr. Bannon, along with the others, took the parole: "We, the undersigned, do pledge our words as gentlemen that we will not take up arms nor serve in any military capacity against the United States, during the present civil war. This parole to be returned upon our surrendering ourselves, at any time, as prisoners of war. While we make this pledge with the full intention of observing it, we hereby protest against the justice of its exaction." [27]

After a considerable number of escape attempts from St. Louis and Archbishop Peter Kenrick's command, Fr. Bannon went into the Confederate army under Gen. Sterling Price. In September 1863, Judah P. Benjamin, Confederate secretary of state, asked Fr. Bannon to undertake a diplomatic mission to Ireland to convince the Irish that the United States was never friendly to the Irish and that the North was simply using its Irish immigrants as cannon fodder in the war. Immigration slowed, although it never totally ceased, but after the Union conscription laws called up Irish workers in the eastern cities, passion for the Union cause that identified the Irish early in the war cooled significantly. Bannon attempted to return to America after his mission in 1864, but the Northern Naval Blockade prevented it. As a result, Bannon remained in Ireland, joined the Jesuits, and died in 1913. [28]

Two other Roman Catholic chaplains served in unusual missions as well as Bannon: Fr. Emeran Bliemel and Fr. Abram Ryan. Fr. Bliemel, a German immigrant to Pennsylvania, served a parish in Tennessee before the war. After hostilities began, Bliemel joined the 10th Tennessee Regiment as its chaplain. He died attempting to give last rites to a dying soldier with the 4th Kentucky. Fr. Abram Ryan survived the war and after it wrote some of the most stirring patriotic poetry of the era. His most famous poem was titled "The Conquered Banner":

> Furl that banner, softly, slowly;
> Treat it gently—it is holy
> For it droops above the dead;
> Touch it not—unfold it never;
> Let it drop there, furled forever.—
> For its people's hopes are fled.

After Fr. Ryan's death, the citizens of Mobile erected a statue, and he was the only Confederate chaplain so honored.[29]

Father Joseph J. O'Hagan, S.J., a native of Ireland, became chaplain of the 73rd New York Volunteer Infantry from Manhattan's East Side, a rough area indeed. Chaplain O'Hagan was captured during the Peninsular Campaign and paroled back to his men. He then served at the battles of Chancellorsville and later at Gettysburg. After a brief stay at the Jesuit house in Fredericksburg, Maryland, to complete his spiritual formation, Fr. O'Hagan returned to the army and marched with his men to Richmond in 1865.

Charles T. Quintard went to Memphis from Atlanta in 1851 to teach at the medical school. He also became an Episcopalian priest in 1854. When the war broke out, he was serving at the Church of the Advent in Nashville, and he became a full-fledged chaplain from there. In the field, Chaplain Quintard tended to both body and soul of the dead and wounded. He served until the war's end and became the perfect chaplain, what one man would call "incarnations of their theologies" and their creeds "no moral elaborations." No chaplain could ask for more than that! He was ordained bishop of Tennessee after the war and received several honors for his medical work.[30]

The question of status remained a problem during the Civil War. Both sides recognized that chaplains were not POWs per se if they were captured, but neither side was totally certain what these men really were: soldiers or noncombatants? More in the South than in the North, chaplains sometimes bore arms. Called "Fighting Parsons," they were certainly combatants, although it was argued that this tradition went back to the Revolutionary War, and many were killed or wounded in battle. Chaplain John Granberry was hit twice, as was Edward Hudson. Chaplain M. Page of the 32nd Georgia Regiment was wounded, and George Smith, another Georgia chaplain, was shot through the neck at the battle of South Mountain. After the fight at Gettysburg, twelve Confederate chaplains were held prisoner at Fort McHenry in Baltimore.[31]

Both sides declared that chaplains, akin to medical personnel, were noncombatants and should not be kept as POWs. Even Gen. Thomas "Stonewall" Jackson believed that chaplains ought to be noncombatants. A policy recognizing chaplains as noncombatants was initiated by a Confederate General Order dated July 1, 1862, and thirty days later the Union reciprocated. This did not mean, however, that all was well or clear for that matter. On April 27, 1863, the Federal authorities issued an order that made it possible to detain captured Confederate chaplains for certain "justifiable reasons," but by July 1863 the North decided that the "cause for holding chaplains had been removed and the original policy was reinstated."[32]

Chaplain Henry Clay Trumbull of the 10th Connecticut Volunteer Infantry was taken prisoner, by accident he claimed, after an action at Battery Wagner near Charleston, South Carolina, in the summer of 1863. His unit was on its way to relieve the 54th Massachusetts USCT, the now famous black infantry regiment that first stormed Battery Wagner.[33] He believed the major of the 10th Connecticut who told him that an armistice had been established to tend to the dead and wounded. However, he was mistaken; only specific areas were agreed upon for the wounded to be brought and tended to. No real armistice had been established, and Chaplain Trumbull and his friend Henry Camp wandered into some Confederates who immediately took them to their officers. Of course, Chaplain Trumbull believed there had been some mistake. The Confederates, on the other hand, believed they had caught some Yankee spies and were not about to turn them loose. Instead, they were sent to Charleston for interrogation and incarceration. In his prison journal, he noted from the book of Jeremiah, "Do not weep for the dead but weep continually for the one who goes away; for he will never return or see his native land but in the place where they led him captive, there he will die and not see this land again" (22:10, 12).[34] At Charleston Chaplain Trumbull and Henry Camp went before Confederate general Beauregard who ordered them to a POW hospital, where Trumbull witnessed several surgeons from Charleston working diligently on the Union wounded. Naturally, the chaplain did his work praying with and for these terribly wounded prisoners. Shortly thereafter, Trumbull and a Union surgeon, Dr. Luck, were taken from the Charleston City Jail to the Richlands Military Prison (for officers) in Columbia, South Carolina (also known as Castle Pinckney). It was there in Richlands that Trumbull waited for exchange.

He notes that he and his companions were well treated at Richlands, that his chief jailer, the captain of the guard, was a Christian man, and that they were guarded by respectful Confederate veterans who had seen combat and were recovering from wounds. "Yes," Trumbull wrote, "it seems odd to preach as a prisoner to fellow prisoners, with a guard standing over me, his rifle loaded and bayonet fixed." True, they suffered from the usual mosquitoes, fleas, and bedbugs common to all Civil War prisons North and South alike, but they had access to money and extra food that they purchased in the local market. On September 1, 1863, Trumbull witnessed an onrush of refugees from Charleston who believed that their city was about to fall. Watching from his window, Trumbull read his text of the day, again from Jeremiah: "Remove out of the midst of Babylon for lo, I will raise and cause to come up against Babylon an assembly of great nations from the north country; and they shall set themselves in array against her; from thence she shall be taken" (30:3, 10, 11, 33:14, 50:87, 9).[35] As far as Chaplain Trumbull was concerned, he knew the end was close for the Confederacy, but it was better to keep this to himself for the moment. His kind jailers brought him books of Shakespeare so he and his fellow officer POWs could put on plays and parts of plays. They also bought some German books so they could learn the language and played chess, anything to combat a POW's worst enemy, boredom.

In mid-October 1863, Chaplain Trumbull learned that his exchange came through. He had to leave his friend Henry Camp behind, but he had no choice in the matter. He left Richlands Military Prison and went by rail to Richmond, Virginia, where he stayed in Libby Prison (Officers) for two days. On November 11, the Confederates summoned him to leave. He was taken to a landing on the James River, placed on board a steamer flying a white flag, and then taken forty miles downstream to meet a Union flag-of-truce boat at City Point.[36] Chaplain Trumbull, like all loyal officers, North or South, felt a great deal of patriotic pride at this moment, and it is common for returning prisoners to weep for joy at the moment of release. Most did and still do.

Chaplin Henry S. White, Methodist chaplain of the 5th Rhode Island Volunteer Heavy Artillery, captured in 1864 in New Berne, North Carolina, who spent a day in the Andersonville compound before being taken to the officers' camp in Macon, Georgia, recalled how intense the recitation of Psalm 23 was for his men in the prison camp: "Every knee bowed as I offered prayer. Such ability to lay hold of the promises I have seldom felt. Home and loved ones, and dear country, and the sacred flag and its noble defenders, as well as our personal salvation and holiness were timeless that then and there had new inspiration, and *we worshipped God*. There is more heart in any worship, I think, than is usual in civilian life; but with us there were reasons we should be solemn and tender before the Lord." Like Chaplain Trumbull, Chaplain White was exchanged after a few months behind the wire. He wrote of it: "In devotion I poured out my soul to God for the President, for Congress, the army and the navy, and for the country, for ourselves and our loved ones at home. It to me was a peculiar service and a solemn hour." [37]

Dealing with in-house prisoners was a serious difficulty for chaplains, especially preparing a man for execution. During the Civil War, execution was the standard punishment for desertion, and the chaplain had to comfort the prisoner up to his execution. Every effort was made to lead the man to accept the forgiveness of God before his death.[38] Chaplains also tried to visit the sick and wounded in hospitals.

Father James Sheeran, C.SS.R., was a totally devoted Confederate chaplain, although he was an immigrant Irishman. Father Sheeran believed that he had obtained permission to visit his 14th Louisiana wounded in Richmond, but he found himself arrested instead. He wrote about his run-in with Union general Philip Sheridan, who actually ordered his arrest and detention at Fort McHenry in Baltimore. In his personal narrative, one of the few written by a Catholic chaplain after the Civil War,[39] he first addressed his status as a Confederate chaplain to the post commandant of the Union hospital that was also treating Confederate wounded: "You make use of the 'chaplain in the Insurgent Army.' I came into your lines as such; I have been treated as such by your superior officer, and demand to be treated as such by you. I will accept no such title. 'Father, I did not intend to offend you.' So, he wrote the letter and introduced me as chaplain of the 14th Louisiana Regiment of Infantry." Fr. Sheeran was then arrested on the order of General Sheridan. Outraged by what he believed was a betrayal of a promise, Fr. Sheeran wrote,

> I asked what charges were preferred against me. I came into your lines with a pass from one of your major generals and now in violation of it I am deprived of my liberty and about to be cast into a dirty prison. I was soon ushered into an old building where I found some of the most respected citizens of Winchester (Virginia) among them several feeble old men averaging from 60 to 80 years, and some of the most vile characters of the Yankee army confined for criminal offenses.[40]

We can see easily that Fr. Sheehan was not imprisoned with other officers in a POW camp but was treated as a political prisoner by Federal authorities. On November 11, 1864, he was transferred from Winchester, Virginia, to Fort McHenry, Maryland. About his stay there in the stables with other political prisoners, he commented, "The interior of this stable prison presented a dismal and most filthy aspect. The posts which formerly divided the stalls are yet standing and serve as the supports of another platform raised some four feet from the ground. These were also used as sleeping apartments. At the extreme end of the building they had already fixed up a bunk for me, and as I entered they kindly led me to my quarters and I gave my bunk the title 'Stall No. 1.'"[41]

He actually wrote a letter to the press dated November 12, 1864, in which he rewrote his note in which he castigates General Sheridan severely: "Let it be known to the Catholics of the United States that General Sheridan has gained another victory, not over the defenseless women and children of the valley, but by throwing a Catholic priest into a dirty prison to be the companion of drunken and disorderly soldiers, and this, too, when some of his own Catholic soldiers are dying without the sacraments."[42] He was finally released from what was known then as the "Baltimore Bastille" and returned to his unit. He was with Gen. Robert E. Lee at Appomattox and signed his parole agreement on April 14, 1865: "I, Rev. James Sheeran—Prisoner of War, do hereby give my solemn Parole of Honor not to make part in hostilities against the Government of the United States, until properly exchanged, and that I will not do anything directly or indirectly to the detriment or disparagement of the authority of the United States until properly exchanged as aforesaid." [43] So ended Fr. Sheeran's military career as a chaplain in the Confederate army. Apparently, after the war, he had some problems with church authorities and left his order to become a parish priest in New Jersey, where he remained until his death.

Chaplains also received orders to tend to enemy POWs in prison camps. On June 16, 1864, Father Peter Whelan first entered CSM Camp Sumter and witnessed for himself an absolute hell on earth. In May 1864, Father William J. Hamilton, a mission priest in Georgia, had visited the same prison near the town of Anderson in south-central Georgia and had been revolted by the conditions there. He urgently asked Bishop Augustin Verot of Savannah to assign a priest to the prison, known commonly as Andersonville, the most infamous prison camp, North or South, in the Civil War. The bishop sent Father Peter Whelan to tend to Union POWs there.

Father Whelan, also an Irish immigrant to the United States, became chaplain at age sixty to the Montgomery Guards, an Irish company raised in Savannah for the First Georgia Volunteer Regiment. Father Whelan was captured with his unit and transported to Governor's Island, New York. As an officer he was placed in relative comfort in Fort Columbus Barracks. However, he spent virtually none of his time there; rather, he spent most of his waking hours at damp and dark Castle William, where the enlisted men were lodged in poor conditions. He appealed to the priest of Saint Peter's on Barclay in Lower Manhattan for help. The priest responded with food and clothes for the Confederates and arranged for Father Whelan to be paroled. He could have gone home immediately, but he stayed with his men until August 1863, when all of them had been paroled and returned to the Confederacy.

Father Whelan had a good idea of what prison life was like well before his assignment to tend to the Northern POWs. He came to Andersonville in June 1864 and remained for four months during the hottest season of the year and the period of greatest mortality. He ministered to the sick and dying in such heat that he had to cover his head with an umbrella. After his departure in late September, he borrowed $16,000 in Confederate money and purchased ten thousand pounds of flour, which was baked into bread and distributed at the prison hospital.

The prisoners never forgot him, and many recalled him in their memoirs. After the war Father Whelan returned to Savannah and his peacetime duties as a priest. Father Whelan ministered to both imprisoned friend and foe as his brothers in Christ. Father Whelan died on February 6, 1871, at the age of sixty-nine, but in 1869 he gave testimony to Congress about what he saw and experienced in Andersonville.[44] After he died his funeral procession was the longest ever seen in Savannah, and news of his death caused mourning among his admirers, North and South. The marker to the memory of Father Whelan at Andersonville and the Father Peter Whelan Assembly of the Knights of Columbus in Albany, Georgia, attest to the fact that he is not forgotten.

We have not covered the experiences of every chaplain who was captured and sent to a prison camp during the Civil War. We have seen, however, that many chaplains were indeed captured along with their officers and men, North and South. Not many Catholic priests left any significant commentary about their captivities, but a few did. We have also seen that not all were angels of the battlefields, although many were. What we did see were some fundamental changes taking place in American society. The Protestants were still the majority of the population North and South, and it was indeed their war. Yet there were major inroads of Catholic immigrants from Ireland and Germany from the 1840s through the late 1850s that required official federal attention to their religious needs. It was surely their fight. After the war, Brig. Gen. Joshua Lawrence Chamberlain, USV, noted one observation he made was that war made good men better and bad men worse. Embellishing Chamberlain and rephrasing him in religious terms, Chaplain White, one of the most elegant writers of his era, encapsulated the feelings of many of his colleagues at the end of his captivity and the end of the Civil War in 1865: "Was the gospel a vast and immutable truth? Was there a heaven, a God? Are these commotions his work; and through and beyond them is there good for man; is there glory for Jesus? Yes. I saw it all and rejoiced."[45]

Four

—·»} {«·—

1898 to World War I

Change during the Wars in Between

Prisoners of war shall enjoy complete liberty in the exercise of their religion, including attendance at the services of whatever Church they may belong to.

—The Hague Convention, 1899 and 1907

BETWEEN 1865 AND 1941, the period between the Civil War and World War II, a great deal took place to solidify the role of chaplains in the American armed services. The Army and Navy expanded and contracted depending upon national and international politics. There is one difference from past wars, however: enemies took no American chaplains as POWs either in the 1898 war in Cuba against Spain or the later counterinsurgency war in the Philippines or during World War I in Europe. This does not mean that the Chaplain Corps disappeared or was silent or nonextant. It became smaller and changed considerably to fit the circumstances in which the United States found itself. This chapter will focus on how the chaplaincy as an institution changed, or, perhaps, functioned as a bridge, so that it could evolve into something new and useful for the next series of America's wars.

The Articles of War of the United States in 1806 said virtually nothing about chaplains except Article 4 that said if they absented themselves from their units for any length of time, they could be fined or dismissed from the Army: "Every chaplain, commissioned in the army or armies of the United States, who shall absent himself from the duties assigned him (excepting in cases of sickness or leave of absence) shall, on conviction thereof before a court martial, be fined not exceeding one month's pay, besides the loss of his pay during his absence; or be discharged, as the said court martial shall judge proper."[1] Did this provision in military law mean anything? It surely set the precedent in 1806 that chaplains were military personnel under orders despite the unmilitary nature of their profession.

If one considers religion and pacifism to be one and the same, one misunderstands what an Army or Navy chaplain is and does. From the Continental army to the nation's contemporary wars, it is clear that the chaplain was no longer a civilian, and the option of being a pacifist no longer was acceptable. True, chaplains in the Revolution wore no specific uniforms, nor did they during the War of 1812 or the Mexican-American War, but they did during the Civil War, and it was the uniform that protected them from capture before 1863 and during capture after it. The Articles of War defined what was not lawful for officers and enlisted personnel, the nature of courts-martial, and what could be given as punishment. It was not a code of conduct or a prescription of any sort. The U.S. military services lived under these Articles of War in various forms until 1951 when the Uniform Code of Military Justice replaced them. There are other sets of rules too: the Law of Land Warfare, the various international conventions (The Hague Convention in 1899 and 1907, Geneva Convention in 1929 and 1949, and various protocols), and existing rules of engagement that American armed forces have to obey in armed combat.

Chaplains came in two basic types at this time: post chaplains and regimental chaplains. The job of post chaplain required the priest or minister to ride a circuit of frontier posts in the western frontier, whereas the regimental chaplain stayed with the regiment regardless of where it went in the field. After the Civil War the country looked west, not south, and both white people from the North and the South as well as black freedmen and women from the former Confederacy headed west. As the U.S. Colored Troops demobilized along with most of the volunteer Union army in 1865, the army kept some soldiers and units on as regulars and formed four new regular regiments: the 24th and 25th Infantries and the 9th and 10th Cavalries. Known as the "Buffalo Soldiers," these new units of black soldiers fought the hostile Indians in the Southwest until they were repositioned to fight the Spaniards in Cuba in 1898.[2]

The black chaplains to these new units, all Protestant ministers, included Henry V. Plummer, 9th Cavalry, who was court-martialed in 1887 for "conduct unbecoming," that is, for complaining that black soldiers were treated badly. Chaplain Allen Allensworth served from 1886 to 1906, Theophilus G. Steward served from 1891 to 1907, George W. Prioleau served from 1895 to 1920, and William T. Anderson served from 1897 to 1910. Four years after Chaplain Plummer's dismissal, a black chaplain made it to the top of the chain—at least temporarily. When the 10th Cavalry sailed to Cuba in 1898, Chaplain Anderson was left in charge of Fort Assiniboine in Montana, making him the first black officer to command a U.S. Army post. When his replacement arrived in June, Chaplain Anderson joined his outfit overseas.[3] During this period, the chaplain's extra duties included being schoolmaster to the outpost's children and to those freedmen who wanted to learn to read and write.

The Spanish-American War (1898) was one of the shortest wars in American history, but it was indeed violent. Beginning in Havana Harbor the night that the new battleship *Maine*'s forward magazine exploded from overheated coal bunkers on February 15, 1898, killing 260 of the fewer than 400 American crew members on board, a war against Spain seemed likely. William Randolph Hearst and Joseph Pulitzer made sure that war happened because their yellow journalism pounded the drums of war instead of reporting the truth. Six weeks after the sinking, a naval court of inquiry declared mistakenly that the *Maine* was sunk by a mine planted near her keel. The court placed no blame, but the press did: obviously, the Spanish did it. Later inspections show conclusively that they did not. In fact, the Spanish navy was first on hand to rescue the American survivors, only one-third of the crew, after the blast. The *Maine*'s chaplain, Fr. John P. S. Chidwick, arrived on deck unhurt and saw the horror of his life: dead and wounded men everywhere and a new warship in its death throes. In the spirit of Chaplain Fr. William Corby before the Gettysburg fight, he gave the crew a general absolution and then set about to save as many lives as he could. W. T. Culverius, a naval midshipman on board the *Maine* at the time, wrote, "Chaplain Chidwick was everywhere. He had a word of cheer to the wounded which soothed their pain. Without thought of himself he helped the helpless and he ministered to the dying."[4] The war lasted all of four months but had powerful outcomes. From Spain, the United States gained possession of Guam, Wake Island, and the Philippine Islands in the western Pacific and Puerto Rico in the Caribbean. In the spirit of the times, the United States finally created an empire despite the loud complaints from the Anti-Imperialist League.

Up to that time, the First Geneva Convention (1864) was the only international law regulating combat. It recognized the importance of the American Laws of Land Warfare of 1863 and addressed the treatment of the sick and wounded more than the treatment of POWs in enemy hands and certainly nothing relating to chaplains or religion at all. The next reform inside the U.S. Army was the screening of military chaplains before acceptance for active duty. All this began when the Episcopal Church, unhappy about accusations about poor-quality clergy in the early days of the Civil War, decided that it had to screen those ministers applying for entry into the military services. In 1899 the House of Bishops established precedents for review and approval of Episcopal chaplains applying for active duty in the Regular Army. The Roman Catholic Church did much the same in 1905, the Methodists in 1906, and others followed suit until a review and approval by all the denominations became common practice by World War I.[5]

Prior to the onset of hostilities in Europe in 1914, a period of overt humanitarianism surfaced that from 1864 onward attempted to ameliorate the horrors of war. No one ever wanted to see or experience again what happened to Union POWs at Andersonville, or anything like it elsewhere. Not only must individual nations negotiate workable solutions to the POW problem internally, but the nineteenth century witnessed the coming together of an international community of nations for the first time to make this nearly impossible task a reality among nations. Nicholas II, the czar of Russia, called on all nations to meet in the capital of the Netherlands, The Hague, in 1898 in order to create a document that every nation could agree to. Hence, The Hague Convention of 1899 was born, negotiated, and signed. They met again in 1907 to complete the job.

World War I broke out in August 1914. Known as the Great War at the time, it was a true horror in the field; it would have been much worse without the

POW conventions. Part of The Hague Convention, 1899 and 1907, addressed the capture of chaplains and implied that chaplains were not actual POWs but protected by their uniforms. Article 18 states, "Prisoners of war shall enjoy every latitude in the exercise of their religion, including attendance at their own church services, provided only they comply with the regulations for order and police issued by the military authorities."[6] Little did anyone realize that large armies needed a lot of chaplains, who, like their soldiers, were killed, wounded, and taken prisoner of war.

Before World War I, chaplains were appointed to individual regiments. During World War I, the chaplain of the American Expeditionary Force (AEF) coordinated chaplains' activities in the Army; however, when the United States declared war in April 1917, only 72 chaplains served in the Regular Army and 74 served with the National Guard. By the close of the war on November 11, 1918, 2,363 chaplains were in service. The chaos of the American military chaplaincy clearly showed itself. Historians agree that the shipment of 2 million American soldiers to Europe in a relatively short period of time showed how arbitrary the chaplain situation was. The General Headquarters of the AEF had no idea how many chaplains were part of the force, nor what denominations they were, nor in what units they were serving.[7] Gen. John "Black Jack" Pershing, commanding general of the AEF, most certainly refused to put up with this kind of bad administration in his massive command. His first attempt to rectify the situation solicited the services of Episcopalian bishop C. E. Brent, whom Pershing knew from his tour of duty in the Philippines. Brent became a chaplain major in the AEF, and Pershing brought him into his staff. The day of chaplains being on their own was over; now Americans looked to the British for organization and basically copied it.

By 1918 American chaplains had uniforms and rank insignia. Senior chaplains trained and supervised junior chaplains while making sure they had what supplies they needed to do their religious work in the field. In addition to uniforms, chaplains received their own insignia, Roman crosses for Christians and the Tablets of Moses for Jewish chaplains. To make all this easier overseas, two schools came into being at home: the U.S. Army Chaplain School at Fort Monroe, Virginia, and in France at Neuilly-sur Suize for those chaplains who arrived in France with no training at all. Chaplain Brent required that all chaplains submit monthly reports of their religious and pastoral activities. The American chaplaincy came of age.

Chaplains accompanied their units into combat and purposefully attempted to maintain morale and fighting spirit on the front, what is termed the Proximity Principle, which requires chaplains to be close to their soldiers during deployment and battle.[8] They ministered to the dying, as they had in earlier wars, and wrote letters home for the wounded and illiterate soldiers in their units. They also collected and buried the dead, a job that grew too great for the few men assigned to the chaplaincy. Later, in World War II and beyond, this grisly work was assigned to the Quartermaster Corps' Graves Registration Units and remains that way to this day. Chaplains continue to conduct burial services, however.

Early in the American experience in World War I, General Pershing found his force not only in need of soldiers but also in desperate need of Catholic chaplains. He had a total of eight in the entire AEF. The Knights of Columbus informed Pershing that they could supply volunteer Catholic chaplains for his Army in France, and did, Father John DeValles being one of the first. He was severely wounded in combat in 1918, sent home, and finally died of his wounds in 1920, much revered.

No examination of World War I and the American Expeditionary Force would be complete with mention of Father Francis P. Duffy, chaplain of the 69th Infantry Regiment of the New York National Guard. One trip to Times Square drives this home. As one comes out of the subway at Duffy Plaza and looks up, one sees a large bronze statue of a World War I soldier. It is Chaplain Fr. Francis Duffy, or "Fightin' Father Duffy," as the soldiers and the press called him, standing there. Much loved? Yes! Revered? Yes! An exaggeration? No. Fr. Duffy was the "real thing" as far as the New York Irish in the 69th Infantry were concerned. They fought hard, in part, because they had faith in the cause, their God, and their chaplain. By the war's end, the 69th Infantry amassed an impressive combat record: 264 days of combat, 844 dead including poet Joyce Kilmer, and 2,387 wounded; in terms of decorations, the 69th won sixty Distinguished Service Crosses and three Medals of Honor.[9] Very few units could match that record after World War I.[10] Fr. Julius J. Babst of the 2nd Division received two Distinguished Service Crosses for gallantry and two

Croix de Guerres from France and became the most decorated chaplain of the American Army during World War I. He saw action and won the Silver Star at Chateau Thierry as well. This chaplain, like Fr. Duffy, was a true hero, and the U.S. Army used his image and story for recruiting from 1919 to World War II.

After the war, General Pershing became chief of staff, the highest position in the Army at that time, and created the position of chief of chaplains in July 1920. John T. Axton, a Congregational minister, was named first chief of chaplains.[11] The National Defense Act of 1920 formally established the Office of the Chief of Chaplains, and Southern Methodist John Brown Frazier was appointed the first naval chief of chaplains in 1917. The pope appointed Most Rev. Patrick J. Hayes as the first American Catholic military bishop or ordinariate, which became the endorsing agency for Catholic naval chaplains. In 1920 there were 107 chaplains of all faiths on active duty in the Navy. Throughout the military services, a spirit of ecumenism spread, and they moved from being competitors for acquiring communicants to a new respect and love for comrades of differing beliefs. This sort of mutual love and respect survived for the most part and extended into the future, to this day.

In 1949 the Second Geneva Convention was ratified and put into place by most of the belligerents of World War II. Japan signed the convention but failed to ratify it at home, saying that it was more lenient, in fact, than its own rescripts for soldierly behavior, punishments, and responsibilities in its own army. The USSR refused to sign or ratify it because it refused to allow any Western nations to inspect Soviet POW facilities—that is, snoop on the Russians internally for any reason, which the convention's provisions required.

In retrospect, both Geneva 1864 and Hague 1899 and 1907 failed also to protect POWs to a satisfactory degree, and The Hague Convention failed to mention chaplains at all. It did make provision for a POW to observe the duties of his faith, whatever it was: "Prisoners of war shall enjoy complete liberty in the exercise of their religion, including attendance at the services of whatever Church they may belong to, on the sole condition that they comply with the measures of order and police issued by the military authorities."[12] Geneva 1929, Article 67, began the process of protecting chaplains: "Members the medical personnel and chaplains while retained by the Detaining Power with a view of assisting prisoners of war, shall not be considered as prisoners of war. They shall, however, receive as a minimum the benefits and protection of the present Convention, and shall be granted all facilities necessary to provide for the medical care and religious ministration to prisoners of war."[13] The international community finally recognized that soldiers have souls as well as bodies, and international law guided everyone's behavior during and after World War II until 1949 when a new revised and expanded Geneva Convention took precedence internationally.

In 1926 chaplains' rank structure was restored after World War I, and the chaplains began to become clergymen again instead of being saddled with extraneous, time-consuming assignments like service-club managers, post-exchange officers, morale officers, education officers, and other extra-duty jobs on bases around the country and overseas. Beginning in 1938, the Roosevelt administration created the Civilian Conservation Corps as a part of the New Deal under the direction of the U.S. Army, and thus the need for an expanded Chaplain Corps grew quickly. By 1941 chaplains in the U.S. military services had real jobs tending to a growing Army, Navy, Coast Guard, and Marine Corps, a spiritual job of tending to the hearts and souls of America's fighting men who were about to head into harm's way again. The Chaplain Corps expanded from 383 active duty chaplains in June 1940 to nearly 10,000 in September 1945.[14] World War II changed everything!

Five

—◦≫◦≪◦—

1942 to 1945

Via Dolorosa in the Pacific and the Sacrifice of the Chaplains

Praise the Lord and pass the ammunition.
—Anonymous

FOR THE FIRST TIME in American military history, every chaplain was no longer a fighting parson as in the Revolution, or an independent operative as in the Civil War, and unlike World War I, the chaplains of World War II were coordinated by experienced authority. Pay and equipment were regulated throughout the U.S. Army and Navy, and the chaplain was free of all those pesky side assignments that sapped his energy from his spiritual profession. The chief of staff of the Army was Gen. George C. Marshall, a friend to chaplains in all the military services, and the chief of chaplains was Maj. Gen. (Fr.) William R. Arnold, USA. Incoming chaplains received training at the Chaplain Schools at Fort Benjamin Harrison in 1942; Harvard University, 1942–44; Fort Devens, 1944–45; and Fort Oglethorpe, 1945–46. A total of 8,183 chaplains graduated from these schools. Navy chaplains trained at the Naval Chaplain School at the Naval Station at Norfolk, Virginia.[1] The American chaplaincy came to maturity.[2]

In his commentary regarding the beginning of World War II, historian Steven E. O'Brien notes, "After the disaster at Pearl Harbor, there was a surge of volunteering for the chaplaincy among Catholic priests, though some bishops still had a degree of reluctance to let their men go. The same situation prevailed with the religious orders, including the largest, the Society of Jesus. The Jesuits had a long history of naval service as well as military service. Of the thirty-seven chaplains imprisoned, twenty-one were Catholic, mostly army chaplains who were serving either in the regular army or the Philippine Scouts."[3]

Life in the American military services for chaplains became a real search for meaning. In some cases horror and shame gave way to numbness and dry, dulled emotions.[4] Beyond the moods of despair and apathy known by all in harm's way, the strength and self-esteem born of faith and service persisted throughout the Pacific theater of operations from the beginning to the end of everyone's time behind barbed wire. According to Chaplain Leslie Zimmerman in his extensive history of chaplains in the Pacific, *Chaplain Prisoners of War in the Pacific, 1941–1945,*

> One rationalized that since suffering was inescapable, meaning must be found to justify that suffering. When the chaplain brought men face to face with the love of God, His concern, and His power, then the chaplain himself found a "why" to live that became a "how" to live. This new outlook became a magnificent commitment by a group of God's servants that has never been fully appreciated by government, military, the American public, or even the chaplains' own denominations.[5]

For the United States, the war began in the Pacific region in December 1941, first in Hawaii (Pearl Harbor), then in the Philippines and Wake Island, and Guam. Beginning at the turn of the twentieth century, the Imperial Japanese militarists demanded domination of the Pacific region and, later, even greater domination in the post–World War I era, in support of the Greater East Asia Co-Prosperity Sphere. As far as the Japanese Imperial Staff was concerned, all the Western colonial nations had to be removed and replaced by the Empire of Japan. "Asia for Asiatics" was the propaganda cry at the time that spread over the region; however, it was actually Asia for Japan, and war was the means to accomplish it. On Sunday morning, December 7, 1941, a "date which will live in infamy," as President Franklin D. Roosevelt said before Congress a few days later, the naval and air forces of the Imperial Empire of Japan attacked most of the American military facilities at Pearl Harbor on the Hawaiian island of

Oahu without any prior warning. Two Navy chaplains died in action that morning: Chaplain Thomas L. Kirkpatrick in the battleship USS *Arizona* when it exploded after a direct bomb hit on its forward magazine, and Fr. Aloysius H. Schmitt on board the battleship USS *Oklahoma*. Fr. Schmitt died as he attempted to push men through a porthole to safety as the ship turned on its side and filled up with water after being torpedoed several times by attacking Japanese aircraft. Both chaplains died heroically that dreadful day. Pearl Harbor was just the beginning; things got much worse. With more than two thousand dead on American soil, the war was on.

The *Via Dolorosa*, or "Way of Sorrows," began on that Sunday morning not only in Hawaii but also in the Philippine Islands, also a possession of the United States at the time, as well as Wake Island and Guam. Although the Japanese did not invade Hawaii, they did invade all the other American possessions. War began on December 8, 1941, in the Philippines when the Japanese bombed Clark Field on the island of Luzon, not terribly far from Manila. Gen. Douglas MacArthur initiated War Plan Orange almost immediately after he declared Manila an "Open City" in order to save it from being bombed into oblivion. After the Japanese invaded northern Luzon at Lingayen Gulf and headed south, MacArthur's defensive position fell apart quickly. American and Filipino forces moved south and west into the Bataan Peninsula, where, according to War Plan Orange, they were supposed to hold off the Japanese until relieved by Americans coming from the United States. By March 1942, the Americans understood that no relief was coming and composed the following doggerel verse that began, "We are the Battling Bastards of Bataan, / No Momma, no Papa, and no Uncle Sam."

On April 9, 1942, 66,000 Filipinos and 12,000 Americans surrendered against their will to the Imperial Japanese Army;[6] the fortress of Corregidor surrendered on May 6, 1942. Thirty-three Army and four Navy chaplains were among those who surrendered: twenty-one Roman Catholic priests and sixteen Protestant ministers. Of these chaplains, twenty made the supreme sacrifice on the *Via Dolorosa*. One was Jesuit Juan E. Gaerlan, S.J., a native Filipino who was murdered by the Japanese army on the Death March.[7] Most of the chaplains on Bataan made the Bataan March from Marivelas to San Fernando and then by an old rickety train to Camp O'Donnell.[8] True, the Japanese army never expected the number of surrendered Americans and Filipinos; nevertheless, their behavior was atrocious. War crimes were committed. Many American chaplains stepped into the breach and became heroes. They had no weapons to lay down; instead, they took their weapons with them into captivity: their Bibles, rosaries, religious medals, Mass Kits, sermons, and, most important, their faith and their soldiers who became their congregations.

Chaplain John K. Borneman commented in the *Army and Navy Chaplain*, a professional journal written by and for military chaplains before and during World War II, that the chaplains of the Bataan surrender might well have voiced the words of Saint Paul in his second letter to the Corinthians, chapter 1, verse 8: "For we would not, brethren, have you ignorant of our trouble which came to us in Asia, that we were pressed out of measure, above strength, insomuch that we despaired even of life." As a Protestant chaplain who suffered with his men the entire war, from 1942 through 1945, he concluded his reflection with a quote from Micah: "And what doth the Lord require of thee, but to act justly, and to love mercy, and to walk humbly with thy God" (6:8).[9] As Richard S. Roper wrote in *Brothers of Paul* (2003), Chaplain Borneman was one of those American chaplain POWs who wanted to push the Japanese to allow the Americans to bury their dead on Corregidor before their evacuation on May 3, 1942. He and other chaplains remained on Corregidor until July, when they were transferred to Cabanatuan, where he remained for the remainder of the war years. The 6th Ranger Battalion rescued Chaplains Borneman, Fr. John J. Dugan, Fr. Eugene J. O'Keefe, and more than four hundred other POWs on January 30, 1945, during their famous raid on Cabanatuan.[10] Surprised, Borneman looked at one of the Rangers. "Where you from soldier?" "Oklahoma." "Oklahoma is a state I'll never forget."[11]

Chaplain Borneman reminds us that "not a single chaplain ever once refused to hold services," and he recalled seeing Chaplain Herman C. Bauman say Mass in the open with full vestments in full view of the Japanese, who opposed the Christian faith for the most part.[12] In his postescape narrative, *Return to Freedom* (1982), Samuel C. Grashio recalled his feelings toward his chaplains behind the wire:

Like so many others in prison camps, I found the chaplains immensely inspiring. They were unselfish when most of the rest of us were assuredly not. They got up at four or five o'clock in the morning to say Mass for their fellow prisoners. They worked hard both to comfort the dying and to make the lot of the living a bit easier. Overall, their conduct more than measured up to the ideals they were supposed to personify. They strengthened my own faith in God and my conviction that somehow, God would not let me die in a Japanese prison.[13]

Chaplain Robert Preston Taylor, a Baptist, and Fr. John E. Duffy walked together on the Death March. Fr. Duffy weakened and often stumbled and even fell down, at his peril from the guards who did not hesitate to bayonet anyone who did not keep up. On the third day of the march, Fr. Duffy collapsed. The local Filipinos stood beside the roads and attempted to hand canteens of water and fruit to the POWs. When caught by the Japanese guards, these good people were punished severely, but they persisted in attempting to assist the Americans and fellow Filipinos suffering from the hardships along the *Via Dolorosa*. Finally, Fr. Duffy went down hard on his knees, and the Japanese guard ran him through with his bayonet. Thinking that Fr. Duffy was dead, the Americans continued on their way. The local Filipinos found him barely alive and rescued him by pulling him off the dusty road and giving him water, and then they took him to their village and tended to him for a year. The Japanese recaptured Fr. Duffy, but, after a trial and acquittal for war crimes (guerrilla activities), they did not punish him for escaping. Instead, they returned him to the Cabanatuan POW camp, where he and Chaplain Taylor were reunited.[14]

Chaplain Fr. John E. Duffy, USA, was a favorite of Gen. Douglas MacArthur, who in 1942 appointed him force chaplain in northern Luzon and later appointed him chaplain of the First Philippine Corps, where he served until the surrender. He had an unusual way about him, according to Sgt. Abie Abraham, who recalled,

> Father Duffy entered the building, walked over to a youngster and said, "Son, I'm going to pray for you."
> "It won't do you any good."
> "Do you want me to hear your confession?"

"No, it's easy for them at churches, all they do is confess and not tell God the truth."

"Give it a try. It will make you feel better."

"I'm not a good Catholic. To get me to church you'd have to drag me with a bulldozer."

A week later, just before the youngster died, Fr. Duffy heard his confession.[15]

Fr. Duffy was one of the lucky POWs who went on board the *Oryoku Maru* in Manila en route to Japan on December 13, 1944. American carrier aircraft attacked the ship off the former American naval base at Subic Bay not knowing that U.S. POWs were on board and sank it just offshore.[16] After escaping from that sinking ship, he and many other survivors were put on board the *Enoura Maru*, a ship that was also attacked by American naval air forces. The *Enoura Maru* did not perish at sea, however, and Fr. Duffy gave last rites to many Americans who were badly wounded in the attack. The American POWs finally arrived in Japan on board the *Brazil Maru*. The Japanese then sent Fr. Duffy to Camp Fukuoka 17, where he continued to serve the POWs spiritually, although he was too ill and too weak to hear confessions or administer the sacraments. On April 24, 1945, Chaplain Fr. Duffy went to the prison camp at Munkden, Manchuria, where he stayed until war's end and liberation.

In August 1945, Fr. John E. Duffy returned to U.S. hands in extremely poor condition. First a patient at Kunming General Hospital, China, then at the Calcutta Hospital, and finally at Walter Reed Army Hospital in Washington, D.C., Chaplain Fr. John E. Duffy finally retired from the Army in 1948.[17] After learning that he and Chaplain Taylor were the only two American chaplains to survive the hell-ship passage to Japan in 1944, he remarked, "Why we know not, but we suspect that even the Lord did not want us."[18] Dan Murr published a biography of Fr. Duffy, *But Deliver Us from Evil* (2008), and wrote affectionately in his epilogue, "Throughout Father Duffy's pain and suffering of surrender, the Death March on Bataan, the bayoneting, the court-martial, the torture by his captors, the hell ships and sickness and the constant staring into the face of death, he miraculously persevered and never lost his faith and trust in God."[19] Fr. John E. Duffy died on June 4, 1958, in San Francisco and is buried in the San Francisco National Cemetery.

Fr. Duffy's best friend in the Philippines was Chaplain Robert Preston Taylor, a Texan, a Southern Baptist, and married man. From the spring of 1940, Chaplain Taylor saw the Army as a vast missionary field. He stated his intention clearly:

My deepest desire has been to represent in the worthiest manner the cause for which Texas and the Southern Baptists stand. In doing so, I have endeavored to proclaim Christ, and Him crucified. Upon my entrance into the chaplaincy I thought to write of the army as a vast field for evangelistic and home mission work. I concluded, however, it would be better to wait and watch the situation for a few months and then write out a personal ministry and experience in the service.[20]

The world changed for Chaplain Taylor on December 1941, when the Japanese struck the Philippine Islands after their attack on Pearl Harbor on December 7, and again in April 1942 when the order to surrender went out to all American and Filipino forces. Taylor wrote,

I guess around 8 or 9 in the morning the surrender flags went up, and we got the word that General King had been ordered to surrender. This was rather a bad moment in the lives of most of us; and you just can't imagine what the feeling is unless you've been there to see the white flag being hoisted and the American flag being lowered in defeat. We were not prepared for it at all, no. To see all those white flags flying was degrading and rather suffocating to all of us in spirit and in feeling.[21]

Much worse was on the way.

After Chaplain Taylor encountered Fr. Duffy on the march, he was sent with the most injured men to the hospital at the camp at Little Baguio, where he joined two other chaplains, Chaplain Dawson, also a Southern Baptist, and Fr. Albert D. Talbot.[22] While working in the hospital, Chaplain Taylor began making contact with some of the outside personnel who were helping the POWs by smuggling food, vitamins, medicine, and money into the camp. In this project, known as "Operation Life," Chaplain Taylor discovered that his outside helpers needed money to purchase medicines and food on the open market. The POWs in Cabanatuan came up with an astounding amount of

Philippine pesos, about eight thousand all told, and the process began to save lives of the American POWs.[23] It became obvious that Chaplain Taylor as well as all the others involved who were subsequently captured by the Japanese in this instance were devoid of any spy-oriented tradecraft and used only sheer faith in their righteous cause to act as their defense and strength. Chaplain Taylor recollected,

> In the hospital we had a smuggling service which brought us medicine, pesos, and news. Our contact in Manila was a person with a code name 'High Pockets.' Receiving these goods through unauthorized channels was the reason that several of us got caught up in this guardhouse business. One day Chaplain Tiffany, who was the key man in the smuggling situation, told me that Clara Phillips was High Pockets.[24]

They most certainly needed courage. After a great deal of torture, starvation, isolation, and inhumane treatment, the Japanese finally returned him to the general population. Chaplain Taylor recalled,

> At first, maybe the first two weeks, they held the group in a little makeshift place with guards around us day and night. Then they came and got us and took us to a remodeled old house. Inside the building they built six or so small cells measuring five or six feet long, four feet wide and five feet high. I couldn't stand up straight in it, but I could lie down by a kind of scrunching up. They put two men into each cell. I became ill. The guards notified one of our camp doctors.[25]

The doctor, Eugene Jacobs, took the Japanese camp physician to see Taylor, and he conveniently coughed up a twenty-inch worm. His ordeal as a jailed prisoner within a prison camp was over.

By the fall of 1944, the Japanese realized that the Americans were retaking the Philippine Islands by force, and if left to their own methods, the Americans would seek out their own POWs and release them quickly. As a result, the Japanese decided to remove all able-bodied POWs from the Philippines to Japan as quickly as possible. They used merchant ships, freighters mostly, to transship the POWs and packed them unmercifully into the ships' filthy holds.[26] In October 1944, along with most of the remaining American POWs at Cabanatuan,

Chaplain Taylor was sent to the Billibid Prison in Manila to await movement. In December the whole Billibid group boarded the *Oryoku Maru*, and in an attack Chaplain Taylor was wounded and at one point became unconscious. He regained consciousness long enough to jump off the sinking ship and swim to the shore, where Japanese guards first shot at and then waited for the living, exhausted but surviving, American POWs to wade ashore. They kept all the American POWs waiting on a tennis court for five days in the blistering sun, without any cover, food, and very little water, until their captors took them north to board the *Enoura Maru* along the Philippine coast. The ship made it safely to Formosa (now Taiwan), where it was bombed by American aircraft and lost. The next ship, the *Brazil Maru*, took what was left of the POWs to Japan. Of all the chaplains who started this trip, only Chaplains Taylor and Duffy survived. The rest died.[27]

Chaplain Taylor's itinerary did not stop in Japan at Camp Fukuoka 22. He then went to Hoten Prison Camp in Mukden, Manchuria. On September 21, 1945, the Russians liberated all the American and Allied POWs in Mukden, and they began the process of coming home. Chaplain Taylor decided to remain in the service on active duty and attained the rank of major general and U.S. Air Force chief of chaplains. There is no doubt that Chaplain Maj. Gen. Robert Preston Taylor, USAF, was an American hero and a man of God.

Father William T. Cummings was a slightly built man, a Maryknoll priest sent to the Philippines in 1940 to teach ethics and apologetics to Filipino students in Manila. He convinced the U.S. Army to take him on as a chaplain just as the Japanese were beginning their attacks in December 1941. As a hospital chaplain, his calling card of sorts became his raised arms in the middle of a bombing attack when he recited the Lord's Prayer. In every instance, the panic stopped despite smoke and dust rising from the floors. Once, on April 7, 1942, a bomb hit an ammunition truck near his hospital, and he raised his arms and said the Lord's Prayer, but he had to stop because the bomb's shrapnel wounded him. After evacuation to Hospital No. 2, he recovered. During the Bataan campaign, Fr. Cummings was given credit for coining the expression, "There are no atheists in a foxhole." Although no one ever heard Fr. Cummings say it during his lifetime, he could not avoid, skirt, or deny that it came from him.[28]

Like many others, Fr. Cummings climbed on board the *Oryoku Maru* in Manila in October 1944. Like Chaplain Taylor, he survived the bombing in

Subic Bay and swam ashore. Of 1,600 American POWs crammed into the ship, only 425 survived the voyage to Japan. Fr. Cummings survived the trip to Formosa on the *Enoura Maru,* but the *Brazil Maru* became his coffin during the final trip to Japan. Sydney Stewart in his eulogy to Fr. Cummings, *Give Us This Day* (1957), witnessed his final heroic moments:

> Slowly he began to pray, "Our Father Who art in Heaven, hallowed by Thy name." The cries of the men became still. I concentrated on the voice that soothed me and gave me strength and the will to live. Then I felt his body shiver and tremble in my arms. He gasped for air, and there was a terrible pain on his face. He gritted his teeth, sighed and went on. "Thy will be done—on earth—as it is—in heaven." I felt him tremble again as if he wanted to cough. His hands fluttered, and his eyelids almost closed. Then with superhuman effort he spoke again. "Give Us This Day." I felt his body go tense all over. He relaxed and his hand fell by his side. I waited, but his eyes looked straight ahead. His eyelids no longer flickered. I knew he was dead.[29]

As previously noted, Fr. Juan Gaerlan, a Filipino Jesuit and chaplain to Filipino troops, died on Bataan. He managed an escape on the Death March with several of his men, but the Japanese tracked them down and murdered them all with bayonets.[30] Fr. Mathias Zerfas, a Franciscan priest who served with the 26th Cavalry, arrived in the Philippines in April 1941 and was assigned to duties first at Fort Stotsenburg and later with the 26th Cavalry, with which he was cited for bravery after exposing himself to heavy enemy fire during the Japanese assault in the northern Philippines in 1942. He was captured and put on the Death March as well. Not an escaper like Gaerlan, he suffered quietly on the march, in Camp O'Donnell, and in Cabanatuan prison camp until orders came from the Japanese to move some POWs to the Davao Prison Camp on the island of Mindanao in the southern Philippines. After a stint in Davao, he returned to Cabanatuan in 1944. In the fall of 1944, the Japanese then ordered as many POWs as possible removed from the Philippines to Japan. In October he boarded the *Oryoku Maru* and survived the bombing and the trip to Formosa in the *Enoura Maru,* but he died there as a result of the American bombing on January 9, 1944.

❧ • ❧

Fr. Zerfas and Fr. Duffy were close friends, and at death's door on the *Enoura Maru*, Fr. Duffy made certain that he gave Fr. Zerfas the last rites so precious to Catholics. Fr. Duffy wrote, "Father Zerfas died about dusk on the evening of January 11, 1945, and we had put him over with the other cadavers. On the 13th the dead were taken from the [ship's] hold and buried in a common grave on the beaches of Takao Bay, Formosa [Taiwan]. No chaplains were allowed to go ashore with him but some of the detail who took care of the internment told me that the spire of the Catholic Church in Takao could be seen from the place where they laid him."[31]

Fr. Zerfas' fellow Franciscans remembered him well. In 1946 his close friend Fr. Joseph Springbot wrote in the *Steubenville (OH) Register*, the diocesan newspaper: "Next Sunday on the anniversary of your death, I shall offer the Holy Sacrifice of the Mass that we your friends in the priesthood may follow your shortcut to heaven over the steep but certain pathway of humanity, devotion, and brotherly love."[32] Fr. Duffy remembered him and wrote,

> Father Matt was one of 500 of us who were in the forward hold of a Japanese prison ship in Takao Bay, Formosa, when we were attacked by naval airplanes on the morning of January 9, 1945. Father Matt had his leg practically blown off at the knee. He was in great agony and shock. After administering the sacraments to him, I moved him to a place where I covered him with rags [to] warm him as he was chilled and shaking badly. Father Zerfas died about dusk on the evening of January 11, 1945. On the 13th the dead were taken and buried in a common grave on the beaches of Takao Bay. No chaplains were allowed to go ashore.[33]

Fr. Zerfas was missed by his comrades while they suffered in Japan at the end of the war and by his Franciscan brothers at home as well. He was loved and served with distinction, as so many chaplains did.

Capt. Fr. Richard E. Carberry, USA, performed his chaplain duties, but additionally, he assisted in one of the major escapes in the Pacific theater. Fr. Carberry began his work in the Philippines assigned to the 45th Infantry, Philippine Scouts, where he was decorated several times for bravery in the jungle trails of Bataan. One Silver Star citation read in part, "Captain Carberry, with utter disregard for his own safety, left his foxhole and dashed some thirty years to the mortally wounded Sergeant Sagging and remained with him rendering spiritual sustenance while enemy shells burst all around. Captain Carberry's faith and fearless attention to duty gave the entire command renewed hope and calmed the shocked personnel at the height of danger."[34]

Yet Fr. Carberry distinguished himself further in his assistance to the American escapers in the Davao Prison Camp in 1943.[35] Determined to escape despite the Japanese threat of executing all the remaining POWs who did not escape and everyone if and when they were recaptured, one group took the chance and made their way to freedom. One of the escapers was Colonel Sam Grashio, a very religious Army Air Force officer who wrote Fr. Carberry's bishop explaining what happened in the prison camp and Fr. Carberry's part in the escape:

> In the course of planning our escape I had suggested that it might be helpful to take along a Catholic priest. Since most Filipinos are Catholics, a priest would be warmly received. He might be able to open many doors for us and secure invaluable aid. I knew Fr. Carberry well; indeed I had often purloined food from the kitchen for him. When I approached him, he was willing to join us. He also gave us considerable useful information and advice.[36]

A problem, however, arose when the senior chaplain in Davao, Fr. Col. Albert Braun, feared that if a chaplain escaped or even tried to escape, the Japanese would use it as an excuse to forbid any and all religious services and activities in the camp. Fr. Braun then informed Fr. Carberry that his duty was to minister to those POW in the camp, not to think about his own life. Thus, Fr. Carberry stayed behind and in the end obeyed his senior officer in the prison camp. A chaplain who earned two Silver Stars and a Bronze Star for bravery under fire, he died on January 4, 1945, in Taiwan en route by ship to Japan.

First Lt. Fr. Carl W. Hausmann, S.J., had been assigned to missionary work in the Philippines in 1933 well before the war broke out in December 1941. He volunteered for the Army Chaplain Corps and had possibly one of the shortest Army careers on record: two days after he took the oath of office, the Japanese army arrived, and Chaplain Hausmann became a POW.[37] Sent to Davao Prison Camp on the island of Mindanao shortly after his capture. The Japanese permitted the Catholic chaplains to say Mass, but they refused to give them the bread or wine they needed for the service. Fr. Hausmann's solution was to use an eyedropper for the wine in his chalice and a small piece of bread for his host for distribution to his congregants. In June 1944, all the POWs in Davao were transferred to Cabanatuan Prison Camp prior to their transshipment by sea to Japan, and there Fr. Hausmann said Mass devoutly. Catholics called him St. Joseph; non-Catholics called him the Holy Ghost. Neither was irreverent; rather, it was a way that the whole POW community came to terms with holiness. Fr. Hausmann showed his devotion to his duty by resisting Japanese efforts to stifle his efforts to conduct his service during an air raid. A guard barked orders at him to cease the Mass, but he refused, Then the guard flew into a rage and began to beat Fr. Hausmann unmercifully, while the POWs began shouting until the guard left the altar.[37] Like so many other POWs, chaplains included, he boarded the doomed *Oryoku Maru*. Fr. Hausmann survived the bombing and swam ashore under Japanese machine-gun fire. He also survived the *Enoura Maru,* and like Fr. Cummings, died on board the *Brazil Maru* in the hold, lying on the floor in the darkness and the filth among men too exhausted, sick, accustomed to death, and near death themselves to have any concern at all.[39] Found were his stole and rosary. In all, eight priests and seven Protestant chaplains died on this trip from the Philippines to Japan, one that most certainly was unnecessary, deadly, and cruel beyond human imagination.

Chaplain Alfred C. Oliver, USA, was the senior chaplain in the Philippines in 1941 and oversaw all the chaplains' service even in captivity. It was his brand of hands-on leadership, sense of duty, and simple caring that rallied all the chaplains to their mission of welfare, morale, and spiritual nurturing. To the chaplains of all the services in captivity in the Philippines during World War II, Chaplain Oliver was a prince among men and an example of what a chaplain ought to be. At the surrender in April 1942, Chaplain Oliver served on the staff of the commanding general on Bataan, Gen. Edward P. King. After the surrender, they were all put into cars and trucks and taken to Camp O'Donnell, arriving there on April 11, 1942. On that day, Chaplain Oliver wrote to the Japanese camp commander, requesting that the POWs be treated in accordance with Geneva '29. Additionally, he requested that Red Cross supplies then on hand be distributed promptly. In his presence the camp commandant told Chaplain Oliver, "I hate all Americans and always will hate you. The only thing I want you to know is when one of you dies, I will then have you bury each other."[40] At Cabanatuan Chaplain Oliver, like Chaplain Robert Preston Taylor and sixteen others, became a smuggler of food, medicine, money, and letters into the camp. When the Japanese caught and punished them severely, some nearly to death, Chaplain Oliver went into solitary confinement and remained there until late August 1944. Released during the 6th Ranger Battalion's raids on January 30, 1945, Chaplain Oliver lived to tell his story, one of the few chaplains who did survive. He died in 1958.

Capt. Frank L. Tiffany, USA, served as a Presbyterian hospital chaplain in the Philippines. As the Americans abandoned Manila in the move to Bataan, the hospital chaplains for the most part did not suffer the Death March after the surrender. They were brought to Camp O'Donnell by truck. When Chaplain Tiffany arrived, he was appalled at the state of affairs: approximately 1,500 Americans and 30,000 Filipinos had died there already.[41] Chaplain Tiffany and his colleagues decided to help the living stay alive. To do that, they had to link up with outside helpers, Filipinos and the few Americans left free in the Philippines after the Japanese occupied the islands in 1942. First, the Philippine Red Cross came into play, and along with some staff and professors from Stetson University in the Philippines, they began to make contact with outside helpers. In February 1943, Chaplain Tiffany moved to Cabanatuan, where he became a leader of the camp underground. After discovery and capture by the Japanese, he was removed from the camp and put into solitary confinement. After his release and return to Cabanatuan, he was put on board the *Arisan Maru*, bound for slave labor in Japan; however, an American submarine torpedoed this unmarked ship in the South China Sea on October 24, 1944. There were nine survivors; Chaplain Tiffany was not one of them.[42]

There were no Jewish chaplains in the Philippines in 1941 when World War II broke out. Dr. Alfred A. Weinstein wrote in *Barbed-Wire Surgeon* (1948), "We Jews had no rabbi. Among those of my faith still alive in camp we found one who could conduct services. Lt. Jack Goldberg, pug-nosed ex-amateur pugilist from New York City, assembled us on Friday nights in his galley. In this tumbledown Nipa shack, surrounded by pots and pans, we reaffirmed the faith of our fathers. On Yom Kippur we met near the little entertainment stage in the open field before the sun went down."[43] Dr. Weinstein noted too that MSgt. Aaron Kliatcho served as a makeshift chaplain for the Jewish soldiers on Bataan. In fact, Kliatcho was not actually in the Army at all. He was a large older man who had served with the Imperial Russian forces and became a POW of the Japanese in the 1905 war before he emigrated to the Philippines, married, and raised a family. The Americans employed him as a counterintelligence agent, and after the Japanese invaded in 1942, they gave him a uniform and the rank of master sergeant.

Sergeant Kliatcho became one of the master smugglers in Cabanatuan. As he cared for the water buffalo (carabao), their drivers became links in a chain that brought food, money, medicine, and other forbidden items into camp. Unlike the Christian chaplains who were caught doing this by the Japanese and severely punished, Sergeant Kliatcho evaded the Japanese, but he was forced to sail on board the *Oryoku Maru* and died with many other American POWs when the naval aircraft attacked the ship in Olongapo Harbor.

Not only were the Philippine Islands attacked in December 1941, but so too were the other American possessions in the Pacific: Guam in the Marianas and Wake Island. Chaplain James E. Davis was captured on Guam and told his story in 1946 in an article in the *Army and Navy Chaplain*. Guam fell to the Japanese invaders in December 1941, and the Americans were removed from the island very quickly. Most of the POWs were taken to Japan and were put into the Zentsuji POW camp on Shikoku Island. Chaplain Davis noted, "Zentsuji was fortunate in its religious program, since most of the prison camps under Japanese custody had no chaplains, although a number of them had some form of religious observance without the aid of a chaplain. The Japanese did not disperse the chaplains among the camps as was done in the case of doctors. In some sectors, Allied chaplains were regarded with suspicion by the Japanese largely as propaganda agents used to whip up the fighting spirit of the men."[44] At Zentsuji, however, according to Chaplain Davis, the expression of religion became a normal thing under abnormal conditions, in part, because the camp had seven chaplains after the first six months of the war.

As the war progressed, so did religious observances in Zentsuji prison camp. Thanks to the International Red Cross and the YMCA, new equipment came into the camp, and Australian Catholic chaplain Fr. Turner managed to get vestments from the Roman Catholic bishop of Japan, who actually visited the camp once. According to Chaplain Davis, there were a lot of religious activities other than regular Sunday services, although this was not the case for the Americans in the Philippines. Chaplain Davis noted interestingly, "On the way home from Japan I met one man who had been a loyal worker in Zentsuji and was transferred to another camp. He said that he had carried on there, giving regular religions talks and performing funerals. This case could no doubt be multiplied. Whenever it was possible, Christian POWs carried on as best they knew how in the spirit of their Master."[45]

The complexities of the interactions between the Filipinos, the Americans, and the Japanese during the invasion and occupation of the Philippines during World War II are nothing short of staggering. The World War II generation in the Philippines had a choice: one could support the Americans who were committed to abandoning any ambitions of keeping the islands as a colony, or one could ally with the Japanese at the risk of being charged with collaboration at the end of the war. Being caught in a major conundrum of being damned if one did and damned if one did not support one side or the other was a very serious issue for Filipinos.

Medical Corps commander J. E. Nardini, USN, a former POW of the Japanese, published a much-needed analysis in 1952 that addressed the issue of survival and death in Japanese captivity Asia during World War II.[46] The author points out that approximately 12,000, or 40 percent, of the 30,000 men of all services survived imprisonment in the Philippines. Why was survival so difficult? Nardini hoped to answer that question. Several reasons surface. First, during active combat, December 8, 1941, to May 6, 1942, the troops were given inadequate food, suffered tropical weather, frequent poor to bad leadership, diseases such as malaria and dysentery, and always vitamin deficiency. Second, the ignominy of capture deeply affected each man, especially because of the Japanese ethos engendered by radical or militant Bushido that denigrated surrender and accorded the POWs virtually no rights that they expected under the 1929 Geneva Convention.

Conditions of captivity, as we have witnessed, varied from camp to camp at different times and depended often on the character of the camp commandants.

Food, however, became the greatest physical problem the POWs had to deal with. The death rate at Cabanatuan, the main POW camp for Americans in the Philippines, was between forty to sixty per day in a population of six to nine thousand, or roughly 1 percent per day, in June, July, and August 1942. Hungry men often did horrible things just to get something to eat, including stealing from one another from time to time. Anything to alleviate the food problem was welcome by everyone, especially from outside sources not connected to the Japanese. In addition to the lack of food was the boredom the men experienced, which, of course, added to racial and cultural prejudices already in place among the Americans. Self-pity made things worse, as did the sense of isolation and abandonment. Punishment, including capital murder of POWs by the Japanese, however, did not weaken these prisoners; rather, it strengthened their resolve for resistance and, if possible, retribution against their captors. Death on a hell ship did not pose a danger to these men nearly as much as starvation or disease.

At the end of the war, Gen. Douglas MacArthur summoned MSgt. Abie Abraham to his office in Manila. Master Sergeant Abraham had no idea what the general wanted and thought it odd that any general wanted to see him. As it turned out, Gen. Douglas MacArthur knew well what Sergeant Abraham had done in the camps throughout the war and asked him to do something special. According to Abraham, MacArthur said, "I would like for you to remain in the Philippines. I want you to retake the Death March route."[47] Given the fact that Sergeant Abrahams had been a POW for so long, rather than simply shipping out for rehabilitation and further duty back home, the general asked him to use his Filipino connections to find all the unmarked American dead on Luzon, including disinterring them, identifying them if possible, and returning their bodies to the central cemetery in Manila. Sergeant Abraham did his duty well, and according to Peter Eisner, there are today 17,206 people buried in the Manila American Cemetery located at the former Fort William McKinley.[48]

It seems safe to conclude that the chaplains captured in the Philippines and Guam played a fundamental role in the survival of all their men in several ways. Former POW Lyle W. Eads wrote, "Those prisoners with children worried about how they were, and worried and worried until they realized one by one that it would not change what was or was not happening, and that it wouldn't help a bit. More turned to God in prayer than ever would have under ordinary circumstances; hard, rough men, men who had for most of their adult life lived apart from God, suddenly had gotten religion and their comfort made them realize what they had missed previously in the years they had felt they hadn't needed Him."[49] The chaplains and their men showed fortitude—strength in the face of adversity—that was a gift to all POWs from their chaplains of all faiths: faith in God and the American military services to come to their rescue in time before their lives were spent and gone and a strong sense of interdependence on each other, especially when the chips were down about as far as they could go. Last, the chaplains showed courage in the face of a savage enemy, hell bent on making these Americans and their Filipino allies suffer as much as humanly possible. If there is a tragedy here, it is the fact that so much of this history has been forgotten or encased in statues, even in the Philippines where it all happened.

Six

—⟫⟪—

1942 to 1945

Resistance in the Philippines

Our most outstanding experience in 1944–1945: the marvelous unity of faith, fellowship and mutual concern shared by religious personnel of all denominations; the sacrificial devotion of Filipinos outside in sending in foods and other gifts to sustain our lives and uplift our spirits.

—Rev. Joseph A. Moore, an Episcopalian internee

IF ONE CONSIDERS the literature created after World War II, little has been said about what the chaplains did as POWs behind the wire. What is certain is that without the help of outsiders, mostly Filipinos who put themselves in extreme danger doing this sort of duty, even more Americans would have died in Camp O'Donnell, Cabanatuan, and Davao Prison Camps and the several internment camps the Japanese created in the Philippines than actually did. Filipino civilians, occupied but not terrified by the Japanese in 1942, decidedly at great peril supported the American and Filipino troops held prisoner by the Japanese throughout the Philippines.

The United States purchased the Philippines and Guam from Spain at the Treaty of Paris in 1898. True, the American government did not ask the Filipinos or the Chamoro people in Guam if they wanted to become colonies, known as commonwealths, of the United States. The people of Guam did not object, but under the leadership of Emilio Aguinaldo, the Filipinos fought a guerrilla war against the U.S. Army from 1899 to 1905. The United States won this contest and began the process of Americanizing the Philippines from 1899 to independence in 1946.[1] By 1934 the United States had decided with the Tydings-McDuffie Act to grant full independence to the Philippines, but Guam remains an American commonwealth to this day in the Mariana Islands chain. Guam was fully occupied by the Japanese from 1942 until 1944 when naval and land forces of the United States invaded and recaptured the entire Mariana group of islands, including Tinian, Saipan, and Guam. As for the Philippines, the result of the political, social, cultural, economic, religious, and military interactions between the Filipinos and the Americans before World War II, there was little question about which side the Filipinos supported after the Japanese invasion.

Catholic Army Chaplain Maj. John L. Curran, OP, a POW then at Camp O'Donnell, wrote a powerful narrative that described the help that the POWs received from the Filipinos outside the prison camps.[2] He commented, "After the death march, which ended around the 19th of April [1942], I happened to be on a detail from Camp O'Donnell and went near the Barrio of Tarlac. While on this detail I encountered about 200 women, all Filipinas, who had various packages of food and medicine for their beloved."[3] At first, the Japanese paid little attention to these sorts of supply activities, in part because they wanted to win over the Filipinos to their way of thinking about so-called Western oppressors. Yet there was no end to the help that the American and Filipino POWs received from these wonderfully generous people, and the cost in lives was nearly beyond belief.

The cost of resisting the Japanese occupation weighed very heavily on the civilian clergy as well as the military clergy. For example, the Columban Fathers were an Irish order of priests, all missionaries, sent to the Philippines and served as curates at the Malate Church in Manila's inner city. There were five priests at this church that doubled as a storage facility for underground supply operatives who sent materials to the POW camps and to the American and Filipino guerrillas in the mountains. After the American Army invaded in 1944 and all but reconquered the Philippine island of Luzon in 1945, all five priests were arrested, interrogated, and murdered by the Japanese. On February 10, 1945, the Japanese came to the Malate convent and took Frs. Kelly, Heneghan, Monaghan, and Fallon away together with a group of several parishioners to some nearby apartments where they executed them, bodies never recovered. The next night the Melate Church burned either from Japanese arson or by

American artillery. Three days later, Fr. John D. Lalor died from some flying debris of an artillery blast, probably American by then. Two hundred others died there too. The American government awarded him the Medal of Freedom posthumously after the war. The citation reads,

> Father John Lalor, Citizen of Ireland. For meritorious service which has aided the United States in the prosecution of the war against Japan in the Southwest Pacific Area, from 1942 to February 1945. During the Japanese occupation of the Philippine Islands, Father Lalor was an important link in the underground that supplied food, medicine, clothing and messages to prisoners of war and internees. He, with other priests of his order, operated a hospital in their school building and were able to feed and give medical care to many. While operating a store outside Nichols Field, he was able to give the prisoners much extra food and necessities, at great risk to his life. He was arrested by the Japanese, later released, and died in the battle of Manila in February 1945. By his outstanding bravery, resourcefulness, and devotion to duty, Father Lalor made a distinct contribution to the cause of freedom.[4]

The other deadly massacre of clergy in Manila took place against the Christian Brothers (Brothers of the Christian Schools, a French teaching order founded in the seventeenth century by Saint Jean Baptiste de la Salle) at La Salle College. The principal was Brother Egbert Xavier, FSC, who worked closely with Fr. Lalor aiding American POWs and the local guerrillas. The local Japanese detachment told Brother Egbert that his men could not be responsible for their protection, and thus they should leave the premises. The Brothers decided to remain at the school. On Monday, February 12, 1945, a Japanese detachment rushed the school and attacked everyone in sight. Forty-one Christian Brothers, students, and family members died that day. Only two clergy survived: Brother Antonius and the chaplain, Fr. Francis J. Cosgrove, an Australian missionary.[5]

After the Death March in 1942, countless numbers of Filipinos and American civilians worked to alleviate the sufferings of the POWs in Camp O'Donnell, later Cabanatuan, and the civilian internment camps in Manila and on the island of Luzon. There were two civilian supply networks at work in Manila at this time: one created and operated by Margaret Utinsky, "Miss U," and the other by another American expatriate, Dorothy Claire Phillips, or "High Pockets," as she coded herself. Neither woman was a trained intelligence professional, and ultimately their lack of spy craft gave them away to the Japanese. Nevertheless, their exploits were exceptional, given the circumstances they were in. Margaret Utinsky was originally married to John Utinsky, a former Army officer who worked as a civilian in the Philippines. She became Margaret or Miss U, instead of Mrs. John Utinsky with the help of Columban Father John D. Lalor, who used the Malate Church cellars as a resistance storage area under the Japanese noses.

In his study of the U.S. Army raid and liberation of the Cabanatuan Prison Camp in 1944, *Ghost Soldiers: The Forgotten Epic Story of World War II's Most Dramatic Mission* (2001), Hampton Sides noted his fascination with the stories of the outside helpers: Fr. Heinz Buttenbruch, Miss U, and High Pockets. Sides described how Claire Phillips operated her intelligence-gathering activities in Club Tsubacki, namely, how she connived tactical information from her Japanese officer clients and then sent it to the American guerrillas in the hills not far from Manila for transmission to Gen. Douglas MacArthur in Australia for action. According to Sides, Claire Phillips' regular customers included many of the most powerful Japanese officers who passed through the Philippines, such as generals, admirals, submarine captains, doctors, merchant-marine captains, and so on, all good potential sources of operational intelligence.[6] All these activities came to a halt in May 1944 when the Japanese high command realized that the Americans were going to attack and possibly remove the Philippines from their control. With invasion in mind, the Japanese authorities intercepted and arrested a whole supply train moving to the Cabanatuan prison camp. The major players inside the camp were Chaplains Frank Tiffany, Robert Preston Taylor, Albert C. Oliver, and Fr. John Wilson. A total of twenty-one POWs were swept up by the Japanese, punished by beatings, starvation, and incarceration in prison barracks. According to Chaplain Zimmerman's official history, the Kempeitai, the Japanese version of the Gestapo, tricked Chaplain Tiffany into disclosing the names of some of those suspected of involvement in the smuggling operations.[7]

Placed in a filthy jail cell in Cabanatuan City, Chaplain Oliver was beaten, tortured, and placed in solitary confinement. He was then returned to the Cabanatuan prison camp and put into a tiny cell too small to stand up or lie down. After several weeks of this, Oliver got caught trying to wash his face with drinking water, and a guard struck him on the neck with his rifle butt, breaking his neck. Returned to the prison population and hidden from the Japanese, Chaplain Oliver stayed in the camp, which in the fall of 1944 contained only those POWs who were deemed too sick or wounded for transport to Japan. Fortunately, the U.S. Army Rangers recovered Chaplain Oliver, along with several other chaplains in the raid on January 30, 1945. Also captured for internal "spying" was Chaplain Leslie Zimmerman, a Disciple of Christ pastor. The Kempeitai interrogated him severely and attempted to obtain the names of the helpers.[8] Miss U caught word of all this and escaped to the mountains before capture and joined the guerrillas, whereas the other group under Claire Phillips, High Pockets, was captured by the *Kempeitai*.

The American Claire Phillips was the married name of Dorothy Claire Phillips Fuentes (among several other aliases). Fr. Heinz Buttenbruch, a German national and a missionary of the Society of the Divine Word, established that her husband, John Phillips, died in Cabanatuan after capture and the Death March in 1942. Following the news, Claire received a note from Chaplain Tiffany, code-named "Everlasting," begging her "not to forget the ones who are left. They are dying by the hundreds," he wrote.[9] Fr. Buttenbruch befriended Claire and kick-started her work supplying American POWs in Cabanatuan, and it is fair to assert that Fr. Buttenbruch was perhaps the single most important outside helper bringing in clothing and supplies into Japanese military and civilian prisons and internment camps during the occupation. He was finally arrested and, like so many people at that time, beheaded by the Japanese in 1944.

How the smuggling system worked was both complicated and simple at the same time. Not knowing exactly what to do in a city under occupation, Claire decided to continue her old profession of being a vivacious nightclub entertainer. With the assistance of a Chinese friend in Manila, Claire opened Club Tsubaki, which catered to entertaining ranking Japanese officers. Claire, along with her girls, all accomplices, mixed with the Japanese officers and extracted operational (who, what, when, where, and how) rather than political intelligence from them. Her intelligence went primarily to Maj. John Boone, USA, who operated a lethal guerrilla force in the mountainous region of northern Luzon, and to the POWs in Cabanatuan.[10] Boone had radio communications with Gen. Douglas MacArthur in Australia who could order American forces to intercept and often destroy Japanese assets based on tactical information garnered by these agents in Manila.

Taking materials into the prison camps was a difficult chore. According to Peter Eisner, by 1943 the Filipino supply units were successfully working under the very noses of the Japanese guards. Whenever a delivery was ready to be taken into Cabanatuan, the Filipino agents waited patiently for the American POWs to come out of the camp on work details.[11] They kept their materials in oxcarts, but the Japanese thought that all this activity, namely, a young woman combing her hair early in the morning in the front of her house, along with an old man parking an oxcart, was perfectly normal. What they did not know was that the women were sending messages that told where the real materials were hidden. Also the Japanese took no real note when the POWs purchased small amounts of food from the Filipino women, but little did they know that all sorts of codes were being used to signal where the really valuable goods were hidden, like medicine, money, and mail. True, all this activity could not feed the thousands of prisoners in Cabanatuan or in any of the other camps so supplied, but it helped not only bellies but also morale among the POWs to know that the Filipinos risked their lives to care for the Americans who suffered so badly behind barbed wire.

The Japanese all but closed down American and Filipino intelligence operations, as the Americans reconquered the Philippines in 1944–45. They captured, interned, and murdered an enormous number of people, the innocent and the guilty alike, many in Santiago Prison in Manila, but places of execution meant little to the maddened, crazed Japanese. After all, they knew they were doomed; taking American and Filipino lives in 1944 meant very little.[12] Claire Phillips, the hunted High Pockets, was seized and taken swiftly to the Kempeitai headquarters, where the Japanese officers began some hard interrogations. Guards stripped her down to her underwear and tied her to a bench, where they began to administer the "water treatment."[13] She refused to answer any questions, and her captors continued administering the torture. She was then taken to the Santiago Prison, where she was put into solitary confinement awaiting execution. Luckily for her, it never came.

This is not the end of the Claire Phillips story, however. Peter Eisner researched and published an insightful book, *MacArthur's Spies: The Soldier, the Singer, and the Spymaster Who Defied the Japanese in World War II* (2017), that shows just how dreadfully complex espionage can be. Eisner found Phillips' personal memoir about her experiences in Manila called *Manila Espionage* (1947), but he also discovered that it was more fiction than fact and, worse, that it was ghostwritten by a Hollywood screenwriter with the aim of making a movie.[14] The film was *I Was an American Spy* (1951), starring Ann Dvorak. A good movie it was not, at least by modern standards, but it did tell the basic story of what High Pockets did in Manila during the war, albeit with the overt use of period stereotypes and a lot of verbal jingoisms.

More important than a mediocre adventure movie was Claire's claim for restitution from the U.S. government for all the money she spent on feeding both POWs and guerrillas. In 1957 Claire Phillips was awarded $1,349.21, only a fraction of what she claimed. Yes, the U.S. government was generous with medals after World War II but not generous with compensation to its war heroes, especially those who told rather tall tales at first and then the truth later. Peter Eisner discovered this as his research dipped into the National Archives and found several sworn affidavits from people whose voices have long been silent. Was Claire Phillips a hero? Yes. Was she a victim of social standards of the time? Yes. Did she do what she said she had done? Yes, indeed, she did. She was one of thousands of Filipinos and Americans who defied and resisted the Japanese occupation and domination of the Philippine Islands, which, sadly, cost them more than five hundred thousand dead.[15]

The Jesuit Fathers were also active in Manila from the Spanish occupation period to the American takeover in 1899. In 1927 the Spanish Fathers turned over their mission to American Jesuits. Most of the American Jesuits remained outside the Japanese prison system until 1944, when they were put into Santo Tomas Internment Camp in Manila and avoided the mass murders inflicted on so many other clergy.

The Reverend R. Sullivan, OMI, told of the scarcity of wine for Mass at the end of 1943 and how many of the Catholic internees contributed their boxes of raisins from the Red Cross food kit to be processed into altar wine.[16] Even on the first day the Japanese used Santo Tomas University as an internment camp, they were astounded at the degree of loyalty the Filipinos displayed toward the imprisoned Americans. They came bearing food, bedding, and many other necessities, and this sort of action continued nearly for the entire duration of the war, although the Japanese attempted to prevent contact between the internees and the Filipinos who assisted them, but they could never stop them.[17]

On February 3, 1945, the U.S. Army liberated the Santo Tomas Internment Camp in Manila and made a deal with the Japanese guard force that if they left the prisoners alone, they could return to their own lines unharmed. Both the Japanese and the Americans saw fit to accept that offer, and the Japanese walked away weapons in hand. In a short time the Japanese troops died fighting the American Army in Manila, and the internees went home alive. Recalling that happy experience in a way was this song written by an internee:

> The day I left my happy home to sail across the sea,
> I never thought I'd end up as a broken-down internee;
> Behind the walls of wire and stone we live with a hustle and boom,
> I'd rather live like a tinned sardine 'cause a sardine has more room,
> Muah, oh glory be!
> Talinum, deliver me!
> Cornbread, deliver me!
> Oh, how I wish that I were free![18]

Rev. Joseph A. Moore, an Episcopalian missionary, recalled, "Our most outstanding experience in 1944–1945: the marvelous unity of faith, fellowship and mutual concern shared by religious personnel . . . of all denominations; the sacrificial devotion of Filipinos outside in sending in foods and other gifts to sustain our lives and uplift our spirits."[19]

Another link in the Filipino chain is an American named Charles "Chick" Parsons, a truly clandestine character who became the direct link between the Philippines and Gen. Douglas MacArthur in Australia. In the beginning of the war shortly after the defeat of the Americans in the Philippines, there were a small number of American soldiers who refused to surrender to the Japanese and became guerrilla fighters in the mountains of Luzon and Mindanao Islands. John Boone, an Army corporal in 1942, fought on Luzon, the main island of the Philippines, while Col. Wendell Fertig, a former civilian engineer and Army

Reserve officer, fought on Mindanao. Gen. Douglas MacArthur at first did not approve of guerrillas, but he soon discovered that he could obtain valuable intelligence from their direct observations of the enemy in the field. MacArthur wrote to a Philippine officer, "Primary mission is to maintain your organization and to secure maximum amount of information. Guerrilla activities should be postponed until ordered from here. Premature action of this kind will only bring heavy retaliation upon innocent people."[20]

It was Chick Parsons' job to coordinate all intelligence and guerrilla activities in the Philippines with MacArthur in Australia. Parsons had been a resident of Manila, a kind of period expatriate who loved the Philippines and spoke Spanish, Tagalog, and some other Filipino dialects. He was an untrained natural intelligence officer, and MacArthur needed him and his valuable services badly. In 1942 Parsons had escaped to the United States and deposited an intelligence summary. He was a naval reserve officer, so the Navy made him a lieutenant commander, more for show than anything else other than being able to talk to people of rank with some authority. In 1943 Parsons had been assigned to the Allied Intelligence Bureau and received several weeks of intensive field training. In early 1943 Parsons found himself on board American submarines servicing supply and espionage missions in the Philippines. His mission was to establish contact and analyze what needed to be done on the ground.[21] But he had to get into the country as soon as possible, to begin what became many naval supply missions to the Filipino guerrillas that lasted until the war's end.

Parsons had become a bit of a roving ghost in the Philippines in 1943. Resisters seemed to see him everywhere, dressed in peasant as well as priestly clothes, in contact with all sorts of people fighting against the Japanese. All the while he had eluded the Japanese by operating off the grid on the southern island of Mindanao. Most certainly, Parsons was in contact with the Luzon and Manila resisters and guerrillas, despite being ordered to stay away from them. What Parsons learned in late 1943 and early 1944 was that the Japanese were beginning to strip the Philippines of anything they considered valuable, including healthy POWs, for transshipment to Japan as soon as possible. Parsons reported to MacArthur that the Filipinos were ready for a fight with the Japanese and were "bitterly disillusioned, and acutely aware that in place of a pleasant democratic way of life, they had gained only misery, hunger, and poverty." Meanwhile, he came ashore from the large supply submarine USS *Narwhal*, to the island of Mindoro with commandos and forty-five tons of supplies, complete with a lot of counterfeit Japanese occupation currency with the intent of counteracting inflated food prices for the people. Parsons also reminded the guerrillas that General MacArthur wanted or ordered them to continue gathering intelligence rather than attacking the Japanese before the American invasion.[22] From Mindoro Parsons then went to Mindanao, where he met up with Colonel Fertig and prepared him as well for the invasion. By mid-1944 progress was substantive, and thousands of American and Filipino guerrillas were ready for action.

Gen. Walter Krueger commanded the American Sixth Army and prepared his invasion plans thinking about how the Filipino guerrillas would respond, especially on the island of Leyte, where the first invasion was set to take place on October 20, 1944. He wanted them to hold off attacking the Japanese until they had begun to withdraw from the Americans points of attack. At that time, McArthur directed the guerrillas to surround and destroy the Japanese forces when and where they could. Meanwhile, at the invasion site on Leyte, after more than 170,000 American fighting men assaulted the beach, Gen. Douglas MacArthur came ashore several times for the cameras; on the radio, he announced, "People of the Philippines, I have returned."[23]

By December 1944 the Japanese decided in response to send the Americans to Japan by ship, a very deadly decision on their part. The story of the hell ships is well known, and, as pointed out in the previous chapter, they became iron coffins of death for so many American chaplains who refused to leave their men at that time. Only 500 American POWs remained in the Cabanatuan prison camp, some at Billibid prison in Manila, and many internees at Las Baños and Santo Tomas. MacArthur knew that these prisoners needed to be rescued as soon as possible.

Manila, once referred to as the "Pearl of the Orient," became an armed fortress and evolved into the only major city in the Pacific theater to be fought over and taken by the American Army in World War II. The Japanese naval infantry, leftover sailors from the sunk battleship *Musashi*, were ordered to defend the *intermuros*, or old city, to the last man, and they did. They ran around the gutters, murdering Filipinos in cold blood, all needless and all brutal beyond belief. The Americans rooted them out one by one; virtually no

Japanese soldier or sailor surrendered or survived. It was a bloodbath, consisting of enormous amounts of needless, mindless, killing that the Filipinos remember well to this day. It ended March 3, 1945.

The Sixth Ranger Battalion, commanded by Lt. Col. Henry Mucci, USA, planned and executed the first prison raid to free POWs in the Philippines at the Cabanatuan prison camp on Luzon. A total of 121 Rangers plus some Filipino Scouts made the raid and freed 513 very startled POWs, including several chaplains who were too sick to go to Japan in the hell ships. The following chaplains were all rescued by the Ranger raid: Chaplains Fr. John Dugan, John K. Borneman, Fr. Hugh F. Kennedy, Fr. Eugene J. O'Keefe, Alfred C. Oliver, and Fr. Albert D. Talbot. Born was the idea of the "Flying Squads" rushing to prison and internment camps in the Philippines, where they freed prisoners everywhere they found them: Billibid Prison (Chaplains Fr. Herman C. Bauman, Earl R. Brewster, Perry O. Wilcox) and Santo Tomas Internment Camp in Manila, Los Baños internment camp, and the Mandaluyong Women's Prison in Manila, where Claire Phillips was kept.[24] High Pockets waited in her cell on Saturday, February 10, 1945, rather than risk being caught in gun battles, and then she saw American soldiers standing in the courtyard. She recalled, "There stood ten of the tallest Yanks I had ever seen! I rushed up to the nearest soldier and timidly touched his arm." When the soldier smiled, she kissed him solidly.[25] A new life was waiting for her, yes, but she wanted to settle some wartime accounts first.

The new life became a very jagged road for Claire Phillips. Many of her close friends in Manila were executed by the Japanese in 1944. On board the *John Lykes*, one of the ships that took civilian survivors back to the United States in 1945, the authorities did not accept Claire's story as truth. She had trouble with the captain after filing a report that she believed that a traveling companion, Margaret Utinsky, broke into her stateroom and took important papers. The Federal Bureau of Investigation entered the fray as well and questioned Claire as to her identity and wartime activities, and her case went all the way to the director, J. Edgar Hoover, in Washington, D.C. On June 17, 1945, she went on the popular CBS radio show *I Was There*. In other words, Claire began to search for buyers of her story before the war was over and later exaggerated her experiences in her ghostwritten memoir, *Manila Espionage* (1947). After all this, both Claire Phillips and Margaret Utinsky made formal requests to the government for restitution of funds they spent during the Japanese occupation.[26] Margaret received $9,280 and the Presidential Medal of Freedom on October 17, 1946. Claire asked for $15,000 in restitution; however, the Truman administration became extremely cost-conscious at this time. She increased her request to $50,000 upon advice of counsel. On March 15, 1950, Claire hit the big time: she appeared on the radio show *This Is Your Life*, and along with the Presidential Medal of Freedom she and her new husband and her adopted daughter all received significant gifts from various sponsors. Claire received $1,349.21 in restitution from the U.S. government in 1957, not very much, and died on May 22, 1960. Her body was cremated, and she was simply gone. Maybe old soldiers do just fade away?

The intent of this chapter was to show definitively how dangerous it was in the Philippines to resist the Japanese occupation. Many modern historians like John Dower and others have charged that the Pacific campaign was a race war from the beginning to the end. For some men under arms and many civilians at the time, this charge may have been true, but for those men and women, clergy and civilians, in the Philippines who had to deal with the Imperial Japanese Army from 1942 to 1945 face-to-face, fear and hatred were real, tangible, and dripping with blood, theirs, their priests' and nuns', their parents,' and their children's. Their capacity for forgiveness seems to be nothing short of a miracle. Many, however, simply buried their feelings into their sense of now and hope for the future. Why bother remembering an unpleasant past? Because one must have the context based on the perspectives that come from an awareness that parents, grandparents, and friends sometime were subjected to real oppression, the kind that leaves real scars on the body and the spirit.

Seven

—·»{ }«·—

1942 to 1945

Captured Chaplains in World War II Europe

I got shot in the ass in the Kasserine Pass.
—Chaplain L. Berkeley Kines, S.J.

HEROISM AMONG CHAPLAINS may have begun in Asia; it continued on the Atlantic side of the war even before anyone actually got there in force. The Chaplain Corps expanded as the American armed forces expanded. After the Japanese attack on Pearl Harbor on December 7, 1941, and President Franklin D. Roosevelt's call for Congress to declare war on December 8, the men and women of the United States abandoned pacifism for the most part and geared up for war. Automobile factories became jeep, tank, and aircraft factories. Continental Can Corporation began to manufacture light machine or "burp" guns. Shipyards on both coasts produced ships in weeks and months instead of years. The United States became not only the mythic "Arsenal of Democracy," but also a very real Allied arsenal. As people said in those days, "There was a war to be won."

The POW status of chaplains was ambivalent at the time. Tracing the problem was Robert R. Wilson, an international lawyer writing in the *American Journal of International Law* in 1943: "The Prisoners of War Convention signed July 27, 1929 leaves the way open for them to continue in their duties, since by Article 16, 'Ministers of a religion, prisoners of war shall be allowed to minister fully to members of the same religion.'"[1] Belligerents by treaty were to consider one another's chaplains as noncombatants and were obligated to return them to their own forces as soon as possible; however, if chaplains so chose, they could remain in captivity to minister to their men. The British chaplains certainly did this, and the Americans followed suit.

In the Pacific we have seen what the American POW chaplains did, and in many cases they died not only at the hands of the Japanese directly but also in one of the hell ships attacked and sunk by the American submarine or naval air force. Sadly, the American submarine commanders never knew if any American or Allied POWs were imprisoned on board one of these ships. All they saw was a juicy target steaming toward Japan. The Japanese refused to mark "POW" on the sides of these transport ships, as they should have done, not only to save their ship but also to save the POWs for needed slave labor in Japan. The trouble was that there was no legal requirement to do so by convention; thus, not marking these human cargo freighters was not a war crime by the standards of international law at the time. It is interesting to note that the Americans did mark the sides of all POW transport ships taking German POWs from North Africa to the United States. As a result, although there were indeed great fears of attack, none was ever attacked by a German submarine or lost at sea.

While the war in Europe was heating up for the Americans, the war in the Pacific marched on violently, and American military chaplains marched with their soldiers, sailors, and Marines. Fr. Stephen Dzienis accompanied the 32nd Infantry Division in New Guinea as it slogged through the jungle after the Japanese. On Guadalcanal Fr. Frederic P. Gehring made history quietly when he said Mass for the men of the First Marine Division, "the Old Breed." Until 1941 Fr. Gehring was ringside in the Sino-Japanese War, where he served as civilian Vincentian missionary, but after Pearl Harbor he volunteered for service as a Navy chaplain. Early in December 1942, the Navy got word that two priests and two nuns were murdered by the Japanese for refusing to carry phony messages to the Marines. Fr. Gehring then volunteered to rescue as many missionaries in the Solomon Islands as possible. He did his best, and Adm. William F. Halsey awarded him the Navy and Marine Corps Medal. The citation read, "The Commander, South Pacific Area and South Pacific Force takes pleasure in presenting the Navy and Marine Corps Medal to Frederic P.

Gehring for distinguishing himself during the early months of the occupation of Guadalcanal. He, by his courage, cheerfulness and willingness, passed through the enemy lines and took a leading part in the evacuation of missionaries on the island. Outside the scope of his routine duties, he made numerous voluntary trips to the front lines and was a remarkable source of encouragement which greatly lifted the morale of front-line troops." Fr. Gehring served for twenty-two months in the Pacific theater. The part of chaplain in this world struggle may best be portrayed by this unforgettable character.[2]

On Iwo Jima, Navy chaplain Fr. Charles Suver celebrated Mass before the Marines raised the flag on Mount Suribachi. During the Okinawa campaign, Chaplain Fr. Joseph T. O'Callahan, S.J., received the Medal of Honor, the first Catholic chaplain to receive it, when the USS *Franklin* was attacked and hit by a Japanese kamikaze aircraft, setting the ship ablaze. It was Fr. O'Callahan who remained calm and, along with his Protestant colleague, helped to save the ship and its crew from total destruction.[3] There were, however, no more chaplains taken POW in the Pacific after the Philippine surrender in 1942.

When the Americans invaded North Africa in 1942, the chaplains came with them. Most people of the World War II generation remember the story of the Four Chaplains of the USAT *Dorchester* who, after the ship's torpedoing en route to North Africa, gave away their life jackets and went down with the ship. Tragically, the explosion knocked out power to *Dorchester*'s radio shack, and the ship lost contact with the three U.S. Coast Guard cutter escorts. The USCGC *Comanche*, however, saw the flash of the explosion and responded, rescuing 97 survivors. The USCGC *Escanaba* circled the sinking *Dorchester* and rescued an additional 132 survivors. The third cutter, USCGC *Tampa*, continued on, escorting the remaining two ships eventually into port and safety.

On board the *Dorchester*, panic and chaos set in as it settled into the sea. The blast killed scores of men, and many more were seriously wounded. Through the pandemonium, according to those present, four Army chaplains brought hope in despair and light in darkness. Those chaplains were Lt. George L. Fox, Methodist; Lt. Alexander D. Goode, Jewish; Lt. John P. Washington, Roman Catholic; and Lt. Clark V. Poling, Dutch Reformed.[4] Men jumped from the ship into lifeboats, overcrowding them to the point of capsizing, according to eyewitnesses. Other rafts, tossed into the Atlantic, drifted away before soldiers could get into them. By this time, most of the men came to the main deck, and the chaplains opened a storage locker and began distributing life jackets. It was then that Eng. Grady Clark witnessed an astonishing sight. When there were no more life jackets in the storage room, the chaplains removed theirs and gave them to four frightened young men. "It was the finest thing I have seen or hope to see this side of heaven," said John Ladd, another survivor who saw the chaplains' selfless act. Ladd's response is understandable. The sacrifice of the four chaplains constitutes one of the purest spiritual and ethical acts a person can make. When giving their life jackets to their soldiers and crew, Rabbi Goode did not call out for a Jew, Father Washington did not call out for a Catholic, nor did Reverends Fox and Poling call out for Protestants. They simply gave their life jackets to the next man in line. As the ship went down, survivors in nearby rafts could see the four chaplains' arms linked and braced against the slanting deck. Their voices could also be heard offering prayers. These four chaplains are remembered today with great reverence, and one visit to the Chapel of the Four Chaplains at the former Philadelphia Navy Yard certainly reinforces it. Writing during the summer of 1943, John Way, OP, in *Dominicana*, commented, "In his role of chaplain, the soldier-priest can truly act as another Christ." Fr. Way goes on to describe what he believes is the chaplain's role in every army: "The soldier-priest is truly Christ's ambassador. At the reception of Holy Orders he was given the power to fulfill the offices of another Christ, to give to others the sacrifice and sacraments by which they live. Thus, when he takes his place in the armed forces of his country, he brings with him the most potent weapons for good, the spiritual sacerdotal character. The Divine Master, whose minister he is, said on one occasion: 'Greater love no man hath that a man lay down his life for his friends.'"[5] There is no doubt that chaplains from the Revolution to World War II have been more than ready to do that.

Chaplain Eugene L. Daniel was taken POW by the Germans in Tunisia in 1943 and spent twenty-six months in captivity in Germany before liberation.[6] Chaplain Daniel noted that there were twenty-one British chaplains in his POW camp. All were Protestants except for one Catholic, Fr. Charlton. Services were performed in the camp with Chaplain Daniel, the only American in this camp, but he was later transferred to Stalag Luft III in Sagan, Silesia, where there were several chaplains, both Protestant and Catholic. In Chaplain Daniel's words, "It is my dominant prayer that together we may learn more of the grace and love of our Heavenly Father."[7] This was certainly done in Stalag Luft III. According to a 1944 report, "In 1943–44, camp chaplain was 1st Lt. Eugene L. Daniel, who won the admiration of both Americans and British. He had complete liberty to look after PWs in the Stalag, and once a month went to visit the two work detachments near Munich. He also received permission to visit the PW hospital. In addition to Chaplain Daniel, Capt. Arkell of the Church of England held services for Protestants. Roman Catholics were permitted to attend weekly Masses celebrated by French priests."[8]

The Catholic chaplain best remembered by the Americans in Stalag Luft III was a British priest, Captain Fr. Wilfred Coates, or Father Wilf, as the Americans called him. Chaplain Daniel wrote, "He was a fine gentleman, and he meant a lot to us, especially to the Catholic boys in our compound."[9] Fr. Coates did run into an ecumenical problem in the camp after President Franklin D. Roosevelt died. He was asked to take part in a service with Protestant clergymen but hesitated, thinking that as a Roman Catholic priest, he should not do such a thing. His brother Bill, also in camp and acting as his orderly, convinced him to take part, mainly because his American boys would not understand his reluctance. At the service Fr. Coates said a short prayer, in which, according to Chaplain Daniel, he referred to Roosevelt as "Thy servant Franklin." Chaplain Daniel commented, "I thought this was really broad-minded, coming from a Catholic and referring to an Episcopalian in a day long before Vatican II."[10] Father Wilfred did receive a commendation from the British Army at the end of the war: "Captain Wilfred Coates, British army Chaplain Corps, rendered exceptionally meritorious service, from January 1944 to April 1945, in administering to the morale and spiritual needs of American prisoners of war confined in the Center Compound, Stalag Luft III, Germany. The initiative, determination, and untiring efforts displayed by Captain Coates contributed materially to the welfare of many otherwise discouraged and dejected prisoners, and reflect high credit upon himself and the armed forces of His Majesty's Government."[11] All the American POWs in Stalag Luft III wound up detained in Stalag 7A, Moosburg, Bavaria, after the long march during the snowy freezing January 1945. Liberation came shortly thereafter in April 1945 when Patton's Third Army crashed through the gates and set them free.

The first American Catholic chaplain to be taken prisoner came in the North African campaign. He was Fr. Stanley C. Brach, whose unit was ambushed by the Afrika Korps on Christmas Day in Tunisia. Fr. Brach spent two and a half years as a POW and after an extremely difficult captivity was finally liberated in Poland by the Russians at war's end.[12]

The battle at the Kasserine Pass became one of the most fearsome disasters for American arms in World War II, and the chaplains found themselves in the middle of the fighting. Protestant Chaplain Orville Lorenz crawled under fire to rescue a wounded soldier. Chaplain Fr. L. Berkeley Kines, S.J., from Maryland, was one of the few wounded chaplains at the Kasserine Pass. Unhappily for him, his rump was a little too high as he crawled around his foxhole, and a German sniper got him in his sights. Poor Fr. Kines got a wound in an embarrassing spot, and he wrote humorously to his superiors, "I got shot in the ass in the Kasserine Pass."[13]

The Allied campaign in North Africa ended with the surrender of the Afrika Korps on May 12, 1943. Gen. Juergen von Arnim, then the commander of all Axis operations in North Africa, accepted the Allies' terms and surrendered some 275,000 German troops unconditionally. The British told the Americans that their island was full and asked President Roosevelt if the United States could take some POWs. The Americans responded that they could take them all and did. More than 425,000 German, Italian, and Japanese POWs came to the United States during World War II and were placed in hundreds of POW camps.[14] Historian Arnold P. Krammer notes that the Americans believed in the Golden Rule—treat enemy POWs as we wish our own to be treated—and sought to treat enemy POWs firmly, fairly, and with as much generosity as possible in accordance with the Geneva Convention of 1929. In historian Arnold Krammer's words,

> The War Department was convinced that the conditions experienced by the 90,000 Americans in German camps, atrocious as those conditions may have been, were often the best that could have been expected in a country which was losing the war. Food, medical supplies, fuel, material for camp construction, all were in desperate short supply. On the other hand, conditions could have been worse. Not only could the German

government have consistently withheld what little food and fuel was available, but it could have prevented the distribution of the massive supplies of supplemental food and medical aid provided by the International Red Cross Committee, the American Red Cross, and the British Red Cross.[15]

Thus, Krammer confirms many scholars' claim that the Golden Rule worked well between Nazi Germany and the United States, although there were no thoughts of it by the Japanese. As one former German POW, Wilhelm Sauerbrei, said to a Houston reporter when the reporter asserted that he must have had it pretty easy, "I'll tell you pal, if there is ever another war, get on the side that America isn't, then get captured by the Americans—you'll have it made."[16] When and where possible, the Americans supplied German-speaking American clergy to tend to the religious needs of German POWs.

The victory in North Africa was impressive, but it was also deceptive. The German army intended to fight hard in Sicily and later in Italy. The Americans were worried but not as much as they were before the North African landings, simply because the army was now blooded and much more skilled in the military arts. Not only could they march, but they could now fight as well. The invasion of Sicily pitted 150,000 Allied soldiers initially against 30,000 Germans and later nearly 200,000 in Italy. Leading the Americans was Gen. George S. Patton Jr.; leading the British was Gen. Sir Bernard Montgomery. Such was the oil-and-water environment where cooperation never entered the vocabulary of either general. The invasion began early on July 10, 1943: thousands of paratroopers landed on Sicily along with four chaplains who jumped with them into harm's way. By the evening of July 22, 1943, General Patton accepted the surrender of Palermo.

What surprised many of the American GIs on the ground was the friendliness of many of the local Sicilians. What they did not know was that the head of the Sicilian Mafia, Charles "Lucky" Luciano, from a jail cell in New York, ordered his colleagues in Sicily to cooperate with the invading Americans.[17] After all, there were now many family connections between Sicily and the United States, and there were a large number of Italian Americans in the American Army. Although many chaplains were Irish Americans, the cadre of Catholic chaplains felt this as well, especially as the Army fought its way north to Messina.

After losing a few chaplains, dead and wounded, the Americans noticed that between all the commotion in the press surrounding the competition of the Patton-versus-Montgomery rush to Messina, about 100,000 German soldiers crossed the Straits of Messina and landed safely in Italy intact and ready to fight. The next step was the invasion of Italy, and the chaplains accompanied their men on the troopships, even though many tired of war by now and hoped for a more quiet life back home.[18]

British historian Alan Robinson comments in *Chaplains at War* (2008) that life in German POW camps was much more constrained that it was in the Italian camps.[19] That the Italians were Catholic for the most part made life easier for British and American Catholic POWs in Italy; however, after the Italians capitulated and changed sides in September 1943, the world turned upside down for a great number of POWs and, of course, their chaplains. The Germans separated officers from their enlisted men immediately, which meant that the chaplains lost contact with the soldiers. British clergy often had to lobby their German captors to allow them to minister to their troops behind the wire. The German authorities often imposed severe restrictions, including the censoring of sermons to make certain the chaplains would not cross political lines, so important to the Germans at the time. This problem also extended to persecuted minorities like Russian and Jewish POWs. It is important to note that British and American Jewish POWs were not separated from their comrades until late in 1944 after the Battle of the Bulge. Robinson does make several keen observations: first, he notes that church membership continued in captivity, much as it did in civilian life; second, he observes that there was competition between chaplains of various denominations; and third, the strengths and weaknesses of chaplains as well as denominations, individual prisoners, and Army structures were not at all lost in the POW camps during World War II.[20]

Soldiers called Italy the "Old Gut," in part because of the terrain, in part because of the kind of war that they fought there from 1943 to 1945. When one thinks of Italy, it is common to anticipate sunshine, good food, happy people, and nice beaches. Well, 1943 was nothing like the travel brochures. It rained a lot, especially in the mountains, where the soldiers were struggling. The mud was sticky and deep so that using light armored vehicles was extremely difficult.

The Italians were not happy with the war, their country, their terrible leadership, the fascists, and then the German occupation and defense they were putting up against the Allies as they pushed north. In September 1943, Field Marshall Pietro Badoglio surrendered Italian arms to the Allies, and Italy changed sides in a hurry. Place-names like Anzio and Salerno, Monte Casino, Naples, and Rome became well known in the American and Allied wartime vocabulary. The main attraction for Catholic troops in Italy, however, was Pope Pius XII in Rome's Vatican City. Jesuit historian Donald J. Crosby explains how young Catholic soldiers, often along with their chaplains, streamed into St. Peter's hoping to see and possibly have an audience with the pope. He describes how Pope Pius XII responded to soldiers and clergy and notes with great pleasure how well everyone got along.[21] The war continued past Rome north, up the "Old Gut," until the German army surrendered in 1945.

Chaplains were lost, dead and wounded, but only John W. Handy was taken in France during the fight at Saint-Lô after the Normandy invasion in June 1944. Subsequently, no American chaplain was taken POW until the Battle of the Bulge in the Ardennes Forest of Belgium and Luxembourg. Historian Lyle W. Dorsett writes, "Chaplains not only died in the Battle of the Bulge, many were captured by the Germans and became part of the massive throng of American POWs who experienced much suffering during the last five months of the war."[22] Dorsett points out that the regular units of the German army took prisoners, about 21,000 Americans all told, and sent many of them, especially two entire regiments of the 106th Division, 75,000 officers and men, to Stalag IX B at Bad Orb, only about thirty miles northwest of Frankfurt am Main. Mark Moore was a Protestant chaplain in the 106th Infantry Division captured at the Bulge fight and made a POW at Bad Orb. His early postwar memoir, *Prisoner of the Germans* (1945), tells his story:

> The Germans marched us many miles towards a rail junction that would lead us to the prison camp at Bad Orb. I was gripped by hunger during one of the halts during the march. We were packed in unsanitary conditions on tiny train boxcars and shipped to the prison camp in Limburg, Germany. British bombers bombed us, but it was by God's hand that we were saved from a direct hit. The only men among us that were killed were those who

tried to use this opportunity to escape. After we arrived at Bad Orb, our imprisonment stretched from days to weeks. The Germans kept us on a 700 calorie per day diet. Our diet was supplemented by precious Red Cross boxes full of treasured foods like salmon, oleo and jelly shipped through Switzerland courtesy of the Red Cross and the U.S. government. Sharing these boxes and our regular ration was a careful process of division and selection. The man who would divide the food would be the last to choose, and we took turns dividing these meager provisions in this way. Despite the pitiful conditions of the camp, the other chaplains and I continued to help the men's morale and spiritual condition by holding services. There were Sunday Worships, Evening Devotions, Morning Devotions, and Bible Study. Many men would attend these services, but others would sit and talk or play cards during our prayer sessions.

While we were certain that we would be freed soon, the weeks passed into months. We thought that 100 days would bring us freedom but it was more than five months until the first possibility of liberation arrived. An American armored (tank) unit had broken forty miles behind enemy lines and moved to liberate us from our captors. After shelling and smashing the German resistance in the vicinity, they arrived at our camp. Our commanding officer brought out an American flag that had been hidden and saved in anticipation of liberation. Disappointingly, the tank unit had only expected 250 men, but there were more than 1500 officers at our camp.[23]

Chaplain Moore was a free man for a little while, but even worse events took place.

Near the Belgian village of Malmédy, the SS murdered about eighty American POWs after their surrender. As this was clearly a war crime, the Americans stopped at nothing in their attempt to bring the German SS officer in charge of the guilty SS unit to justice. In 1946–47 the Americans tried Jochen Peiper, an SS officer known as "Blow Torch," for his war crimes on the eastern front against the Russians. He was found guilty of the Malmédy massacre and given a sentence of death. His sentence, like so many others, was reduced, and by the mid-1950s, Peiper was a free man. In 1976 Jochen Peiper died in a suspicious house fire in France, where he worked as a children's book translator. No one was ever charged for any crime. However, in 1944 the American soldiers and their chaplains lost respect for the SS as soldiers. Fr. Leo Weigel found himself with some SS wounded, and after a trooper attempted to insult his American rescuers, Fr. Weigh gave him a right cross in the teeth.[24]

At least seven Catholic chaplains fell into German hands as POWs during the Battle of the Bulge in 1944. Jesuit Fr. Paul W. Cavanaugh and several thousand enlisted men of the 106th Division were surrounded and taken POW on December 19, 1944. Loaded into freight cars, the Americans just sat there in the freight yard, locked in the vulnerable freight cars: no food, no water, no guards, no movement, nothing. The train finally took them to the POW camp Stalag IX B at Bad Orb. Realizing his friends and he were in a POW camp on Christmas Eve, Fr. Cavanaugh gave the sermon of his life, realizing that both the Americans and the Germans were Christians: "Lord, grant peace to the world. Grant that the peace which Christ who is called the Prince of Peace, came to bring us may be established all over the world. Amen."[25] When Fr. Cavanaugh was finished, he found that the men had calmed down and were asleep finally. They had to wait now for liberation, which came in the spring of 1945, but not before the men of the 106th Division suffered a great deal. After the war, Fr. Cavanaugh was asked to recount his experiences behind barbed wire and wrote a personal memoir about his captivity, *Pro Deo et Patria: The Personal Narrative of an American Catholic Chaplain as a Prisoner of War in Germany* (2004).[26] One of Fr. Cavanaugh's most memorable experiences was in Stalag IX B at Bad Orb, where he met an Italian POW priest-chaplain who had been taken prisoner during the summer of 1943, just after the capitulation of Italy. The Italian chaplain introduced him to some French priests, also POWs, and they worked together, one priest saying Mass while the others heard confessions. He recalled,

> It was no cathedral; but no consecrated church ever held a more grateful crowd of worshippers than the cold barracks of Bad Orb, where the priest lacked vestments and the dirty table of an altar left much to be desired in the way of fine linen. Around that rude setting hearts filled with faith, hope, and love; faith in the sublime mysteries enacted under the visible

forms of bread and wine, hope in the power of the redeeming sacrifice to free us from the hands of our enemies, and love born of fellowship with the suffering Christ in cold hunger and privation.[27]

On the Protestant side, in 1945 William Turner's B-24 took hits on both inside engines, and he and his crew out bailed out far from Vienna. Taken to a POW camp near Nuremberg, he learned that the German POW system had all but broken down completely. There was nothing left in the camp for the prisoners. They received few rations, and the Red Cross supply system was stopped by Allied bombing campaigns as well. Turner recalled that his group of POWs was "without benefit of a chaplain."[28] One of the officers had a Bible and led Sunday and Wednesday-evening services by reading scripture and singing hymns from memory such as "The Old Rugged Cross" and "Rock of Ages." On April 6, 1945, the Germans removed all the POWs to a camp north of Munich, where they were liberated by American troops on April 29.

At Oflag XIII-B, the POW officers' camp at Hammelburg in south-central Germany, there were nine chaplains, seven Protestants, and two Catholics. Services were held regularly, despite the difficult living conditions and scarce food rations. The POWs at Hammelburg witnessed one of the POW camp raids, Task Force Baum, ordered by Gen. George S. Patton Jr. to liberate the camp where his son-in-law Col. John Waters, who was captured in North Africa, was held. The raid failed, and a large number of raiders were killed in action; the rest became POWs in Hammelburg.[29] A similar raid against Stalag IX-B at Bad Orb went much better and freed a large number of Allied POWs in 1945.

Perhaps the best-known POW chaplain in the European theater during World War II was Chaplain Fr. Francis L. Sampson, the "Paratrooper Padre." Beginning as a high school teacher, he joined the Army in 1942 after the war broke out for the United States and decided early on that he wanted to be a paratrooper, even though he had little or no idea what he was getting into: "Had I known this beforehand, and particularly had I known the tortures of mind and body prepared at Fort Benning for those who sought the coveted parachute wings, I am positive that I should have turned a deaf ear to the plea for airborne chaplains. I had already begun to enjoy the prestige and glamour that goes with belonging to an outfit."[30]

On June 6, 1944, Fr. Sampson jumped with his 101st Airborne Division behind German lines of Utah Beach at Normandy and landed in a deep stream of water, where he lost his Mass Kit and everything else he carried. He recalled, "As soon as we were over land, the ack-ack was terrific. The plane was hit many times. As we stood up and hooked up, the plane was rocking badly. The Germans were waiting for us." After landing in the water, he managed to retrieve his Mass Kit and a few other things and met up with some other paratroopers. Along with a Chaplain McGee, he set up a makeshift medical station, but Fr. Sampson volunteered to set out to find a real medical station for their wounded. They managed to get the walking wounded on their way, but Fr. Sampson decided to remain with the seriously wounded and kept a white flag handy in his attempt to keep the German soldiers from committing any atrocities.[31]

At dawn the next day a German unit arrived at the farmhouse and, in a foul mood and frightened that so many Allied soldiers had arrived, interrogated Fr. Sampson and decided to execute him on the spot. Knowing this, it was time to say his prayers. Fr. Sampson got so rattled that he recited the Prayer Before Meals before a German officer appeared and recognized that Fr. Sampson was a Catholic chaplain. The officer then sent sent him back to the farmhouse to tend to the wounded Americans.[32] Although it was a very generous gesture by that German officer, it is safer to say that Fr. Sampson got lucky.[33] His next encounter with the German army face-to-face was not as fortunate.

When the Paratrooper Padre of the 101st Airborne Division met the German army the second time, the Battle of the Bulge raged in Belgium, and his luck gave out. Although Fr. Samson learned that the Germans had captured the regiment's medical supplies, he decided to make an attempt to salvage some of it. He recalled, "I loaded my jeep with a couple of chests of much-needed equipment, and was ready to head back to the regimental aid station. A soldier there told me, however, that there had been quite a skirmish last night. He thought there were still some wounded left there. We drove over the hill to see, and just over the crest of the hill we ran into Germans—hundreds of them. We were captured."[34] Retained as a POW, Sampson was sent east to a POW camp near the town of Neubrandenburg, north of Berlin.

In the camp, Stalag II-A, Mecklenburg, Fr Sampson said Mass daily and offered a nondenominational service twice weekly.[35] By this time, the SS had taken over the administration of all the military POW camps and changed the rules to include separation of Jews from Allied Gentile soldiers. The Americans and the British found this unacceptable and often complained bitterly to the camp administration. Fr. Sampson played a role in all this, but the SS control of POW camp policies held until liberation in late April and early May. In mid-April, after nearly four miserable months of wartime imprisonment for the POWs, the Russian Second Belorussian Front approached the nearby town of Neubrandenburg from the east.[36] The German inhabitants knew well what all this meant: chaos, rape, theft, murder, and destruction. The Americans became aghast at the behavior of the "liberating" Russian soldiers, seriously drunk most of the time and intent on doing as much harm to any and all Germans as possible.

At this uncertain time, Fr. Sampson had developed a good rapport with the local parish priest in town, but his worst day came when he came to the parish church to visit his friend and his family, mother, and sisters and found them all simply devastated, raped, and destitute in every way. Shocked but powerless to stop the Red Army from committing war crimes against a defeated enemy, Fr. Sampson had to move on. American Army personnel arrived at the camp and eventually managed to separate Americans from the Russians, sending Fr. Sampson west to American lines, where he became well known as their own Paratrooper Padre. His war was over. In a report from the U.S. Army Command and Staff College at Ft. Leavenworth, Kansas (1969), the author states, "On April 1945, Chaplain Sampson and four other chaplain-retainers, conducted an Easter Sunday service for thousands of POWs. American, Russian, English, French, as well as prisoners from other nationalities, prayed with one voice for true brotherhood and deliverance from their harsh taskmasters. That particular Easter service was most significant, for it served as an inspiration to the men for acts of human kindness and righteousness for years to come."[37] He returned home via Paris and Camp Lucky Strike, as did all POWs in Europe; however, Fr. Sampson returned to active duty during the Korean War and remained an Army chaplain until he retired as a major general and Army chief of chaplains in 1971.

Fr. Paul Cavanaugh, S.J., had a very different and much more troubling end of war experience than Fr. Sampson did. In March 1945, his group of Americans from the 106th Division moved from Stalag IX-B at Bad Orb to Stalag XIII-C at Hammelburg. They left at two in the morning on March 28, 1945. In a few days, the guards simply vanished, leaving the entire group of POWs to fend for themselves. They decided to head south to Bavaria and near Nuremberg found themselves under a flight of B-17s dropping bombs directly on them. Of course, the bombers had no intention of bringing such terror on their own men, but in this case the fog of war is again pure hell. There were subsequent attacks and some direct hits near the American POWs. Fr. Cavanaugh kept his head, as he anointed every dead and wounded near him. He also found his best friend dead, a Protestant chaplain with whom Cavanaugh went through chaplain school.[38] It was one of the worst days of his life. After thirty-seven days of marching south across Bavaria, the group of POWs finally arrived at a point of freedom. On May 3, 1945, the men wandered into the village of Gars-am-Inn on the German-Austrian border and there met a convoy of the 14th Armored Division. They were free men again.

By May 1945 so many Army chaplains had seen too much combat that they began to simply wither from fatigue. They saw a Germany that was all but destroyed and a German people who had all but lost their faith in anything. Both the American soldiers and the Germans, both military and civilians, shared the "thousand-yard stare" that describes the soldier's state of mind after seeing and experiencing too much combat. Nazi Germany surrendered to the Allies on May 8, 1945. Celebrations took place everywhere across Europe and America, some lasting quite a while. Many Allied soldiers knew that chances were excellent that they would have to face the Japanese on their home islands in bloody battle, although that seemed pretty far off at the moment. For the German people it was *Stunde Null* (Zero Hour); for the Americans, after losing more than 500,000 dead in Europe alone, including twenty-three chaplains, it was the beginning, so they thought, of a life without war.[39]

Eight

—»›‹«—

1943 to 1946
Chaplains and Enemy POWs

You will understand our impatience and even our astonishment at the
fact that, more than ten days after greeting our liberators, the 34,000
detainees of Dachau are still prisoners of the same barbed-wire fences.
—Fr. Michel Riquet, S.J., to Gen. Dwight D. Eisenhower, May 1945

PART OF THE MISSION of the American Chaplain Corps of all services is to tend to enemy POWs. This mission was carried out by many chaplains both in the United States and at the more than five hundred POW camps, in European camps for German POWs, and for wounded German soldiers in their own hospitals. In June 1944, Fr. James A. Gilmore, S.J., went ashore on Normandy beach after the invasion. According to Gerard F. Giblin, S.J., after Fr. Gilmore's appointment to General Hospital 50, the first general hospital in the combat zone hosted a group of German POWs freshly brought in. Fr. Gilmore was very surprised to hear them give the servers' responses in perfect Latin as he said Mass for them.[1]

After the invasion, Jesuit Father George L. Earth was put in charge of captured German POW clergy, thirty-six Catholic priests and thirty Protestant ministers, during his chaplain service in Marseille, France.[2] Jim Graves of the *National Catholic Register* wrote about Divine Word Father Henry Marusa, a U.S. Army chaplain who hit Omaha Beach in Normandy, France, in 1944, with the second wave of Allied invaders and was nearly killed multiple times in the following weeks. On September 12, 2020, Graves wrote that Father Marusa offered Mass every day, "unless the firing was too heavy." He did this from the hood of his jeep, so the men would be able to see him better, and was able to complete a liturgy quickly—a necessity in the midst of combat. In September 1944, Father Marusa was assigned as chaplain to the POWs at a camp in Rennes—partly because he spoke fluent Slovak, which Russians could understand, and could make himself understood in German. For a year, he acted as priest to fifty thousand Germans and ten thousand Russians. "Oh, what a blessing," he recalled. "It was wonderful work."[3]

Chaplain (Col.) Herbert E. MacCombie, the 36th Infantry Division, had an unusual experience with enemy soldiers he never expected to meet, German chaplains captured in the Alsatian Vosges mountains in 1944. He reported,

> The 142nd Infantry has captured two German majors of the Chaplain Corps at Chateau de Koenigsbourg. They were brought to me for interrogation. When they arrived, we found there were two German chaplains. They were accompanied by a third man, a Catholic priest who had been drafted into the service and assigned as a medical corps enlisted man. Apparently, the Germans drafted all clergymen, but only made chaplains of those who would support the Nazi regime. While Chaplains were not supposed to be held as prisoners of war, it was evident that we could not release them in the midst of battle. I was instructed to evacuate them to the POW enclosure of the Seventh Army. We fed the three prisoners, and they were evacuated by the Provost Marshal.[4]

In Stalag II-A Mecklenburg, German guards approached Chaplain Sampson, seeking pastoral help. Nearby was a large German military hospital, and the Catholic guards asked him to go to the hospital to anoint dying German soldiers. Fr. Sampson went to the hospital and anointed those German Catholic soldiers who needed the sacrament, what Catholics called the "last rites" at that time. When the Red Army entered the town of Neubrandenburg, they set it on fire and burned it to the ground, torching the hospital where he anointed all the German soldiers.[5]

Perhaps it stands as one of the paradoxes of war in the twentieth century, but chaplains understood their task first as one of saving souls for God and only second that of helping to win the war for the Allies. Rev. Paul Link, C.PP.S., records in his book *For God and Country* that Fr. Sabastian Kremer, who served as an auxiliary chaplain at Crile General Hospital in Parma, Ohio, recorded this story about his service to German POWs:

> The first group of prisoners were rather indifferent and quite arrogant, but those in the camp at present are devout, respectful and courteous. They set up the altar, decorate it with flowers, serve the Mass, and in general, are very edifying. During the Mass they sing congregational, sometimes even four-voiced without benefit of organ. On Easter Sunday seventy-two were present, and sixteen of those approached the sacraments. On ordinary Sundays about fifty attend the Mass which I say at four o'clock in the afternoon. The age of the prisoners are [*sic*] from teens to middle thirties. Most of them are from Baden, Wurttemburg, the Tyrol, and the Rhineland. In all there are about 200 prisoners here, thirty percent are Catholic, Twenty percent Protestant, and the rest have no religious affiliation.[6]

Fr. Link noted that Fr. Kremer enjoyed his work, in part, because he liked giving his sermons in German, his mother tongue, to the prisoners. On October 23, 1944, the *New York Times* reported that members of the clergy in Germany, both Catholic and Protestant, were included in the draft for the German people's Home Guard army. Only Jesuits were exempt because they were considered unfit to bear arms in the Reich. The Nazis were reported to have been afraid the religious propaganda that the Jesuits might spread among the German troops. As a result, the Allied chaplains encountered German clergy who were formally uniformed in the German army and some who were not. This became a problem, but not an unsolvable one.[7]

The question was this: How anti-Christian were the German military authorities, and why was American captivity a breath of fresh air for those captured chaplains? To answer this in part, one can look into the writings of Doris Bergen, whose book *The Sword of the Lord: Military Chaplains from the First to the Twenty-First Century* (2004) is a collection of essays from a conference at Notre Dame University in 2000 that sheds some light on this issue. First, the Nazi Party's religious guru was Alfred Rosenberg, one of the vilest human beings on the planet at the time. His so-called religious book *The Myth of the*

Twentieth Century (1935) dubbed the Old Testament as a collection of pimps and cattle traders and said that real men did not pray.[8] To any person of faith, Rosenberg's book is a kind of anti-Christian apostasy that causes one to ask what sort of people could believe this rubbish. According to Bergen, "German chaplains were supposed to present themselves as paragons of Christian manliness, role models for those soldiers around them."[9] Fr. Charles Meyer ran into this kind of Nazi thinking at Fort Leonard Wood in 1943 when he encountered one nasty German POW. He reported,

> When I entered one compound the leader confronted me with the remark that I was no longer permitted to hear confessions in his compound. It had always slipped his mind before, but no one except a German army chaplain is permitted to hear confessions of German soldiers. I spoke to him for about a half hour, and during that time I gave him rope to hang himself. This man called himself the Fuehrer of his compound, and had established dictatorship. He had his henchmen. The authorities have promised he and any other of his kind [would] be removed.[10]

Fr. Meyer was anything but done with his Nazis, however. Reporting on Thanksgiving Day 1943 that he met a German POW priest who described the real problems and issues he had to face with older, more seasoned members of the Africa Korps: "I now have an assistant, a German priest who is a prisoner of war, a private in the Medical Corps. I asked if he had the opportunity to say Mass in the German Army. He stated that even on Easter his group did not have Mass. He did hear confessions, however, when the chance presented itself, and also gave general absolution. There are a few among the older prisoners who are very fervent."[11] That world was turned upside down after the Americans separated the German POWs into Nazi and anti-Nazi camps in 1944. When the German POWs arrived in the United States in 1943, the U.S. Army found a good number of priests and ministers in their prison camps who were drafted into the German army, and in American captivity they could finally deal with their ministries openly and freely.

Things were brewing in Oklahoma in 1944 when the U.S. Army looked into the religious life of German POWs there. In an article published by the Catholic magazine *America*, Stephen A. Leven wrote,

It is none the less gratifying to know that un-official estimates in most German prisoner-of-war camps show that 48 to 53 per cent declare themselves to be *Evangelisch* (Trans. Evangelical, the equivalent of "Protestant"), 35 to 40 per cent profess to be Roman Catholics, and only the 10 to 15 per cent remainder affirm no religious affiliation or declare they are *Gott-Gläubig* (God-Believers) in about equal numbers. The *Gott-Gläubig* are also sometimes called "Rosenberg's boys." They affirm belief in God and the need of prayer but they vigorously repudiate all Jewish influence in religion, even that of Christ. That so many have remained even nominally Christian is no small matter.[12]

Leven goes on to say,

The problem of providing the Mass for those who wish to attend has not been easy in any camp. In only one prisoner-of-war camp in the States was there a Catholic Army Chaplain for a short while. At the present time there are only Protestant chaplains. In some of the camps there were German priests among the prisoners from the very beginning. These were not Chaplains in the German Army, though the policy was to have an official Chaplain in each German Division. The priests were members of the Medical Corps. They carried their credentials and served in much the same capacity as the American Civilian Auxiliary Chaplains. Their work was directed and in some measure coordinated by the official Division Chaplains. Through transfers, an effort has been made to provide a prisoner-of-war Evangelical minister and a prisoner-of-war Catholic priest for each large camp.

Because of the great interest of the Most Reverend Bishops in Oklahoma and the charity of religious and secular priests of the diocese, every camp has had Sunday Mass shortly after its initial activation. The German priests that this writer has encountered are all zealous and earnest young men. They have the Faculties of the German Military Ordinariate and they are also given the Faculties of our Military Ordinariate. They do incalculable good, since they share the life of their fellow-prisoners in every particular. They are not obliged to go out on work details, but they are subject to the same restrictions as other prisoners, since they were acting as common soldiers in the German Medical Corps. Their life is not easy, and yet they are cheerful and try to be satisfied with their lot. Only to God can all the good they do be known. Much fruit is quickly apparent, but even more will appear when the prisoners return to their home land.[13]

In 1945 the Society for the Propagation of the Faith, a major Catholic organization worldwide, published a coffee-table picture book titled *The Priest Goes to War.* In it are photos and data that supported the Catholic Church's efforts to keep the faith vibrant and relevant during wartime. One page shows photos of priests serving German POWs working in Michigan. The text reads,

> Spiritual ministration to the prisoners of war is provided in the Geneva Convention [1929], and the American authorities have made conscientious efforts to provide chaplains according to the expressed religious preference of its prisoners. More than a hundred priests of enemy nationality have been captured by our troops. The use of these priests as chaplains has greatly facilitated matters and has lessened considerably the demand on commissioned chaplains for this work.[14]

This raises the fascinating question: What was the status of clergy in the German army? As we have seen, some were recognized chaplains, but they could not have any political (i.e., anti-Nazi) blemishes; others were either parish priests or seminarians who were drafted into the army, many of whom worked as medics. Any clerics who opposed the Nazi regime were arrested by the Gestapo and put into several concentration camps, Dachau being the main one for clergy.[15]

Nazi Germany had signed a concordat with the Vatican in 1933 that protected many of the prerogatives of the Catholic Church in Germany, but it failed to protect its people and clergy very well. Thus, it is fair to say that the church both supported (overtly) and defied (covertly) the Nazi regime from its beginning in 1933 to its end in 1945. Prior to 1933, the church excommunicated anyone belonging to the Nazi Party out of hand, and it is also fair to say that Hitler may have feared very little in Germany, but he did fear the power and influence of the Catholic Church. In 1934 Hitler imposed an oath of loyalty on the German army that forced every officer and man to swear by God fealty to Adolf Hitler, "the supreme commander of the armed forces and that, as a brave soldier, I will be ready at all times to stake my life in fulfillment of this last."[16] Thus, German Christians were in a terrible position: they were damned if they practiced their faith correctly and double-damned if they opposed the regime for any reason. German clergy were in an even worse position, in that the regime restricted all clerical activities other than the actual liturgical service itself. Preaching was perilous, and any sort of activities outside of the church itself was forbidden: no Catholic politics, no Catholic Youth activities, no Catholic press, nothing. It was then a small wonder that anyone retained their Christian religion with the Nazis breathing so heavily down their backs, and it is nothing short of a miracle that Germany retained at least some of its Christian bearing after the war ended.

The Americans liberated several concentration camps late in World War II. What surprised the Americans when they liberated the concentration camp at Dachau, a camp near Munich, the capital city of Bavaria, was the discovery of a prison block in the camp that contained only clergy, mostly Polish Catholic priests but also other clergy of different nations, faiths, and denominations. When General Patton's Third Army liberated Dachau on April 29, 1945, they discovered nearly 30,000 living inmates. They also discovered the "Death Convoy" formed in the concentration camp at Buchenwald (near Weimar and Jena) on April 7, 1945, and after wandering around a bombarded and wrecked Germany, it arrived in Dachau on April 28, 1945. Out of the 4,480 deportees crammed into the wagons of that convoy, only 816 survivors were counted at its arrival in Dachau.[17] Eloi Leclerc wrote, "Most of them died of exhaustion, some of dysentery; others of erysipelas. Their woolen, inflamed faces were completely disfigured. Delirious with fever, these unfortunate men shouted at night, asking for something to drink. The SS quieted them by hitting them with the butt end of a rifle. And in the morning they lay there as *rigor mortis* set in."[18]

After discovering a large number of murdered inmates in the Buchenwald boxcars that arrived a short time before they entered the camp, the Americans began taking what they believed was legal retribution. Guard after guard was simply executed in a spree of killing. For the American soldiers there, it seemed perfectly justified to shoot these SS guards to death for what they had done to thousands of innocents, clergy included. Charges against these American soldiers were brought later, but were quietly dropped by Gen. George S. Patton.[19] For the

American chaplains present, the 1,240 living, surviving clergy interested them the most. What they witnessed was a true cultural and religious horror. They learned that the German and Austrian clergy were there because they resisted the regime, some from the beginning of the Nazis' rise to power in 1933. For example, in 1935, members of the Catholic Church formed the Committee for Aid to Non-Aryan Catholics, which helped converted Jews who were targeted by the Nazis. This was done in a letter circulated throughout Germany and then confiscated by the police from printing houses, libraries, rectories, and display cases in churches.[20]

In 1937 the caldron heated up between the Catholic Church and the Nazi government with the publication of the papal encyclical *Mit Brennender Sorge* (*With a Burning Desire*), written by Vatican secretary of state and former papal nuncio to Germany Eugenio Cardinal Pacelli and signed by Pope Pius XI. It damned everything the Nazi Party stood for as well as damning how the Nazis usurped the provisions of the concordat, and finally completely damning Nazi racial policies against Jews, Gypsies, and others. As a result, the Nazi press lashed out against purported church embezzlement, pedophilia, and sexual perversion in monasteries. Joseph Goebbels was delighted; the church was outraged, and the descent into a new hell began in Germany. From 1940 to 1945, 447 German clergymen went to, passed through, or died in Dachau for their anti-Nazi beliefs and preaching.[21]

Of the Polish clergy captured in 1939–40, the vast majority were sent to Dachau because not only did they resist the Nazi defeat and occupation of Poland, but they were also part of the Polish elite whom the Nazis decided to eliminate. Father Stefan Biskupski, detained in Dachau from December 14, 1940, gave this analysis of why the Polish clergy were persecuted, imprisoned, and killed:

> All Polish culture—its history, its rich literature, its magnificent art—all
> of it had value only because it was deeply based in Catholic principles. So
> much so that it all ceases to be intelligible if it is detached from Catholi-
> cism. The Church had to be destroyed, therefore, in order to destroy the
> culture of the Polish nation. And to do that, the Polish clergy who were
> inseparably tied to the people, had to be destroyed.[22]

Others were there for similar reasons: Czech and Slovak clergy because they were Slavs or subhumans to the Nazis and French, Dutch, Italian, and Belgian priests because they refused to be pacifists or allies of the Nazi occupation. Added to 2,579 Catholic priests, lay brothers, and seminarians who came from thirty-eight nations were 109 Protestant, 30 Orthodox, and 2 Muslim clergymen.[23] Writing in 1960, the auxiliary bishop of Munich, Dr. Johannes Neuhaeusler, himself a prisoner first in the large camp called Sachsenhausen (near Berlin in the small city of Oranienburg) and then in Dachau later, described the American liberation:

After the entry of the small American advance party, an immense joy filled the hearts of the prisoners. All went to the roll-call square which instilled such terrible memories for them and thanked the liberators. Soon the flags of various countries were unfolded from the living quarters and from the former administration buildings. The papal flag flew from the priests' barrack. In the chapel the *Te Deum* was sung. An altar was erected outside the priests' block and Holy Mass was biblically celebrated. During the night, comrades erected a huge cross on the roll-call square. The sacrifice of the Mass was offered on the following day for all the deceased. And then came the great farewell and their return to freedom and homeland, to family and profession.[24]

Their suffering intensified as liberation got ever closer in 1945. Rumors of extermination flooded the camp area, as they did in all POW camps among the POWs. Whereas the POWs attempted to arm themselves and developed plans to resist what they called Nazi "Death Squads," the clergy just prayed their way through it all. Father Bedrich Hoffmann recalled, "From February 3 to 11, special divine services were celebrated in the chapel to avert dangers. Typhus was raging in Dachau. The bombardments threatened the camp, and there were many other dangers. During these devotions, the priests prayed not only for themselves but also for all the detainees."[25]

The Nazi SS also attempted to move large numbers of prisoners east or west to keep them from being liberated by the Allies. They also held what they called *Prominente*, or elite VIPs whom they wished to use as bargaining chips if they gained the opportunity to bargain with the Allies. They were all liberated in time; none were lost. In Dachau a wholesale massacre was planned by the SS guard force for the evening of April 29, 1945. According to Chaplain Fr. John M. Lenz in his wonderful account of the American liberation of Dachau, "The prisoners were to have been assembled on the parade ground and then mowed down by machine-gun fire. The camp itself, together with the sick and any other survivors was then to have been destroyed by flame-throwers. But to the Americans on that very afternoon, God had willed it otherwise." The prisoners had seen American reconnaissance aircraft circling the camp and began shouting, "The Americans are here." As the troops came into the camp, the prisoners went nearly mad for joy and swarmed any soldier they saw. They laughed, cheered, and cried, and hardly believed that their liberators had arrived.[26]

In brief, when dealing with the losses of clergy in Dachau, it does not include clergy or nuns shot, beheaded, or tortured to death by the Nazis all over Europe. According to Pauly Fongemie's work, "In the first sixteen months of the war, 700 Polish priests died and 3,000 more were sent to concentration camps; more than half did not return. In Dachau, 868 Polish priests perished. The Poles indeed had the right to be vindictive, but most of the clergy never were."[27] In 1972, former prisoners put up a plaque that reads, "Here in Dachau every third victim tormented to death was a Pole, and one in every two Polish priests imprisoned here laid down his life. Their sacred memory is venerated by their fellow prisoners, members of the Polish clergy."[28]

In the end, Dachau prisoners pervaded a sense of gladness for the newly found freedom given to the inmates by the American Army. Some priests went to the crematorium to pray for the dead; others needed to go outside the confines of the camp just to get some fresh air. Father Alexandre Morelli recalled, "I remember as one of the most vivid joys in my life that unprecedented moment when for the first time in two years, a few minutes after the liberation of the camp in Dachau, the large gates opened, and, inebriated with freedom, I could walk freely on the ground of the surrounding courtyard, thinking that I was dreaming, striking this land of Germany with my foot to make sure that it was not a dream."[29]

Liberation, however, did not mean instant freedom for all the inmates to leave for home. The Americans feared typhus, and they imposed a very strict quarantine. Fr. Joseph Hoying commented, "After hostilities ceased, the chaplains were asked to give whatever assistance they could to displaced persons, crowded into camps by thousands. In two camps where I had Mass, the people were mostly Polish, and 98% Catholic. Some had not attended Mass or seen a priest from three to five years." Fr. Hoying was surprised to meet a priest in Dachau who was an American citizen and reported, "His family moved to Poland just before the war. He spent three years in the prison camp. Although only fifty, he looks seventy."[30]

Apparently, the Americans had developed no real plans for the liberation of concentration camps that held large numbers of international prisoners. POW camps were easier to administer and manage. The first task was to bury the dead. Mass graves were dug near the Leitenberg, an open hilly area a few miles from Dachau. For days peasant carts arrived at the camp to take bodies to a new cemetery at Etzenhausen where crosses marked Christian prisoners and a Star of David marked Jews. Once a week the American Episcopalian chaplain collected a Catholic priest and a rabbi to say prayers for the dead at the cemetery.[31]

The military authority was already in place among the inmates; all any authority had to do was to reimpose it. The civilian camps were larger, messier, devoid of any real discipline except for SS discipline, and nearly impossible to manage from a military point of view. The Americans may have had the best of intentions, but demanding that all the inmates, including clergy, stay in place for any length of time was a difficult, if not impossible, task. In a letter to Gen. Dwight D. Eisenhower, Supreme Commander, Allied Expeditionary Force, Fr. Michel Riquet, S.J., wrote,

> You will understand our impatience and even our astonishment at the fact that, more than ten days after greeting our liberators, the 34,000 detainees of Dachau are still prisoners of the same barbed-wire fences, guarded by sentinels whose orders are still to fire on anyone who attempts to escape—which for every prisoner is a natural right, especially when he is told that he is free and victorious. In the barracks that are visited every day by the international press, some men continue to stagnate, stacked in these triple-decker beds that dysentery turns into a filthy cesspool, while the lanes between the blocks continue to be lined with cadavers—135 per day—just like in the darker times of the tyranny that you conquered.[32]

No discussion of the Priest Block in Dachau is complete without at least a cursory look at the experience of Fr. Jean Bernard, the secretary-general of the International Catholic Office for Cinema from 1934 to 1940. Deported as a deportee from Luxembourg in 1941, he was released for a few days, ostensibly to go home to Luxembourg to bury his mother. His release, however, was for only ten days, and then he had to return. The film *The Ninth Day* (2004) tells the story shockingly well.[33] Fr. Bernard was finally released for good on August 6, 1942, and the film remains a must-see for any student of World War II history in general and Nazi atrocities against religion in particular.

Eventually, the camp was evacuated and turned into a jail for Nazi war criminals on their way to trial. For other people, it became a Camp for Displaced People or a "DP" Camp that held all sorts of homeless, and in many cases stateless, people who could not, or decided for political or social reasons not to, return home. Polish priests knew, for example, that the communists were gaining control of Poland under the Red Army, and they faced another form of political oppression. Germans and Austrians had their own chaos to face: Germany in ruins, occupied, and chopped into several opposing parts; Austria occupied by the Red Army except for Salzburg and Linz, where the Americans commanded people and events. Fr. John Lenz reflected on what he called "The Lessons of Dachau," not a sermon he preached but one preached by the German Benedictine Dom Maurus Muench, OSB, in 1953 when the victims were still alive and thinking about what all this meant to them: the German people and their faith. Fr. Muench talked about faith and the future and how Christian Germany suffered hunger and misery when the clergy of Dachau carried their crosses: "The prisoners of Dachau had lost everything; those who accepted this sacrifice as the will of God learned to know an inner peace and joy which no amount of cruelty, starvation, and disease could banish, and enjoyed a freedom that took no account of barbed wire. . . . How different might things be, we thought, if Hitler and his henchmen could for one night of conscience-ridden material luxury barter one night of the peaceful luxury of the soul." Fr. Muench was not quite finished. He reminded his audience, "Of the 2,700 clergy who were interned in the Dachau concentration camp, 1,034 died as opponents to the Nazi pseudo-religion. He called his brothers to go forward in the spirit of sacrifice and endurance to preach the gospel of God's love. May we attain life everlasting, together with 'all men of good will.'"[34]

Despite the call for goodness and the will of God, a very tired Europe and a war-weary America faced the beginning of the Cold War; however, it was not Cold in central and eastern Europe. The communists in Poland, the Baltic countries, Bulgaria, Romania, Yugoslavia, and eastern Germany imposed communist control, persecuted all religions as they did in Russia after their revolution, and used national prison-camp systems to incarcerate the opposition. Priests were taken to prison camps and gulags, and people who desired to practice their age-old faith were again denied access to it. In Asia the Cold War in Korea became a hot war in a few short years and caught the U.S. Army completely by surprise, certainly unready for another conflict.

Nine

—»} {«—

1950 to 1953

Captured Chaplains in Korea

"Do you remember Father Kapaun?" "Yes, a wonderful man."
—Lloyd Pate, president, Korean War POW Association, 1999

DURING THE PERIOD BETWEEN 1945 and 1950, the Cold War era, the American chaplaincy improved considerably, first by awarding a distinct "Military Occupational Specialty of Chaplain's Assistant" to enlisted personnel and training them at the U.S. Army Chaplain School. Second, in 1947, the U.S. Air Force became a separate armed service, and a sizable number of Army chaplains transferred to the Air Force. Last, chaplains' responsibilities expanded into the realm of morality and citizenship even more than they had in the past. Chaplains were giving lectures in character guidance throughout the force, and by and large, they were well received.[1]

The start of hostilities in Korea in June 1950 caught most American officials off guard, and those in charge of the U.S. Army Chaplain Corps were no exception. For the previous five years, America's military focus had been on divesting itself of the huge force employed during World War II. There were 8,141 Army chaplains on active duty as the war ended in 1945; by the end of 1947, only a little more than 1,100 remained. In 1949 nearly five hundred of those transferred to the U.S. Air Force. On the eve of the North Korean attack on South Korea, there were 706 active-duty Army chaplains, with more in the National Guard and U.S. Army Reserve. With war again a reality in 1950, the American armed forces expanded rapidly. Having just gone through the painful process of involuntarily releasing chaplains from active duty and forcing them into reserve status, the Chaplain Corps now reversed the process and recalled reserve chaplains to active duty. Chaplain authorizations more than doubled in the coming years, topping out at 1,618 in 1953.[2]

Heroism among chaplains in captivity may have begun during the American Revolution; it continued during all of America's wars, including the Korean War. The United States recovered from World War II's losses by generating new families at a breakneck pace. Europe, however, remained devastated and divided between American and Soviet domination economically, ideologically, and militarily. West Germany and Japan were recovering nicely thanks in great part to the Marshall Plan,[3] East Germany became the German Democratic Republic, a Soviet satellite and a repulsive nation-state. The Chinese communists won their civil war against the Nationalists, shifting mainland China from ally to enemy in a very short time in 1949, leaving only Formosa (now Taiwan) as a much smaller Chinese ally. North Korea and South Korea divorced each other in 1946–47, and Kim Il Sung, North Korean communist dictator and premier, yearned to dominate the entire Korean Peninsula regardless of the cost to anyone. Syngman Rhee, president of the Republic of Korea (South), adopted a hard-line anticommunist and pro-American stance as president and strived to control the entire Korean Peninsula too. War was imminent.

The United States paid little attention to Asian affairs, except for Japan, and stripped its military capacity in the Republic of Korea (South Korea) to about two hundred advisers in its Military Advisory Group in 1949. The United States also mistakenly declared Korea to be out of its sphere of influence, thus allowing Kim Il Sung to approach Joseph Stalin with his plan to unite Korea under communist tutelage. At the time, Stalin, worried more about Europe than Asia, feared that the United States could attack from the west if he made overtures to attack east to west. Berlin became the battleground in the late 1940s, and the Berlin Airlift settled the issue for a while. Still, few diplomats or military leaders were looking east. Korea remained a mystery; hardly anyone in Washington knew where it was!

The North Koreans, aka the People's Liberation Army, attacked South Korea on Sunday morning, June 25, 1950. The South Koreans fought bravely, but the North Koreans had large numbers of Russian T-34 tanks that easily slashed their way south. Trouble was that the South Koreans had no heavy American antitank weapons; instead, they had only small arms and machine guns, neither of which proved effective in stopping tanks of any size. It was about as unbalanced a fight as one can imagine, and the communists won handily at first.

The first chaplain to serve in Korea deployed with the initial American ground force to enter the conflict, Task Force Smith, a battalion of the 24th Infantry Division's 21st Infantry Regiment. According to Mark W. Johnson, U.S. Army Chaplain Corps, writing in April 2013, the battalion's chaplain, Carl R. Hudson, had been looking forward to a routine tour of garrison duty in Japan upon his assignment to the unit a few weeks beforehand. Chaplain Hudson and the rest of the task force's 540 soldiers left Japan in a hurry and had little time to do anything after settling into a defense position just north of the town of Osan during the early morning hours of July 5, 1950. A large force of North Korean tanks and infantry attacked just a few hours later. By early afternoon Task Force Smith was completely overrun, its survivors scattered. Chaplain Hudson, along with the battalion's surgeon and a large group of walking wounded, spent most of the following night and day making their way southward to the safety of the nearest American unit.[4]

Other chaplains of the 24th Infantry Division had experiences similar to Hudson's during that difficult month of July 1950. Narrowly escaping as one American position after another fell before the North Korean advance, they survived with the exception of Chaplain Fr. Herman G. Felhoelter of the 19th Infantry Regiment. With his battalion falling back as the American position along the Kum River collapsed, Felhoelter volunteered to remain behind with a group of critically wounded men. A North Korean patrol came upon the group and executed the prostrate soldiers and their praying chaplain. He was the first of twelve chaplains to die in action or as a prisoner during the Korean War. The second also perished in July 1950, when Chaplain Byron D. Lee of the 35th Infantry Regiment (25th Infantry Division) was mortally wounded during an attack from an enemy aircraft.[5]

For the opening battles of the Korean War, as with most wars, those who are already in uniform at the start of the conflict bore the burden of the opening battles. Amazingly enough, no chaplains were captured during those confusing initial months of the Korean War, despite all the American setbacks. That situation changed within a few months, however, especially after the successful landing in Inchon in western South Korea and the decision to invade North Korea. The 1950 Chinese surprise counteroffensive in the late fall generated heavy casualties on both sides. For the Eighth Army in northwestern Korea and X Corps on the eastern side, it seemed the communist Chinese were everywhere, attacking in strength beyond anyone's imagination. Within a month, Fr. Emil Kapaun was made a POW; three more chaplains also became POWs: Kenneth C. Hyslop (19th Infantry Regiment), Wayne H. Burdue (2nd Engineer Battalion, 2nd Infantry Division), and Lawrence F. Brunnert (32nd Infantry Regiment, 7th Infantry Division). Two other chaplains were killed during those weeks: Samuel R. Simpson (38th Infantry Regiment, 2nd Infantry Division) and James W. Conner (31st Infantry Regiment, 7th Infantry Division). The fate of the captured chaplains was unknown until the release of surviving American prisoners in 1953. Not one of the chaplain POWs survived their incarcerations.[6]

The eight chaplains lost in 1950 were all members of the prewar Chaplain Corps. Six were veterans of World War II. Chaplains Burdue, Lee, and Simpson had served continuously since the 1940s without a break in service; Hyslop, Kapaun, and Felhoelter also served in World War II, but were released from active duty in 1946. Within two years, however, they decided to continue their service to God and country; all three volunteered for recall to active duty in 1948. Conner and Brunnert joined the others in the prewar era, being commissioned in 1948 and 1949, respectively. None of these eight veteran chaplains knew what the year 1950 would bring, but all rose to the challenges that came with ministering to soldiers under fire. Only a few received public recognition for the actions that ultimately cost them their lives: Chaplain Conner received the Silver Star, Fr. Felhoelter the Distinguished Service Cross.[7]

Early in the war, the North Koreans captured a number of civilian religious personnel, all civilian missionary chaplains. Fr. Philip Crosbie, an Australian missionary and one of these civilian prisoners during the Korean War, in his perceptive book *Pencilling Prisoner* (1955) wrote, "The eruption of the forces of Northern Korea across an arbitrary, invisible border, on the morning of 25 June 1950, the suffering and destruction that have followed, will have appeared to some as inevitable episodes in the struggle between Communism and the West. To those who have come to know Korea and to love its people, they are episodes that must appear as one of history's most tragic ironies."[8] That this fight became a tragedy remains one of the largest understatements in the history of the twentieth century. Its sadness is nearly beyond belief.

No country in the history of the Cold War was more innocent than Korea. Having been a colony of Japan resulting from the Japanese victory over the Russians in 1905, Korea sat ripe for the taking. It was a settled agricultural country, Buddhist, and not terribly politically active. However, the Japanese were hard colonizers and generated serious anti-Japanese nationalist movements both from the left (communists under Kim Il Sung) and from the right (nationalists) under Syngman Rhee. Kim Il Sung had joined the communist Chinese front and fought the Japanese in China during World War II. When the war ended, the communists sent Kim south to communize Korea. Was he successful? Yes, in part, because the communist movement represented Korean anti-Japanese nationalism strongly and stubbornly. Kim Il Sung became the "great leader" in the north and a force to be reckoned with in the south.

The South became the Republic of Korea under the authoritarian leadership of Syngman Rhee, a Princeton University–educated Korean Christian who had worked for the YMCA and the political underground against the Japanese in the 1920s and 1930s. The Japanese occupiers, much like the French in Indochina, worked tirelessly against both political resistance organizations, communist and nationalist. It was not until the Allies, Americans in the South and Soviets in the North, forced the Japanese out of Korea when the Koreans finally turned on each other. For the next three years, from 1950 to 1953, the Koreans not only fought each other on the field of battle on the ground and in the air, but also murdered each other as political prisoners, essentially as "enemies of the people" in their terminology.

Some of these "enemies of the people" were Christian missionaries who came to Korea to serve God and the people of Korea. To the communists, they were philosophical and political enemies, but more important in 1950 they were

Western foreigners, invaders who had to be held in captivity and then expelled if they survived their lives behind barbed wire. Fr. Crosbie commented,

> We were interrogated many times in the months that followed, and as often as not in the small hours. There was always a refresher course in one's life history—name, nationality, country where born, date and place of birth, progression etc. Special attention paid to the authority who had sent us to Korea, and for what purpose,—what weapons we had in the house when arrested, and where we had hidden them. It was taken for granted that we were agents for our countries, and that our houses were crammed with weapons to fight their battles.[9]

In Fr. Crosbie's view, the communists believed that all Christian missionaries whom they captured in the first days of their invasion of South Korea were dangerous enemies who needed to be exterminated one way or the other.[10]

Fr. Crosbie became a political prisoner of the North Koreans along with a host of other civilian missionaries, including several nuns in their seventies, who came from several European countries. What the communists wanted were confessions from their prisoners, and the Americans learned about this later. Fr. Crosbie noted, "Day and night, 'conversion' went on among the unfortunate Korean prisoners. I watched the sickening spectacle of hungry, thirsty, dog-tired men being threatened and scolded and shouted into a state of desperation, their minds battered till their thoughts were drowned in the relentless waves of communist jargon loosed up them hour after hour. . . . Confess, Confess!"[11] When all these prisoners arrived in Pyongyang, North Korea's capital (aka the Democratic People's Republic of Korea), they were put into five different rooms, what they called the "schoolhouse rooms." Room One contained the British Legation; Room Two held more British, Swiss, French, and Columban Irish missionaries; Room Three held the French Legation in Seoul; Room Four held the American Methodist Mission, all women, including five Carmelite nuns and three Catholic laywomen; and Room Five held a cross-section of Protestant missionaries, mining engineers, managers of the Trader's Exchange in Seoul, and two Catholic clergy, one priest and one bishop. In the course of time, a prominent journalist arrived in Pyongyang, Philip Gigantes Deane, a Greek native who became a British subject during World War II.[12] Then everyone received orders to board a train that headed north; no one knew where, of course.

At one stop, everyone was put off the train, and soon they were saddened to observe UN POWs marching slowly in a very long line, all heading north as they were. An American sergeant approached the civilians and said, "This [soldier] we are burying was a Catholic, maybe one of you [Catholic priests] would come and recite the funeral service." Absolutely, but the communist Korean guard said, "No, we don't believe in such things; it is not necessary for anyone to go." Fr. Crosbie noted with distain that the communists never allowed any of the priests to say Mass, whereas the Japanese allowed them to do that during their World War II internment.[13]

This group, along with the POWs, began a long march north to make room for the hundreds of thousands of Chinese troops who began coming south across the border in the fall of 1950. They began the march on October 6, 1950, and as they inched their way north, it became ever colder by the day. The old nuns suffered badly from the cold, including Mother Therese, but when this group of captured clergy saw the POWs marching from Manpo, a frontier town on the central Korea-Manchuria railway line, north, their hearts sank. As Fr. Crosbie wrote, "These lads were in no condition for walking." On the move again on October 31, 1950, the internees and the POWs met the Tiger, a North Korean major who forever has remained nameless. The civilian internees witnessed American POWs marching north. Fr. Crosbie noted, "As the men passed by, my gaze went sometimes to their faces, sometimes to their feet. Some of those feet were bare, and some were already bleeding. Some feet paced steadily, if warily, on, but weaker men, dragging on the shoulders of their comrades, put ghastly, shuffling syncopation on the somber rhythm of the march." Crosbie developed a theory about the Tiger's philosophy of the march north: "The Tiger had decided on specific places for our overnight stops; then our late start and the delay near Manpo upset his schedule which enraged him, that he drove us mercilessly on in an attempt to catch up, and that his failure drove him to greater fury, and blinded him to any regard for health or even life."[14]

Then the Tiger ordered the marching column to "Halt." He drew his pistol and singled out an American POW. After covering his victim's eyes, he executed him out of hand. With blood in his eyes and evil in his soul, the Tiger then said to the American POW officers, "Why did you allow men to fall out against my orders? I will shoot these five men for disobeying my orders." The British Lord High Commissioner took up the man's defense and pointed out that he had acted in good faith to the Tiger's orders. "Then I will shoot the man whose section most men were allowed to fall out," said the Tiger. Lieutenant Thornton of Texas stepped forward and stood before the Tiger, helpless. The Tiger then turned to some North Korean soldiers walking by and asked, "What should be done to a man who disobeys the People's Army?" "Shoot him," they shouted back. "You see," said the major to Lieutenant Thornton. "You have had your trial, a People's Trial, People's justice. Now I will kill you." "In Texas," said Thornton, "we call that lynching, not justice."[15] The Tiger then drew his pistol, flicked up the back of Lieutenant Thornton's cap, and shot him through the head.[16]

The march ended for everyone on November 8, 1950, with around a hundred dead left along the way, Lieutenant Thornton being only one of them. Everyone faced three years behind barbed wire. Fr. Philip Crosbie left North Korea on May 25, 1953, went through China to Russia, and ended his trip at the Australian embassy in Moscow. As far as he was concerned, he marched toward the City of God to profess and live his faith before God and man. Of the American Army chaplains who served in the Korean campaign, eleven died in combat or as POWs. One additional chaplain was presumed dead, and it is possible that several others were killed as POWs.[17]

❮•❯

Father Emil Kapaun of Pilsen, Kansas, the most decorated military chaplain in American military history, was born in 1916, ordained a Catholic priest in 1940, and entered the Army in October 1944 as a young chaplain. Despite all the physical and mental challenges he faced, he liked army life and gave as much, if not more, than required of a young Catholic priest in wartime. He especially liked being required to minister to soldiers of all faiths. Upon completion of his initial chaplain training, he went to Camp Wheeler, Georgia, where he looked after 19,000 troops, military families, and civilians living on the post.[18] There was indeed plenty to do, and he found the soldiers quite willing and always worthy of his concern and action. He was finally shipped overseas toward the end of World War II and served in the Burma-India theater, where he often met with missionaries who had been prisoners of the Japanese. He also reported that on one occasion, American GIs had constructed a church and a school for missionary sisters.[19]

When the war came to an end, the time arrived on June 4, 1946, for Fr. Emil Kapaun to leave the Army, and, like the millions of newly civilianized GIs, he went home. By June 1948, he had earned his M.Ed. degree and began his last assignment as a parish priest. Back to the Army in 1948—next stop, Fort Bliss, Texas. Fr. Kapaun was just one of those chaplain priests who enjoyed being in the Army, but most of all, he thrived on being in the company of soldiers. By 1949 his group finished its training at Fort Bliss, and they were sent overseas.[20] By mid-January 1950, Fr. Kapaun and his friends found themselves on board the troopship *General H. M. Patrick* on their way to Japan and later to war in Korea.

The 1st Cavalry's introduction to the Korean War took place at Incheon, Gen. Douglas MacArthur's brilliant Army and Marine Corps end run around South Korea to hit the North Koreans on the west coast in a major surprise amphibious landing. The objective was to seize Seoul quickly and cut off the North Korean army from their home country and supply lines in the North. Like all military plans, reality sets in quickly, and the destruction and death that Fr. Kapaun witnessed daily rattled his nerves and his men's nerves as well. In a letter he wrote, "This fighting is nerve-wracking. Many of my soldiers crack up—they go insane and scream like mad men. This is war! What a hard thing to understand."[21]

Word of Fr. Kapaun's intense devotion to the unit's men spread throughout the 8th Cavalry, and, in short, the soldiers revered him as a tireless and fearless chaplain because he followed the guns, much as chaplains before him had done from the American Revolution to Korea. It was only when he exposed himself too much to hostile fire that his comrades warned him to get down. Time after time he lost his jeep and Mass Kit as they came under fire and were destroyed, yet the Army or his men always found another one and even a bicycle for him to use.[22] October 30, 1950, however, changed everything.

The battle at Unsan, North Korea, had raged, this time with communist Chinese soldiers attacking the Americans in great numbers. Hordes of Chinese soldiers attacked the Americans and surrounded them, with wounded and dead everywhere. Most of the 8th Cavalry soldiers who fought at Unsan were killed, wounded, or captured by the Chinese communist soldiers.[23] Fr. Kapaun implored his captors not to hurt the helpless wounded. The home-by-Christmas spirit that had pervaded American lines at that time had burned out, and this batch of POWs began their march north. Fortunately for them, the Tiger was not one of their overseers, yet they marched in the ever-increasing cold north to the communist Chinese POW camps along the Yalu River.

Hunger stepped into the American POW groups very quickly. What the POWs could not know at the time was that among the communist captors, there was a method going on: starve the men into submission physically, then hold food out as the reward for any behavior they perceived as favorable; reward the POW a little with some food, then ask for more and more. The Chinese communists did not seek turncoats; rather, they wanted to instill a sense of doubt into the minds of their Allied POWs. They came finally to Camp 5 at Pyoktong, what surviving POWs call the "PU," for the putrid smells at Pyoktong "University."

Camp 5, Pyoktong, also known as the Valley, sat along the Yalu River that formed a border between northern Korea and Manchuria. Fr. Kapaun's favorite welcome to newcomers was *Ni illegitimi carborundum est*, or "Don't let the bastards grind you down."[24] By November, the starvation process had begun to set in, and Fr. Kapaun became what he believed was the "Good Thief," or the character of Saint Dismas, the patron saint of virtuous thieves, in order to retrieve some much-needed food for the POWs. His coconspirator was Lt. Walt Mayo, a World War II veteran, who started a ruckus with other POWs as a decoy.[25] So Fr. Kapaun decided to sneak out of his hut and search for some loose food. The good chaplain then worked with the other POWs to deceive the guards into thinking there was a fight while Fr. Kapaun grabbed some chow from the guard's food stores. William L. Maher, in his biography *A Shepherd in Combat Boots*, described it as follows:

> As the men formed ranks into ranks to march to the supply building, Kapaun sneaked in at the end of the line. When the work party neared its destination, he disappeared into the bushes and crawled around to the far side of the shed. The Americans started fighting among themselves and temporarily distracted the guards. The chaplain darted into the building and grabbed a sack of cracked corn. Then he slipped back into

the surrounding undergrowth and waited until he could carry his spoils back to the area where the POWs lived.[26]

Theft? No. Survival? Yes. In an oral history, William H. Funchess, a POW Camp 5 veteran, recalled that Fr. Kapaun of the 1st Cavalry Division had acquired some cornstalks, scraps of wood, and some corncobs. He started a fire, grabbed some snow, and built a small fire in order to melt it into good drinking water. Then Fr. Kapaun offered each prisoner about a third of a cupful, the first drink of clean water that Lieutenant Funchess had had since his capture on November 3, 1950.[27] The men idolized their chaplain; the guards despised and feared him. Aside from providing food, he helped in many other ways, such as making socks, cleaning wounds, and sharing the last of his pipe-tobacco ration so everyone could get a puff. They still needed food and medicine more than anything else.

Once the communist Chinese evaluated their starvation effects, they began the next phase of their captivity program: indoctrination. To do this, the captors began to separate the POWs into groups of like-minded prisoners. "Progressives" were those very few POWs who agreed with the communist lecturers and interrogators that the Americans were warmongers who served Wall Street and that the United States should simply end the war by pulling its troops from Korea, go home, and sin no more. "Reactionaries" took a diametrically opposite position and supported the United Nations and U.S. war efforts completely. Lloyd Pate was one of those "Reactionaries" who wrote a self-published memoir and participated in the Korean War POW Association's annual reunions. Known to all his friends and fellow veterans simply as "Pate," he remained a force to be reckoned with until his death in 2013.[28] He wrote in his revised memoir, *Reactionary* (2000), "We just looked at each other. We finally realized we were both Americans and approached each other. I finally recognized who he was, Father Kapaun. We sat there and talked for a few minutes." They were attempting to break into a Chinese food-storage building that the guards kept locked. Frustrated that they had to break the lock, Pate noted,

> I don't think that even St. Elmo could help us on this. I asked him who St. Elmo was, and he said he was the patron saint of thieves [actually Saint Dismas]. I said, "You Catholics have a saint for everything." He smiled and said, "We try to cover our asses." I knew I was just a dumb

old Baptist. I saw him a few more times after that and would ask him how Saint Elmo was doing. He would smile and say, "He's having to work overtime."[29]

Most certainly, there was no love lost between the reactionaries and the progressives among the UN POWs; their respective members hated one another. In reality, the vast majority of POWs were neither progressives nor reactionaries; rather, they were in the middle, and their mantra was "Be Cool."

Fr. Kapaun was never caught in the middle of this struggle. He served everyone. His biographer, historian William L. Maher, writes that Kapaun refused to give in to the godlessness of the communist propaganda that the captors spewed day after day. He responded that "God was as real as the air that they breathed, but could not see." "One day," he said, "the Good Lord will save the Chinese and free them from the course that has set upon them. The Good Lord, as He fed the thousands on the mountain, will also take care of us."[30] Then the guard took his rosary beads. In response, Fr. Kapaun made a new one from strands of barbed wire. He drove his communist captors crazy to a point where they looked for ways to apply some kind of physical retribution, anything to make him suffer.

By the spring of 1951, nearly all the POWs suffered dysentery from the bad water in the camp, while their immune systems began to fail from the lack of proper food. This was without a doubt similar to the kinds of treatment and consequent suffering that the Americans had endured and suffered at the hands of the Japanese during World War II. It is possible that approximately 1,700 US POWs died in Camp 5 during early 1951, but when the death toll rose to twenty-four a day by the end of February, the Chinese became alarmed.[31] As far as the Chinese were concerned, they had to get rid of Fr. Kapaun. His influence on the POWs was just too intense, too engaging, too religious, and too dangerous for them to deal with. Yet, as odd as it may be, Fr. Kapaun became the principal cause of his own death. He gave away too much food, too much clothing, and too much of himself to survive captivity very long. Lewis H. Carlson's interviews of Robert Jones, an eighteen-year-old Army enlisted soldier, explains what became of the POWs who became incapacitated in Camp 5: "I was being visited regularly by Father Kapaun who tried to cheer me up even though he had the same condition I had."[32]

Fr. Kapaun died on May 21, 1951, in the prison hospital ward, alone, starved to death by the Chinese communists. The U.S. Army awarded him the Bronze Star, Purple Heart, Distinguished Service Cross, and finally the Medal of Honor in 2013. His citation reads,

> For conspicuous gallantry and intrepidity at the risk of his life above and beyond the call of duty while serving with the 3d Battalion, 8th Cavalry Regiment, 1st Cavalry Division during combat operations against an armed enemy at Unsan, Korea, from November 1–2, 1950. On November 1, as Chinese Communist Forces viciously attacked friendly elements, Chaplain Kapaun calmly walked through withering enemy fire in order to provide comfort and medical aid to his comrades and rescue friendly wounded from no-man's land. Though the Americans successfully repelled the assault, they found themselves surrounded by the enemy. Facing annihilation, the able-bodied men were ordered to evacuate. However, Chaplain Kapaun, fully aware of his certain capture, elected to stay behind with the wounded. After the enemy succeeded in breaking through the defense in the early morning hours of November 2, Chaplain Kapaun continually made rounds, as hand-to-hand combat ensued. As Chinese Communist Forces approached the American position, Chaplain Kapaun noticed an injured Chinese officer and convinced him to negotiate the safe surrender of the American Forces. Shortly after his capture, Chaplain Kapaun, with complete disregard for his personal safety and unwavering resolve, bravely pushed aside an enemy soldier preparing to execute Sergeant First Class Herbert A. Miller. Not only did Chaplain Kapaun's gallantry save the life of Sergeant Miller, but also his unparalleled courage and leadership inspired all those present, including those who might have otherwise fled in panic, to remain and fight the enemy until captured. Chaplain Kapaun's extraordinary heroism and selflessness, above and beyond the call of duty, are in keeping with the highest traditions of military service and reflect great credit upon himself, the 3rd Battalion, 8th Cavalry Regiment, the 1st Cavalry Division, and the United States.[33]

Kapaun was named a "Servant of God," the first step toward canonization, by the church in 1993. If the "Venerable" title is bestowed, the church would begin the process of investigating alleged miracles attributed to Kapaun.[34] A panel of archbishops and cardinals met on March 10, 2020, to vote on whether Emil Kapaun is worthy of the title of "Venerable," which is the second step in the process toward sainthood in the Catholic Church. The pope will make the final determination. His remains, buried among the unknowns at the National Memorial Cemetery of the Pacific in Hawaii, initially, were positively identified on March 2, 2021. If he is canonized by the Roman Catholic Church, he will not be the first chaplain to achieve sainthood, but he will be the second one to have received the Medal of Honor, joining World War II chaplain Fr. Joseph T. O'Callahan, S.J., of the USS *Franklin*.

What we have witnessed, when this part of the Cold War went hot, affirms the reality that all the chaplains in Korea, civilian and military alike, maintained their respective senses of religious mission to serve God in service of the believing, and often unbelieving, laity. This meant that military chaplains like Frs. Kapaun and Felhoelter, remained with their wounded even at the cost of their own lives. No chaplain, civilian or military, who lived and suffered through the captivity experience in North Korea ever failed that difficult test of the highest degree of devotion to God, country, and the men they served in a combat environment. It is a sad truth that not one chaplain survived communist captivity in North Korea. We mourn and honor them to this day.

❧ • ❧

Once the war ceased in 1953, the Chaplain Corps continued to serve its military members and even expanded its scope to include service to military families who joined servicemen assigned to advisory teams around the world. Crises erupted in Lebanon, Berlin, Cuba, and other hot spots, and American military chaplains were always there. Unique in this period were large retreat houses instituted in Berchtesgaden, Germany, and Seoul, South Korea, where groups of laymen and chaplains gathered to consider and reflect upon spiritual and moral values. According to the U.S. Army's history of the chaplain corps, "Speakers of the most distinguished caliber representing every denomination were provided for these periods of study and meditation."[35] Such seeming tranquility served as a respite from all the international chaos at that time, but such a respite came to an end when the war in Vietnam crept into history.

Ten

—⊹⊱⊰⊹—

1959 to 1973
Vietnam and Beyond

*I was struck by the serenity of the scene and the incongruity of
my presence there among the very people we'd been bombing.
"God," I prayed, "I'm going to need you. Please stay with me."*
—Capt. Gerald L. Coffee, USN (Ret.)

FROM 1959 TO 1965 chaplains were sent to Vietnam to minister to the
American servicemen acting as advisers to the armed forces of the Republic
of Vietnam. After that, the chaplains arrived as members of military units.
Fr. Joseph T. Ryan arrived in Vietnam before the buildup in 1965. Two years
later, on July 4, 1967, Chaplain Ryan was saying Mass in a thatched hut the
Marines had built for him. Assisting him was LCpl. George Pace, USMC.
The Vietcong had fired a mortar round at the hut, and it landed close by, so
close that shrapnel struck Pace fatally and wounded Fr. Ryan. Cdr. Herbert
L. Bergsma, CHC USN, explains what the Marines lost that day in *Chaplains
with the Marines in Vietnam, 1962–1971* (1985):

> The corporal had served the chaplain to whom he was assigned as yeoman,
> messenger, driver, and bodyguard. The chaplain had come to depend
> heavily upon his assistant and to know and appreciate him as a faithful
> Christian friend. The next day, 4 July, the chaplain, Fr. Joseph Ryan, went
> to the Dong Ha Memorial Chapel for his daily 4:30 pm Mass. His clerk,

Corporal George A. Pace, had rigged the altar, and made other required preparations while the chaplain heard confessions. He offered the Mass for "Peace in the World" and spoke for a few minutes about the meaning of our Declaration of Independence. Just after the Communion hymn, another artillery shell exploded near the chapel. He later remembered: My clerk and I were both thrown to the ground. I turned him over in my arms, and he looked at me in amazement. He said, "I am hit" and lapsed into unconsciousness. Our congregation scattered into our area. George was hit right through the heart and was bleeding profusely. I realized that I had to take a chance and go out of the bunker if we were going to save him. They had him in the operating room from 1710 to 2000. At 2000 he was doing very well. His blood pressure was stabilized, his heart was beating steadily, and all conditions were favorable for recovery. Chaplain Ryan reported later, "It was in the hands of God, and we remained at his bedside imploring God to spare him. About 2100 George stopped breathing and once again the doctors did everything in their power to get his heart beating, but God had called him home." Death was constant those days in Vietnam, but never common.[1]

Chaplain Ryan later became Archbishop Joseph T. Ryan for Military Services and kept that post until he retired in 1991.[2] Perhaps it is safe to say that once a chaplain, always a chaplain.

In 1965 President Lyndon B. Johnson ordered the U.S. Army and U.S. Marine Corps to begin offensive operations. By 1966 units such as the 173rd Airborne Brigade and one battalion of the 101st Air Cavalry Division, the 1st Infantry Division, and numerous other combat and support units arrived too. The 25th and 4th Infantry Divisions arrived soon after, ready for combat against the communist Vietcong and/or North Vietnamese units in the field. The business of war evolved quickly from part-time to full-time. The number of chaplains increased as well, to more than three hundred army chaplains in 1966. As the numbers of American troops, Marines, airmen, and sailors increased, so too did the need for chaplains to serve them. Because the war in Vietnam took on different qualities in country, it became several wars fought simultaneously: a guerrilla war against the indigenous communist Vietcong cadre in the South, a very tough fight against the regular North Vietnamese army units in the northern part of South Vietnam, and a political war among the South Vietnamese on their home turf. As in previous wars, chaplains found themselves in the middle of firefights, tending to their soldiers, most without worrying about the politics surrounding them. About one Catholic chaplain's sermon, a war correspondent noted, "His sermons are brief and often mention the value of suffering as a means of understanding what Christ himself endured."[3]

Many chaplains rode helicopters to spread-out units in order to bring religious services to the troops in the field. In 1970 Easter services in the city of Hue involved thirty-three Protestant and nineteen Roman Catholic chaplains. More than two thousand men, mostly Marines, were flown into Hue for the event. By 1973 only thirteen American army chaplains had died in Vietnam.[4] No chaplain was taken or kept by the enemy as a POW during the war in Vietnam from 1959 to 1973 nor beyond in subsequent wars in the Middle East. In that sense, Vietnam was similar to World War I in that the Americans worked extremely hard to protect their chaplains in the field. This does not mean, however, that chaplains avoided being killed in action or murdered by the enemy.

Chaplain Vincent R. Capodanno, USNR, a Maryknoll priest, ministered to men of the USMC and died in action of shrapnel wounds while he attempted to rescue a badly wounded corpsman.[5] Chaplain Herbert L. Bergsma's history of chaplains in Vietnam, *Chaplains with the Marines in Vietnam, 1962–1971* describes Chaplain Capodanno's death eloquently:

> At 0200 on 5 September 1967, this chaplain received an unofficial report that Lieutenant Vincent R. Capodanno, CHC, USN, had been killed in action late Monday, 4 September 1967. Colonel Sam Davis, Regimental Commander of the 5th Marines, confirmed this officially at 0730 this date. A preliminary report was forwarded up the chain of command. But the fact that the man was a chaplain was of more than passing interest and concern to many, for men of God were not routinely found in the casualty reports of combat actions. No Navy chaplain had as yet been killed in Vietnam. As the story of this chaplain's last hours of life gradually emerged to fill the outline of spare facts first reported by the division chaplain, it became apparent that Chaplain Vincent Capodanno's

actions on that day had been inspired by an inordinate devotion to his men and to God. For his ministry to Marines during a combat situation that ultimately cost him his life, Chaplain Capodanno was awarded the Medal of Honor on 7 January 1969.[6]

Chaplain Bergsma then continued his description of Fr. Capodonno's actions more insightfully:

Chaplain Capodanno's action on that day symbolized an idea of the ministry to men in combat that transcended the immediacy of personal sacrifices and illuminated a concept of ministry which became unique to Vietnam, the ministry of adaptation that enabled the chaplain to be present as much as possible where needed. In 1965, Father Capodanno volunteered to serve as a Navy chaplain and requested duty with the Marines in-country. He served with a Marine infantry battalion for twelve months and was thoroughly devoted to this kind of duty and to his men and requested a six-month extension. It was during the fourth month of this extension that he was killed in action in Quang Tin Province.

Chaplain Capodanno was compelled to be with his men according to the dictates of his conscience and an overwhelming desire to serve his "grunts." The priorities of ministry, as interpreted by him, did not allow another course of action. His conviction and dedication to a ministry, practically applied, cost him his life on the afternoon of 4 September 1967, yet both his life and his ministry were fulfilled by serving the Marines he loved. One chaplain confirmed this with a delightful anecdote. Lieutenant Conon J. Meehan (Roman Catholic) wrote: With the death of Vincent Capodanno fresh in my mind, I am tempted to include a eulogy of him in this report. But it is not necessary.

The advancing Marines radioed to the command post that they were in danger of being overrun and wiped out. At this news Chaplain Capodanno left the command post and hurried to the positions of the 1st and 2nd Platoons; in the meantime an order was given for the engaged Marines to fall back to form a defensive perimeter on the hill. Lance Corporal Lovejoy, a radio operator, remembered that he was lying in the dirt, having been forced down by a burst of automatic weapons fire when the chaplain ran down the hill, grabbed a strap of the radio, and helped him to pull it up the hill. Twice they had to hit the dirt as grazing automatic weapons fire traversed the hill in front of them. When they finally made it within the perimeter on top of the hill, Chaplain Capodanno began to minister to the wounded and dying. Lance Corporal Lovejoy reflected afterwards that he would never have made it up the hillside alive if it had not been for the chaplain's assistance. Later during the firefight Chaplain Capodanno was giving the last rites to a dying Marine when riot control agents were employed to help blunt the enemy fire. At the beginning of the engagement some of the Marines had dropped their gear, including their gas masks, at the bottom of the hill. The chaplain surrendered his mask to one of the riflemen, casually remarking, "You need this more than I do," and continued despite murderous fire, to assist the wounded.

After caring for about seven men, Chaplain Capodanno maneuvered forward in a crouching running into a position forward on the hill; as he ran, a mortar impacted about 20 meters from him. The explosion seemed to affect his arm for he carried it stiffly thereafter and spatters of blood were observed on his sleeve. But he did not break stride, and continued to the side of Sergeant Peters, who had just fallen. Chaplain Capodanno said the "Our Father" with him." Under critical analysis the reasoning behind this kind of human behavior, behavior that led in Chaplain Capodanno's instance to the giving up of his life, appears complex and not easily understood.[7]

Another chaplain, serving with the U.S. Army, gave his life in battle too; he was Maj. Fr. Aloysius Paul McGonigle, USA, a Jesuit priest who volunteered to serve his men during the battle for the city of Hue during the Tet Offensive of 1968. Most military historians rank the battle for Hue with battles like Manila during World War II in its intensity. Leaving his desk to tend to his soldiers was the reason he became an Army chaplain, but in January 1968 a Vietcong bullet in the brain stopped Fr. McGonigle's attempt to help a wounded Marine near the Imperial Palace in Hue.[8]

Another "Paratrooper Padre" was Maj. Fr. Charles Watters, USA, a New Jersey priest who had attended Seton Hall University and was ordained in 1953. He joined the Army as a chaplain in 1965 and served with the 173rd Airborne

Brigade in Vietnam and was among the men who made the only parachute jump in the Vietnam War. On November 19, 1967, Fr. Watters was killed in action in a friendly bomb run against the North Vietnamese army that struck his location by mistake. He was among forty-two other soldiers killed in action that day. Such was the case among many in the fighting in South Vietnam and previous wars as well.

The role and function of chaplains among the POWs in North Vietnam took on a completely different paradigm, one of deeply felt religious service to one another, over time. Those captured Americans, POWs were for the most part officers and airmen, who tended to their own and each other's religious needs over the years in North and South Vietnam. For many of these officers, the religious experience was more civil than liturgical, and many had no need for religious expression. No chaplain was taken POW by the North Vietnamese army in the field in South Vietnam, nor had any chaplain been among the shoot-downs over North Vietnam.

The American POWs had no chaplain in Hanoi or anywhere else in North or South Vietnam to service formally any spiritual needs behind the wire. In North Vietnam the only Christians were leftover Catholics who failed to go south in 1954–55 when they had the chance. The Americans were given a chance to attend a Christmas Mass once in Hanoi, but they learned quickly that the communists used this Mass as a propaganda event to show how well they treated the Americans. The POWs in Hanoi often prayed together in their cells, but it is very difficult, if not impossible, to argue that religious faith played a vital role in their survival. With that said, when alone in solitary confinement, speaking to God saved the sanity of many POWs, in part, because such an act allows one to bare one's soul to God directly and frankly.

For many Americans in Hanoi, men like Jeremiah Denton became POWs of the North Vietnamese and others by the Vietcong in South Vietnam, Cambodia, and Laos. Religion itself became a tool of individual survival, especially if faith and religion were part of the prisoner's life before becoming a POW. For many American POWs, the religious experience was at a minimum, while for others it served as a vital connection to a force much greater than themselves, or their captors for that matter. Religion, like politics, in the military services remains a personal affair.

Joseph C. Plumb was a naval aviator shot down over North Vietnam on May 19, 1967. He wrote about his religious experiences as a POW in Hanoi in his personal captivity narrative, *I'm No Hero* (1991): "One of the first pieces of communication I had received in solitary was from Bob Schumacher. With tugs on the wire, he announced, 'Church call is five coughs.' I tugged back, 'Do we all go to church together?' 'Yes.'"[9] Rather than participating in an organized service, Plumb and the other POWs in the Hoa Lo Prison (Hanoi Hilton) in Hanoi gathered to say the Lord's Prayer, the Pledge of Allegiance, and the Twenty-Third Psalm ("The Lord Is My Shepherd"). That was enough for some POWs but not all of them.

Up to 1970, the North Vietnamese forbade any religious activity except for the propaganda shows they sponsored. However, after 1970 when the POWs were brought together in Hanoi from several camps, their world began to change. They mixed with fellow prisoners they had known only through tapping messages on walls without seeing faces in Camp Unity.[10] After some cajoling, the Vietnamese captors gave the POWs a Bible. Some POWs were atheists and wanted nothing to do with it; others were thankful to have it in their midst. Plumb and other POWs observed that some of their guards at least had been trained in Christianity or were simply curious about the American officers' respect for it. Plumb stated what his relationship with his faith in God meant to him: "I consider my confinement in prison to be spiritually beneficial. I was given the opportunity that few men have—the time to pause, to reflect, and to establish priorities. Stripped of all my material wealth, the only beacon I could home in on was my faith in an unchanging God."[11] For Plumb and others, it seems that the old meaning of the captivity experience, enshrined in the redemptive Jeremiad of the seventeenth century, became a reality for them in Hanoi.

In his book *Beyond Survival: A POW's Story* (1990), Capt. Gerald L. Coffee, USN (Ret.), another pilot shot down over North Vietnam, wrote, "I was struck by the serenity of the scene and the incongruity of my presence there among the very people we'd been bombing. 'God,' I prayed, 'I'm going to need you. Please stay with me.'"[12] During the period in 1967 when the POWs were tortured daily, Coffee wrote that he focused on the part of Psalm 23 that says, "Thou prepares a table before me in the presence of mine enemies; you anoint my head with oil; my cup runneth over."[13] Gerald Coffee returned to the United States with the other POWs from the Vietnam War in 1973. In a talk he recorded, he said, "Faith was the key to my survival. Faith in my fellow man and in my prison comrades, faith in myself, faith in my country and, of course, faith in my God, truly the foundation for it all."[14]

Jeremiah A. Denton was shot down on July 18, 1965, in his A-6 Intruder over North Vietnam while flying a bombing mission off the USS *Independence*. In 1973, after spending seven and a half years as a POW in North Vietnam, he was the first man off the plane at Clark Air Force Base in the Philippines that brought the POWs from Hanoi and was told he had to say something. He did, and his words became legend: "We are honored to have had the opportunity to serve our country under difficult circumstances. We are profoundly grateful to our commander-in-chief and to our nation for this day. God Bless America."[15]

Denton described himself as an "average product of middle America and its values." He wrote, "Although I had lived a far from perfect life, my heart and soul belonged to God, country, and family long before the Navy got hold of me. My religious upbringing and my mother's strong influence shaped my character." His mother was a strong Catholic and taught him well, but was he ready for the ordeal he was about to experience at the hands of the communist North Vietnamese? His narrative is a story steeped in wisdom and sensibility about what happened around him. He learned or perceived that the course of the war always determined their treatment.[16] Interrogations went on day and night, but the North Vietnamese wanted only propaganda, not military information. Eventually, when the POWs figured this out, they began to give them stories, a lot of stories, that today seem utterly fictitious, but for the men in Hanoi's cages, they were enough to keep the torturers away. Denton, however, was a hard-liner in the sense that he insisted that all those around him kept their responses brief and to the point: name, rank, and serial number in accordance with the Geneva Convention of 1949 and the American Fighting Man's Code of Conduct.[17] As he was deep into torture, starvation, and isolation, Denton wrote, "I prayed. God became more than faith. He became knowledge, and I appealed to Him. Then I became ashamed. Why hadn't I embraced Him so thoroughly before?"[18]

The North Vietnamese took Denton to an interview room in early May 1966, this time full of Japanese press people instead of interrogators. It was time for him to be a threat, something a POW is now trained to become.[19] They sat him down to newsmen who attempted to interrogate him gently. Denton saw this as an opportunity, so he blinked his response in Morse Code, spelling out T . . . O . . . R . . . T . . . U . . . R . . . E several times until his captors removed him from the room. After several torture sessions, the Vietnamese returned him to the prison known as the Zoo. He won that round. As a result, Denton gave a lot of thought to the process the North Vietnamese were using: they wanted to break every American into becoming completely dependent on their captors and, by so doing, pliable and responsive to their calls for propaganda. Simple? Yes, in a way. The trick here is to bounce back, to forgive oneself and one's colleagues for giving the enemy anything. In Denton's words, "Bounce back became a way of life." Then, later in 1966, Denton experienced a truly miraculous event. As he hung from the ropes in a Vietnamese strappado—a medieval form of torture that the Vietnamese learned probably from the French decades ago—for five days, he was nearly at the end of his endurance. He wrote, describing this experience, "I offered myself to God with an admission that I could take no more on my own. Tears ran down my face as I repeated my vow of surrender to Him. Strangely, as soon as I made the vow, a deep feeling of peace settled into my tortured mind and pain-wracked body, and the suffering left me completely. It was the most profound and deeply inspiring moment of my life." Jeremiah Denton survived his captivity and returned to the United States with honor, enough to be selected for rear admiral, then after retirement from the Navy to Capitol Hill as a senator from Alabama. Upon thinking about his devotion to God and his country, he wrote, "Our coins bear the inspiration: 'In God We Trust.' Our Bible reassures us: 'The Lord is just and merciful.'"[20] Who could ask for more from an American who spent many years serving his country in "difficult circumstances" behind barbed wire?

Capt. Howard Rutledge, USN (Ret.), a naval aviator like Jeremiah Denton, also spent seven years behind the wire in Hanoi during the Vietnam War. His captivity narrative, published in 1977, is a deeply committed testament to his faith. He wrote,

I cannot explain with reason or proof why my faith was central to my survival. But it was. Other men went in unbelieving and came out the same. I didn't, and for me my faith in Christ made all the difference. When one is dying from starvation, a bowl of sewer greens is a gift from

God. Before every meal during my captivity, I offered a prayer of thanks. To thank God for life seemed the natural thing to do. Now I know the truth. Prayer really works! I still don't pray aloud very well. But I have tested prayer and found God hears and answers.[21]

Shot down on November 28, 1965, Rutledge flew his missions in an F-8 Crusader aircraft from the USS *Bonhomme Richard* in the Gulf of Tonkin. It was a tough day: shot down and captured by North Vietnamese civilians bent on revenge. It is no wonder that Rutledge believes that it was God's hand that saved his life that day: "I was a prisoner of war. I had no idea what my fate would be, but the Lord had made Himself abundantly clear. I breathed my second prayer of thanks that day."[22]

Like all the other POWs in Hanoi, Rutledge went through the North Vietnamese system of isolation, starvation, interrogation, communication torture, propaganda, and ultimate release in 1973. He knew what the communists wanted and, like other hard resisters, was determined to make them work for anything they got from him. In a very real sense, he knew where he was and wrote reflectively, "The enemy knew that the best way to break a man's resistance was to crush his spirit in a lonely cell. All this talk of Scripture and hymns may seem boring to some, but it was the way we conquered our enemy and overcame the power of death around us." Yet overcoming the power of their captors took a great deal of perseverance and determination and, for these men, help from God. For sixteen months, hard resisters like Cdr. James Stockdale, Jeremiah Denton, and Howard Rutledge were put into what they called Alcatraz, the punishment block of the Hanoi Hilton that had cells reminiscent of medieval times. Rutledge wrote, "Each cell had a sleeping slab and a walking area no more than four feet square. When the guards closed the door, the light really did go out. In the winter the cells were refrigerator cold, and in the summer they were stifling. To make matters worse we spent fifteen hours a day in shackles. We were unshackled on the Tet holiday and at Christmas."[23]

On November 21, 1970, the North Vietnamese moved all the American POWs to one central location in Hanoi, what the POWs called Camp Unity. Actually, it was a part of the Hanoi Hilton with one cell block of forty men each to house everyone together. The POWs were thrilled to get together, now having the opportunity to put faces together with names they had communicated with for years through the walls. They also held church services immediately. On February 7, 1971, the guards came to the church service in Cell Block 7 and tried to halt it. The "Church Riot" then took place: the guards attempted to stop the American church service, and the Americans kept conducting it. According to former POW Guy Gruters, "The next man in line stood up and said, 'Gentlemen, our service was interrupted, let us start again.'" Another POW, Ed Mechenbeier from Ohio, responded to the North Vietnamese, telling them, "It doesn't matter what you do, including killing every one of us, but as long as one man is alive, we are having that church service."[24] After the American POWs ended the service by singing "The Star-Spangled Banner" in full voice, the communists separated the junior from the senior officers, putting the seniors into small cells with shackles and filth all around therm. This treatment for the senior officers lasted until news of the Geneva Protocol of 1973 reached them. The idea of returning home with honor won out for all these men, for many because of their faith in the United States, for others because of their resistance based on their faith in God, the United States, and each other. In their last service in Hanoi, the POWs sang the doxology together:

> Praise God from whom all blessings flow;
> Praise Him, all creatures here below;
> Praise Him above, ye heavenly host;
> Praise Father, Son, and Holy Ghost.

In Hanoi without the benefit of clergy, the POWs became their own chaplains.

Most Americans understand the wars in Korea and again in Vietnam to have been part of the Cold War that began after World War II, turned hot in 1950 and 1959, respectively, and ended when the American commitment in Vietnam ended in 1973. However, a few Americans participated in another part of the Cold War, one that pitted Christianity against Marxist-Leninist Stalinism in the Soviet Union from its beginnings in 1921 until its fall in 1991.

From 1929 to 1945 eleven Roman Catholic priests were trained at the Russian college or seminary in Rome, founded in 1929 and known as the Russicum, and sent to the Soviet Union secretly. Pope Pius XI began a letter, "To all Seminarians, especially our Jesuit sons," calling for men to enter a new Russian center being started at Rome to prepare clerics for possible work in Russia. In 1922 the communists declared them to be enemies of the people, and the priests then became outlaws. The Soviets termed the Catholic Church to be a "Den of Spies" and proceeded to arrest as many priests as they could identify. Despite Stalin's hatred for all things and people Christian, graduates of the Russicum kept coming into the USSR and increased the population of the gulag system considerably from 1923 onward. The American Jesuit Fr. Walter Ciszek, S.J., recalled his interrogation in Lubyanka Prison in Moscow when and where his Soviet interrogator poisoned him after charging him with being a spy for the Vatican: "I never again was fooled, never trusted any Soviet official, of whatever rank. After that, I prayed every morning and every evening, 'Lord, deliver me from my enemies and their evil operations.' It was a spontaneous reaction and a heartfelt prayer; only in God would I ever put my trust. From then on, I felt stronger and comforted. No matter what the danger, I always felt His help and a growing confidence in Him." He wrote again about his understanding of God's Providence while he was in Lubyanka: "I never lost sight of God's Providence. I knew that nothing was too small or insignificant in life when looked on from the standpoint of His will. At least, I tried to keep sight of that. Lubyanka was a hard school, but a good one. I learned there the lesson which would keep me going in the years to come: religion, prayer, and love of God do not change reality, but they do give it meaning."[26]

By the time all this persecution came to an end, eleven dossiers of priests were found in the Soviet KGB (Intelligence Service) archives, including the Jesuit Fr. Pietro Leoni, a former chaplain to Italian troops in the Ukraine during World War II. In 1945 Fr. Leoni was taken captive in his Ukrainian parish, tried, and sent on a ten-year sentence to the gulags. Another Italian priest, Fr. Gedeone, went to Russia from the Russicum in 1936 and was the last priest sent to the Soviet Union. Any priest caught at this time was either shot outright or poisoned, although some were spared death and deported back to their home countries. Fr. Leoni was released from the gulag in 1954, and he returned to Italy.[27] It was not until October 1963 that Fr. Walter J. Ciszek, S.J., the only American in this group, was returned to the United States.

Fr. Ciszek's homecoming was unique in its simplicity, on the one hand, and its complexity, on the other. A Mr. Kirk from the American embassy in Moscow had come into his life as his liberator, although he did not know it at the time.

Perhaps Fr. Ciszek had become somewhat too Russianized after more than twenty years in the Soviet Union, and Mr. Kirk startled him by saying, "'Now, Fr. Ciszek, you're an American citizen.' 'Really,' he asked just stunned. 'Yes, you are an American citizen again.' 'Yes, it's a fairy tale but a fine fairy tale,' smiled Mr. Kirk, 'and it's true.' It was too sudden. All at once I felt free and loose; it was as if a great weight had suddenly been lifted and the bones in my spine had sprung into shape like elastic. I felt like I ought to sing." Fr. Walter Ciszek, S.J., was on his way home after many years of service to his faith and his order in the Soviet Union. In prison and work camps as a political prisoner, little did he know before his death in 1984 that the Soviet Union would melt away in 1991, and the Christians there experienced a Great Awakening, to borrow a term from American religious history. In the October 26, 1963, issue of *America,* the Jesuit magazine, Fr. Ciszek released a brief statement that read in part, "I went into the interior of Russia of my own free will, spurred by my conscience and a desire to do good in the line of my vocation. In spite of seeming failures, I cherish no resentment or regrets for what has transpired in the past years."[28]

This is indeed an astonishing statement of reconciliation and a stunningly beautiful good-bye to the good people he met in Russia. This is not to say that the Russian Republic under Vladimir Putin became an ally of NATO or at least friendly to the West. Old hostilities like bad habits are difficult to break. But for all those men and women captured in wartime in Vietnam and Eastern Europe, faith during the Cold War was just as strong and powerful as it was earlier in the century. Indeed, ideas generate actions, and this is very true for those men of God who were made prisoners of war or of state. Many put their faith first as the tool of their defense against an evil ideology, and most won their battles for freedom, faith, and hope for a future in the hands of their Maker.

Eleven

—◆»〉〈«◆—

War on Terror
Conclusions and Reflections

The work of the chaplain did not stop when he became a prisoner. It increased rather than lessened our responsibilities and opportunities for doing spiritual work.
—Chaplain Mark R. Moore, USA

AFTER A TRIP THROUGH AMERICAN military history from a unique point of view from the French and Indian War fought before the American Revolution to the war on terrorism, each conflict found men of God serving as chaplains to American soldiers, sailors, airmen, and Marines often at the point of the spear. It is an approach that takes on several historical questions: What is the chaplaincy? Why does it exist? How does it function in multicultural societies, past and present? What kind of meaning can we derive from the selfless acts of these men, and what are the connections beginning in the past and working up to the future? Such a qualitative methodological approach to history has no easy answers nor any easy definitional handles to apply to it; however, one can hope that readers might find such a methodology helpful, sometimes direct, sometimes indirect, but always completely human. In short, there are no laws of history such as exist in physics to rely on in order to derive scientific truth. All we can do is gather what evidence we can and let the truth, mostly gained through human religious experience, like cards, fall where it may.

Archival sources were not at the heart and soul of this study as they are in other kinds of historical works. When one intends to tell a story, going into mountains of archives certainly can be impressive; however, other than the Jesuits, or Society of Jesus, and the Dominicans to some extent, not much is available in archives of the various churches or religious orders in the United States. Personal narratives and studies are available, both formally published and self-published, and as many as possible appear in these pages, in part, because personal captivity narratives are indeed primary data. The work of a long list of chaplains and scholars who have studied and commented on what their peers and many who came before them did comes also into play as source material. Thus, this study of wartime chaplains for the most part exists by examining the lives and, in many cases, the deaths of chaplains who served as men of God to American military personnel in battle, on death marches, in prison camps, and in the many different kinds of work that chaplains render to God and their charges. The intention of this book is to tell the often complicated story of what American chaplains did on the field of battle and as POWs during wartime. When the times had no war during the interim periods in history, the chaplaincy matured and changed as a service force within a military institution.

Covering a span of three hundred years, this book stretches from American national antiquity to the present time. When examining chaplaincy in the French and Indian War, enemies and allies seem rather far off to modern readers. To the Americans, the British were the allies and the French the enemies. Their Catholicism was an enemy too. Yet it is important to pursue the nature of faith that Americans have had before and since the beginning of the republic and document the chaplains through all these eras who show in part what Americans valued in the past, present, and possibly into the future. By examining denominations that pervaded the American colonies before and during the Revolutionary period, one can see how they conducted themselves: Congregationalists in New England, what the Puritans called themselves from the eighteenth century to the modern era; Anglican or Episcopalian in the American South; Presbyterians and Evangelical Lutherans in the middle states. We have examined how ministers joined their local militia units to fight and preach, and if the song title "Praise the Lord and Pass the Ammunition," so popular during World War II, could be imagined with muskets and sail, the idea that clergymen acting as a chaplains to militia units prior to or during the American Revolution as an unarmed member of a military unit was not thinkable. Preachers defended themselves just as their parishioners did. They functioned as soldiers and chaplains at the same time. Today, of course, chaplains are noncombatant protected personnel; they carry no weapons, and they will serve the religious needs of friend and foe alike, at least they have done so during the Revolution, Civil War, World War I, World War II, Korea, Vietnam, and beyond.

Both continuity and change showed themselves as we pass through America's wars. The development, both positive and negative, of America itself in terms of its religious tendencies relied on the practitioners of those faiths. During the Revolutionary years and following decades, there were very few Catholics in the British colonies or in the United States after separation. There were some but relatively few; most lived in French Canada at that time. The French Canadian unit Livingston's Regiment, recruited in Canada in 1775, sought out sixty-year-old Father Louis Lotbiniere of Quebec as chaplain who served for the entire length of the war. Gen. Benedict Arnold offered him rations, firewood, candles, and a monthly salary, but along with every member of the regiment, he was ex-communicated by the bishop of Quebec who forbade any of his parishioners or clergy to join the American side of the fight. Fr. Lotbiniere lived on his meager pension and died nearly penniless and all but forgotten in Philadelphia on October 11, 1786.

Chaplains during the American Revolution suffered the same privations and dangers as the men in their respective commands. At times, they were executed in the field or sent to prison hulks by the British, just like the soldiers they fought with. They were appointed into chaplaincies in the Continental army by the Continental Congress and into state militias by state governments. Were they remembered well? No, but records of these units do recall the service of their chaplains, perhaps because Gen. George Washington desired his army to be religious, at least on the surface. Many of his senior officers were men of faith, as well as many of his subordinate junior officers as well. It remains a simple happenstance that a belief in God, eternity, heaven, and hell, as they were stated in the Bible, especially the Old Testament, was common fare for the soldiers of the American Revolution. Did this fundamental belief in God continue after the Revolutionary period in the American armed services? Yes, it did, although it took some rather odd turns as the Early Republic period continued all the religious characteristics of the United States, especially as they manifested themselves during the War of Independence.

Curiously, the Americans who lived following the Revolutionary period saw no real need for a large federal army when state militias seemed to be sufficient for defense of the nation. Finding any writings about chaplains in regular or militia American army units was nearly impossible. A few exceptions exist: one is Kenneth E. Lawson, *Reliable and Religious: U.S. Army Chaplains in the War of 1812* (2012). Lawson wrote the history of the chaplaincy when things began turning against the Americans in battle after battle against British and Canadians forces. Having only ill-trained militias began to take its toll, yet despite the seeming success in the Battle of New Orleans and the end of the War of 1812, there was no real social or religious revolution in the United States. It came after the war in two forms: the Second Great Awakening in the 1815–16 period and the Irish and German Catholic migration of the 1840s and 1850s from Europe to the United States. Both events changed a great deal of feeling, mores, and events in America.

The Second Great Awakening was an important event in that it rebuilt a faith-based country that was beginning to leave the faith of the previous generation for an unknown and uncharted future. In effect, it became a renewal of sorts and a leap into a more democratic kind of Protestantism than what had preceded it during the Revolutionary period. The rise of the Baptists both in the North and in the South, took place, as did a rise in American Methodism.[1] Other Protestant denominations began to give way to the new ones, and the country saw a rise in nonliturgical denominations and the beginning of the shrinking of liturgical ones like Lutherans and Episcopalians. In effect, the Second Great Awakening gave rise to an inward, self-defining kind of faith that Americans relied upon to define what it was to be an American. Then came the Potato Famine in Ireland and the Irish Catholic immigration to the United States beginning in 1845 that introduced a kind of nasty cultural chaos that in part defined the hatreds of the nineteenth century.

The influx of millions of Irish Catholics to the East Coast of the United States changed the culture at its core, not at once and not easily. Native Protestant Americans saw the Irish not only as unwelcome foreigners but also as hordes of ignorant, often illiterate, Catholic barbarians, totally dependent on their Rome-based clergy to guide their lives and religion. Thus, they were worthy of no consideration at all. The women got work as maids, the men as unskilled laborers. "No Irish Need Apply" appeared on signs in windows, except when and where the U.S. Army needed soldiers for the war in Mexico. To the immigrant Irishmen, soldiering in the American Army looked pretty good, except that there were no Catholic chaplains to serve their religious needs. Having been intimidated in Ireland by the British, being again intimidated for their faith in America became unacceptable for some Catholic soldiers serving in Mexico. They deserted, and some formed the San Patricio Battalion in the Mexican army.

Many Catholics remained out of the American mainstream culturally from the period of the Mexican War, 1846–48, until well into the future, perhaps until World War II, when all Catholics became Americans instead of "papists." Beginning with the problems in Mexico with the Irish Catholic soldiers, President James A. Polk, indeed a practical man, sat down with Bishop John Hughes of New York City in 1847 and asked for a solution, imperfect as it turned out, but at least Polk showed respect for his Catholic soldiers and for their religious needs by appointing two Jesuit priests as chaplains to his Catholic soldiers in Mexico. The executions of the San Patricio deserters ordered by Gen. Winfield Scott was the last mass execution in American military history with the exception of the Santee Sioux executions in Mankato, Minnesota, in 1862. Catholics in the United States increased in numbers, especially with German immigration after the unsuccessful Revolution of 1848 against Prussia. Coming to the United States in a large second wave, the Germans also brought their clergy with them to the New World. With citizenship earned before the Civil War, Lutherans became Republicans, while Catholics became Democrats. Modern historical scholars in Germany like Wolfgang Hochbruch of the University of Freiburg remind us proudly that both Lutherans and Catholics joined the Union army during the war because they both opposed slavery.

As the Civil War approached, all the clergy developed strategies and precedents that the chaplains embraced in the field for their soldiers as they provided pastoral care. The numbers became impressive. Benjamin L. Miller notes that "2,398 men received commissions as U.S. Army, Navy or hospital chaplains of U.S. Volunteers. Of these 40 percent were Methodists, 17 percent Presbyterians, 18 percent Baptists. Others included African-American clergy, Irish Catholic priests, Scottish Congregationalists, and German Lutherans." In the Confederate armies, Miller counted 1,308 chaplains, but only 42 percent of these were fully ordained ministers: 47 percent Methodists, 18 percent Presbyterian, 16 percent Baptists, 10 percent Episcopalians, and 3 percent Roman Catholics.[2] Miller also notes that both sides experienced a great deal of missionary work, mostly people and societies who delivered religious tracts and literature to the troops. In the North, this effort was led by the huge United States Christian Commission. Nothing like it existed in the South.

One can readily see when examining religion during the Civil War era that it was just a sea of faith both in the North and in the South. Protestant services consisted typically of prayer and Bible reading by the minister followed by a sermon based on the reading. Then the congregation sang hymns and recited psalms. The Catholics attended Mass reverently, often preceded by confession before communion. Miller writes that "both Catholics and Protestants saw their clergy as exemplars of virtue and dignity in a problem world."[3] Both believed earnestly that without their clergy, they could lose their souls. This was especially true in prison.

Captured and imprisoned soldiers prayed hard. Chaplains in Union prisons like Fort Delaware, Point Lookout, and others pointed out that the Confederate prisoners were deeply devout and often "begged for additional preaching."[4] In the Confederate prison at Andersonville, Georgia, Catholic chaplain Fr. Peter Whelan served his Federal soldiers faithfully until the prison closed in the late fall of 1864. Before evacuation, one of the strangest revelations of the power of prayer took place. In nightly prayer meetings, the Union prisoners prayed for water, fresh potable water, they could drink and not die from it. All they had was a small creek that the prisoners used as a toilet and was completely fouled. One former prisoner, William N. Tyler, recalled that one day after a prayer meeting, "there occurred one of the most fearful rains I ever saw. It washed out the stockade as clean as a hound's tooth. Right between the deadline and the stockade it washed a ditch about two feet deep and a spring of cold water broke out. The spring is there yet . . . called Providence Spring. We had good water from then on."[5] During the Civil War, one can see from the literature left by the chaplains, soldiers, prisoners, and nearly everyone who took part in that war that soldiers required the comfort of faith regardless of the side on which they fought. Confederate chaplain Fr. James Sheeran spent time as a POW at Fort McHenry in Baltimore in late 1864 and found himself surrounded by Protestant prisoners who wanted preaching rather than Catholic liturgy. With hints of ecumenicalism in the air, he had no choice and decided to preach against gambling and profanity.

Little could be said about chaplains in the Spanish-American War or World War I other than Chaplain Fr. John Chidwick of the USS *Maine* in 1898 and Chaplain Fr. Francis P. Duffy of the 69th Infantry Division in World War I. Both Father Chidwick and Father Duffy showed their honor and heroism in the face of great adversity and were greatly respected by their sailors and soldiers during their lives and after their deaths. No American chaplain was taken POW either in 1898 or later in the Philippine Insurrection. During World War I, more than four thousand captured Americans had to depend on British clergy in German POW camps; however, this period was one of change and maturity of the American chaplain corps.

Between World War I and World War II, the United States dealt with an evolving political situation in the Far East, and by the middle 1930s began to build up forces in the Philippine Islands against invasion by Japan. By 1940 at least the high command of American forces knew that the Japanese were going to attack but had no firm idea when or where. That anyone in Manila, Guam, Wake Island, Pearl Harbor, or even Washington, D.C., could believe that Imperial Japan was going to attack everywhere nearly at the same time was not thinkable. On December 7 and 8, 1941, the United States got caught napping everywhere, with the exception of Wake Island, where the Marines resisted the Japanese attacks rather well until overwhelmed by the enemy. As a result, American forces lost thousands of men, a naval force in the Pacific, an army and an air force in the Philippines, Marines on Wake Island, and, ultimately, the largest surrender of troops in American history on the Bataan

Peninsula in April and the surrender of Corregidor Island in May 1942. That a host of American chaplains stood their ground in the face of this sort of enormous adversity was simply amazing, perhaps a miracle.

Never before in an armed conflict had Americans been treated so badly as they were by the Japanese. Chaplain Leslie Zimmerman encapsulated what the chaplains faced: "The morale and spirit of the Japanese Army were established on two rigid principles: first, that a soldier never retreats; second, that he shall never be taken prisoner. Faced with retreat or surrender, the Japanese soldier was expected to commit suicide. It is no wonder that they regarded American prisoners as 'kichibu' (beastly), subhuman, the foul water flowing from the sewage of Caucasian corruption. Prisoners were beneath contempt and not worthy of any consideration or compassion."[6] Thus, the chaplains were caught in the middle: they were uniformed officers in the Army and Navy, yet they were noncombatants. There were thirty-eight Army and four Navy chaplains taken prisoner when orders came for surrender to the Japanese in the Philippines. Of these chaplains, twenty-one were Roman Catholics, seventeen Protestant. Twenty died either in prison camps or on board Japanese transport ships, termed "hell ships" by both POWs and historians. They died as they lived, in service to their soldiers and sailors.

Chaplains were lost, dead and wounded, during the invasions of North Africa in 1942, Italy in 1943, and France in 1944. Beginning with the tragic loss of the Four Chaplains on board the *Dorchester* in 1942, the greatest number were taken POW during the Battle of the Bulge in the Ardennes Forest of Belgium and Luxembourg just before Christmas 1944. Unlike the Japanese who were universally hostile to Western Christianity, non-Nazi, non-SS Germans remained Christian for the most part, and, again for the most part, they obeyed the Geneva Convention of 1929. The SS were criminals. Not Christian either in spirit or in active service, they were Nazis to the core and followed the anti-Christian prescription of Alfred Rosenberg's *Myth of the Twentieth Century*. They murdered POWs, especially those enemy soldiers they believed were racially inferior to themselves, in Poland, Russia, and Americans in Belgium during the Battle of the Bulge in 1944. They also operated the concentration camps and made life deadly not only for millions of European Jews but also for the clergy in the Dachau Priest Block until liberation in 1945.

The problem that continually surfaced in the German POW camps was one of rank. The German armed services were painfully aware that rank had its privileges and attempted to enforce this policy when and wherever possible, both with their Allied POWs and with themselves in Allied captivity. Internally, German POW policy rested on the capturing entity, Army, Navy, or Air Force, and, like the British and Americans, the Germans separated captured officers and enlisted soldiers and sent them to different compounds or to different facilities. The chaplains petitioned their captors to hold services in the enlisted compounds. Many senior German camp commandants granted permission for American, British, and French chaplains to go into their neighboring enlisted compounds to hold services, while some refused. Chaplain Mark R. Moore of the 106th Division, captured during the Battle of the Bulge in 1944, relates his story about his stay in the officers' camp in Hammelburg: "The work of the chaplain did not stop when he became a prisoner. It increased rather than lessened our responsibilities and opportunities for doing spiritual work."[7] It really depended on how steeped in Nazi ideology the commandant was. It is also good to keep in mind that after the Great Escape in March 1944, the SS took all the German POW facilities away from the different military services and put them under stricter SS racial rules. Thus, from April 1944 to the end of the war, the German POW camps changed administrative control and became much harsher and more Nazi than they had been before that time. Heinrich Himmler and his monsters controlled the concentration and POW camps. They were much nastier jailers than the German army, navy, or air force were, and at the war's end, many German SS officers and troops paid for their war crimes by facing the firing squad or the hangman. Others escaped into the wind until years later when the German judicial system finally caught up and prosecuted them. In Germany there is no statute of limitations on war crimes.

Chaplain Moore tells us about the four kinds of activities that Protestant POW chaplains engaged in. First, Sunday worship services had to be written out and submitted to the camp authorities. Of course, many chaplains had a difficult time submitting their sermons and saw this as a form of censorship, which it was. Second, they conducted evening devotions held in individual rooms. Some were successful; others were not and depended on the cooperation of the POWs in the rooms. Third, morning devotions were at first meant to reinforce the chaplains' own faith and inner lives. When the POWs learned about these devotions, often they asked to attend and did in relatively large numbers. Fourth, Bible study groups started because some of the younger officers wanted to enter the ministry after liberation and repatriation.[8]

In some cases, as was the case with Fr. Francis Sampson, held POW in eastern Germany, the American POW chaplain befriended a local priest or pastor who often supplied the American chaplain with liturgical supplies for services. For Fr. Sampson, it was a heartbreaking moment when he witnessed how the Russian troops were taking revenge against German civilians when they arrived. He saw drunken rape and pillage to an industrial degree and could do absolutely nothing to stop it or to help his German friends. He was glad to be out of Russian hands in 1945 and going home. Other chaplain POW stories tell of narrow escapes from friendly bombings in railroad yards and while saying Mass during the unsuccessful Task Force Baum raid on their POW camp at Hammelburg.

The World War II POW experience for chaplains was no walk in the park, but in Europe there was a better chance of survival than there was in Japanese hands. Upon their return to the United States on board the *General Gordon*, Chaplain Moore asked some of the men returning with him to New York if they would like to have a Thanksgiving service in front of the Statue of Liberty. They held their service. Chaplain Moore recalled that one officer told Mrs. Moore, "For a time we thought artillery shells were breaking around us and then we suddenly realized we were hearing our hearts pounding within us."[9]

In Korea Fr. Emil Kapaun serves as an icon for all the chaplains who served and became POWs from 1950 to 1953. Unfortunately, none survived captivity, including Fr. Kapaun. Statistics aside, Korea became the first war where and when Americans met captors who were ideologues with guns, perhaps the first time since the Revolution when the British accused the Americans of being rebels and certainly not POWs with any rights at all. Of the two adversaries, the North Koreans and the communist Chinese, the North Koreans were more terrible in their treatment of POWs than the Chinese. One can argue that they acted more like the Japanese at their worst than the Chinese who treated their POWs more as starving "students" than despised chattel. Former POWs tell us that the Chinese wanted to create doubt in the minds of their prisoners, doubt about capitalism, American democracy, American fairness, doubt about American racism against black troops, and doubt, of course, about Wall Street and the American war in Korea. The communist Chinese starved UN POWs first, then they took advantage of any "Progressive" POWs who wanted to invest their allegiance in the communist world, usually for better food, as twenty Americans did in 1953, but doubt more than allegiance was predominant. Chaplains, of course, got in the way of all that, so the Chinese simply eliminated their opposition by attrition. Fr. Emil Kapaun became a victim of that kind of war of attrition. President Barack Obama awarded him the Medal of Honor posthumously, and many devotees are advocating for a declaration of his sainthood in the Catholic Church.

Captivity during the Vietnam War was similar in some respects to the Korean War, although the numbers were much smaller than those in Korea or World War II by comparison. No chaplains were ever taken prisoner of war in Vietnam, although the number who served in Vietnam from 1963 to 1973 was large, 1,286 in 1963 to 1,900 in 1973, with the U.S. Army having roughly 1,500 in the country at any one time.[10] The POWs in Hanoi served as chaplains to each other. They had no other choice. True, not every American POW in Hanoi was a religious man, but many were, as reflected in their postwar narratives. POWs such as Jeremiah Denton, Charles Plumb, James Stockdale, Gerald Coffee, Guy Gruters, and many others explain how different forms of faith, religious and secular, gave them the strength to suffer what became the longest period of military incarceration in American history. Vietnam was similar to World War I in that the Americans worked hard to protect their chaplains in the field. This does not mean, however, that chaplains avoided being killed in action. The "Paratrooper Padre" (Fr. Francis L. Sampson) of World War II evolved into the "Grunt Padre" (Fr. Vincent R. Capodanno) of Vietnam. Fr. Sampson lived through his war; Fr. Capodanno died in his. Bullets and shrapnel have no conscience; only people do. Fr. Capodanno, much like Fr. Kapaun, in Korea continues to serve as the icon for all chaplains who served heroically in Vietnam and was also awarded the Medal of Honor posthumously.

The war on terrorism began on September 11, 2001, with the unprecedented attack on the World Trade Center in New York City. There is little doubt that it served as the war of the present generation of Americans and allies. President George W. Bush declared on October 11, 2001: "The attack took place on

American soil, but it was an attack on the heart and soul of the civilized world. And the world has come together to fight a new and different war, the first, and we hope the only one, of the 21st century. A war against all those who seek to export terror, and a war against those governments that support or shelter them."[11] As of 2016, the U.S. Department of Defense reported that 6,907 soldiers were killed in action in Afghanistan and Iraq, with another 52,514 wounded.[12] Although definitive numbers remain elusive, approximately 3,000 chaplains served on active duty, serving approximately 175 different religions.[13] None was taken POW by the enemy either in Iraq or Afghanistan. Yet some died, and many walked away permanently stressed by the experience.

Fr. Timothy Vakoc was stationed in Mosul, Iraq, in 2003, a time when suicide bombers were killing civilians and roadside bombs were killing American soldiers and marines. Fr. Vakoc was well known and well loved in the 44th Corps Support Battalion in Mosul and stayed on the road giving comfort and reassuring American soldiers despite IEDs (improvised explosive devices) designed to kill everyone in his vehicle. In a letter he wrote to his sister, he scribbled, "The safest place for me to be is in the center of God's will, and if that is in the line of fire, that is where I will be."[14] One day, as Fr. Vakoc was returning to the 44th Corps, his vehicle struck an IED, and he was severely injured, with a traumatic brain injury among other wounds. He died in 2009 of his injuries.

Chaplain Fr. Joel Panzer served in Iraq with the 25th Infantry Division outside of Tikrit, Iraq, in 2011. Speaking with Joan Desmond, writing for the *National Catholic Register*, Fr. Panzer noted, "As a Catholic chaplain, I have two roles: I'm a unit chaplain to all 800 soldiers in the 25th Infantry Division Headquarters, Catholic or not. But as a priest, I am a high-demand low-intensity chaplain. That means I travel out to other units in our area who don't have their own priest. I travel and offer Mass in the entire area of responsibility covered by the 25th Infantry. Most chaplains would not do that. And, yes, frequent travel in a combat zone increases the risk that you may be injured or killed."[15] Fr. Panzer managed to experience most of the challenges that chaplains before him had dealt with: physically dangerous situations, pastoral care, and stress that deployed soldiers experience, especially under fire. Chaplain Henry McCain served as a Latter-day Saint chaplain in Iraq for two year-long tours, the first from 2004 to 2005 and the second from 2007 to 2008. In speaking to Chad S. Hawkins, Chaplain McCain recalled a serious combat experience:

An Apache helicopter had been shot down, and we knew we had to get to them. They had crashed in an unsafe area during an intense time of the war. I remember someone saying, "You all are going to die. It's too dangerous for you to go out there." As our convoy proceeded, we passed other convoys—each one burning and abandoned. Once we located the chopper, we began to secure the area. I wanted to know who the soldiers were and pay them proper respects, so I ran to the chopper. It was still on fire, so all I could do was grab the dog tags off the pilots. I now had the names.[16]

Chaplain McCain noted that "I will never forget their names. These pilots had been shot down while trying to save other soldiers in a convoy."[17] No one can ask more from a chaplain than that. In 2007 the Army chief of chaplains went to Iraq to bring encouragement and support to his cadre of military clergy in the field. Army chaplain Maj. Gen. David H. Hicks, USA, responded, "People ask me as a spiritual leader, as the chief of chaplains, what do I think about the war." He replied positively: "I am quick to respond very positively because I believe what we are doing is right. Our soldiers on the battlefield understand the connection between what happened on 9/11 and what they are doing on the battlefield today. It's larger than just 9/11, and that's why I connect it to the battlefield because we're fighting a global war on terrorism."[18]

The war on terrorism came to an end in 2022 with the withdrawal of American and NATO troops from Afghanistan. From what we have uncovered from the American Revolution to the battlefields in Iraq and Afghanistan, American chaplains stood beside their soldiers, sailors, airmen, and Marines, doing their best to keep God, and all that God means to them, intact even in the chaos of war and battle. In a world where life meets death sometimes on a daily basis in the most horrid of ways, keeping things right with God is not an abstract notion. From the beginning to the end, we can see that acts of faith take place before our eyes with a sense of reality present in the spirituality at the tip of the spear, the point of a gun, the target of an artillery barrage, the prison camp, or wherever the border between life and death may be at the moment. There may be atheists in foxholes, but that is also where the men of God are.

❧ NOTES ❧

Preface

1. Chaplain J. A. Knight, USNR, "Prisoner of War Evacuation from Japan," *Army and Navy Chaplain* 16, no. 4 (1946): 8.
2. Commander Herbert L. Bergsma, CHC, USN, *Chaplains with the Marines in Vietnam, 1962–1971* (Washington, DC: Headquarters, U.S. Marine Corps, 1985), 68.

Introduction

1. See Michael McCormick, "The Liturgy of War from Antiquity to the Crusades," in Doris L. Bergen, *The Sword and the Lord: Military Chaplains from the First to the Twenty-First Century* (Notre Dame, IN: Notre Dame University Press, 2004), 105–23; and David S. Bachrach, "The Medieval Military Chaplain and His Duties," 69–88. This is an unusually excellent collection of essays, well worth studying in detail.
2. Eugene Franklin Williams, *Soldiers of God: The Chaplains of the Revolutionary War* (New York: Carlton, 1950), 11. See also Daniel P. Jorgenson, *Air Force Chaplains*, vol. 1 (New York: U.S. Government Printing Office, 1962), 4–5; Edith Delaware, *Saint Martin* (New York: Macmillan, 1962), 58; and Dom Aidan Henry Germain, "Catholic Military and Naval Chaplains, 1776–1917" (PhD diss., Catholic University of America, 1929), iii–iv. See also "St. Martin of Tours," Catholic Online, https://www.catholic.org/saints/saint.php?saint_id=81.
3. See Warren B. Armstrong, *For Courageous Fighting and Confident Dying: Union Chaplains in the Civil War* (Lawrence: University Press of Kansas, 1998), 122.

Chapter One. Chaplains of Muskets and Sail

1. Eugene Franklin Williams, *Soldiers of God: The Chaplains of the Revolutionary War* (New York: Carlton, 1950), 33–34.
2. See Rev. Mr. John Norton, *The Redeemed Captive: Narrative of the Capture and Burning of Fort Captivity of All Those Stationed There to the Number of Thirty Persons* (1746; reprint, Albany, NY: S. G. Drake of Boston, 1870).

3. Norton, 35, 51.

4. Williams, *Soldiers of God*, 34, 36.

5. Charles H. Metzger, "Chaplains in the American Revolution," *Catholic Historical Review* 31, no. 1 (1945): 37.

6. Williams, *Soldiers of God*, 37.

7. See U.S. Army, *United States Army Chaplain Corps*, pamphlet 165-1 (Washington, DC: Headquarters, U.S. Army, 1974), 3.

8. Kenneth E. Lawson, *Reliable and Religious: U.S. Army Chaplains in the War of 1812* (Washington, DC: Department of the Army, Office of the Chief of Chaplains, 2012), 10.

9. Herman Norton, *Rebel Religion: The Story of Confederate Chaplains* (St. Louis: Bethany Press, 1961), 14.

10. See Metzger, "Chaplains in the American Revolution," for an outstanding description of these sorts of complaints from brigadiers about the appointment of their chaplains. They could rarely agree about anything, much to Washington's consternation.

11. Williams, *Soldiers of God*, 44.

12. Williams, 49.

13. "Military Chaplains," *Christian Science Monitor*, October 30, 2007.

14. Williams, *Soldiers of God*, 75.

15. U.S. Army, *United States Army Chaplain Corps*, 3.

16. Howard Lewis Applegate, "Duties and Activities of Chaplains," *Picket Post*, July, 1958, 10, in Williams, *Soldiers of God*, 85.

17. See Metzger, "Chaplains in the American Revolution," 47.

18. Williams, *Soldiers of God*, 99–101.

19. Rogers McLane, ed., *American Chaplains of the Revolution* (Louisville, KY: National Society Sons of the American Revolution, 1991), 1. Escaping because of the certainty of death is known as the Principle of Intolerable Cruelty, first articulated during the French and Indian War by Barbara Leiniger, a Swiss captive of the Seneca who escaped successfully. See Robert C. Doyle, *A Prisoner's Duty: Great Escapes in U.S. Military History* (Annapolis, MD: Naval Institute Press, 1997), 1–13.

20. Joel Tyler Headley, *Chaplains and Clergy of the Revolution* (New York: Charles Scribner, 1864), 224, 230–31; McLane, *American Chaplains of the Revolution*, 4.

21. McLane, *American Chaplains of the Revolution*, 28. See also Headley, *Chaplains and Clergy of the Revolution*, 161. Hunter was one of the founders of the U.S. Naval Academy at Annapolis, Maryland, and served as a senior chaplain and teacher until his death in 1823.

22. Headley, *Chaplains and Clergy of the Revolution*, 204; McLane, *American Chaplains of the Revolution*, 9. The Recollects were a branch of the Franciscan order. See Metzger, "Chaplains in the American Revolution," 52; and Thomas J. Craughwell,

Heroic Catholic Chaplains: Stories of the Brave and Holy Men Who Dodged Bullets While Saving Souls (Charlotte, NC: Tan Books, 2018), 13.

23. Headley, "Chaplains and Clergy of the Revolution," 276–79.

24. Headley, 206–7, 202–4.

25. McLane, *American Chaplains of the Revolution*, 33, 13.

26. McLane, 30.

27. McLane, 24

28. McLane, 24.

29. Williams, *Soldiers of God*, 280.

30. McLane, *American Chaplains of the Revolution*, 37.

31. "Military Chaplains," *Christian Science Monitor*, October 30, 2007.

Chapter Two. 1812 to 1848

1. U.S. Army, *United States Army Chaplain Corps*, pamphlet 165-1 (Washington, DC: Headquarters, U.S. Army, 1974), 6.

2. Kenneth E. Lawson, *Reliable and Religious: U.S. Army Chaplains in the War of 1812* (Washington, DC: Department of the Army, Office of the Chief of Chaplains, 2012), 10.

3. Ibid., 28. See also R. Taylor, "The Capture of Detroit 1812," The War of 1812 Website, http://w.w.w.warof1812.ca/batdetroit.html (assessed on April 19, 2020).

4. Lawson, *Reliable and Religious*, 136.

5. Ibid., 99.

6. William F. R. Gilroy and Timothy J. Demy, *A Brief Chronology of the Chaplain Corps of the United States Navy* (Washington, DC: Department of the Navy, 1983), 10.

7. See National Park Service https://www.nps.gov/people/alexander-cochrane.htm

8. Lawson, *Reliable and Religious*, 113.

9. Ibid., 115.

10. See Christopher Conway, "The U.S. Mexican War," *Oxford Bibliographies*, Last Modified: September 25, 2018, DOI: 10.1093/obo/9780199913701–0132 (accessed April 24, 2020).

11. Ibid. For an excellent analysis of the Mexican side of this war, see Ernesto Chávez, ed., *The U.S. War with Mexico: A Brief History with Documents* (New York: Bedford St. Martin's, 2007).

12. See John C. Pinheiro, *Missionaries of Republicanism: A Religious History of the Mexican-American War* (Cambridge, MA: Oxford University Press, 2014), 6.

13. Ibid., 6–7.

14. Robert Ryal Miller, *Shamrock and Sword: The Saint Patrick's Battalion in the U.S. Mexican War* (Norman: University of Oklahoma Press, 1989), 161–63.

15. Dennis J. Wynn, *The San Patricio Soldiers: Mexico's Foreign Legion* (El Paso: Texas Western Press, 1984), 3. See also https://www.biography.com/military-figure /antonio-lopez-de-santa-anna#:~:text=Antonio%20L%C3%B3pez%2de%20 Santa%20Anna%2C%20born%20on%20February,staving%20off%20Spain %E2%80%99s%20attempt%20to%20recapture%20the%20country.

16. *U.S. Army Chaplain Corps*, 6.

17. See Charles W. Hedrick, "On Foreign Soil: The Tragedy of a Civilized Chaplaincy," *Military Chaplain's Review* (Winter 1992): 68. See also Charles E. Smith, "The Work of the Civil War Chaplains" (master's thesis, University of Arizona, 1965), 75, for a good review of President Polk's difficulties with chaplains in 1847.

18. See James K. Polk, *The Diary of James K. Polk* Vol. 1 (Chicago: A. C. McClurg, 1910), np.

19. See Daryl Densford, "First Army Catholic Chaplains," The Chaplain Kit, https:// thechaplainkit.com/history/army-chaplaincy/first-army-catholic-chaplains/ (accessed on April 22, 2020).

20. See Thomas J. Craughwell, *Heroic Catholic Chaplains* (Charlotte, NC: Tan Books, 2018), 19–36 for short biographies of both Frs. Rey and McElroy.

21. Miller, *Shamrock and Sword*, 158.

22. Ibid., 159.

23. Ibid., 86–89.

24. Ibid., 89.

25. Ibid., 101.

26. Craughwell, *Heroic Catholic Chaplains*, 36.

27. Miller, *Shamrock and Sword*, 102–3.

28. Ibid., 107–8.

29. There are historiographic problems, especially in older accounts of the Mexican-American War. Some accounts written near to 1848 lionize the American officers and never even mention the San Patricio problem at all. One of these is J. Frost, L. L. D. *The Mexican War and Its Warriors: Comprising a Complete History of All the Operations of the American Armies in Mexico* (New Haven, CT: H. Mansfield, 1850; Reprint Bowie, MD: Heritage Books, 1989). There are many others like this one.

30. Hedrick, "On Foreign Soil," 85.

Chapter Three. Civil War

1. Charles Edward Smith, "The Work of the Civil War Chaplains" (master's thesis, University of Arizona, 1965), 28–29. See also Benjamin L. Miller, *In God's Presence: Chaplains, Missionaries, and Religious Space during the Civil War* (Lawrence: University Press of Kansas, 2019), for an updated historiographic approach to this issue.

2. U.S. Army, *United States Army Chaplain Corps*, pamphlet 165-1 (Washington, DC: Headquarters, U.S. Army, 1974), 8.

3. See William Corby, CSC, *Memoirs of Chaplain Life: Three Years with the Irish Brigade in the Army of the Potomac*, ed. Lawrence F. Kohl (New York: Fordham University Press, 1992).

4. See Chaplain Charles Cardwell McCabe, "Memoirs, 1863–1865," in *The Spirit Divided: Memoirs of Civil War Chaplains*, ed. Benedict R. Maryniak and John Wesley Brinsfield Jr. (Atlanta: Mercer University Press, 2007), 185–203.

5. Warren B. Armstrong, *For Courageous Fighting and Confident Dying: Union Chaplains in the Civil War* (Lawrence: University Press of Kansas, 1998), 30.

6. Maryniak and Brinsfield, *Spirit Divided*, 186.

7. Armstrong, *For Courageous Fighting and Confident Dying*, 35, 104.

8. U.S. Army, *U.S. Army Chaplain Corps*, 9, 10.

9. William F. R. Gilroy and Timothy J. Demy, *A Brief Chronology of the Chaplain Corps of the United States Navy* (Washington, DC: Department off the Navy, 1983), 20–21.

10. Gardner H. Shattuck Jr. "Faith, Morale, and the Army Chaplain in the American Civil War," in *The Sword of the Lord: Military Chaplains from the First to the Twenty-First Century*, ed. Doris Bergen (Notre Dame, IN: University of Notre Dame Press, 2004), 109.

11. William B. Kurtz, *Excommunicated from the Union: How the Civil War Created a Separate Catholic America* (New York: Fordham University Press, 2016), 69.

12. Benjamin J. Blied, *Catholics and the Civil War* (Milwaukee, 1945), 111, in Smith, "Work of the Civil War Chaplains," 32 ff 9.

13. Blied, 70.

14. See Kurtz, *Excommunicated from the Union*, 76, for an excellent and thorough description of most of the acts of general absolution performed by Union chaplains. This was not done in the Confederate army by Catholic Confederate chaplains.

15. See Kurtz, 80–87, for a description and discussion of the various orders of nuns who served on the Civil War battlefields.

16. Shattuck, "Faith, Morale and the Army Chaplain," in *Sword of the Lord*, ed. Bergen, 109–10.

17. Herman Norton, *Rebel Religion: The Story of Confederate Chaplains* (St. Louis: Bethany Press, 1961), 34–35.

18. See Drew Gilpin Faust, "Christian Solders: The Meaning of Revivalism in the Confederate Army," *Journal of Southern History* 53 (1987): 63–73. See also Robby Wray Burke Jr., "Confederate Chaplains, The Great Revival, and the Prolongation of the Civil War" (master's thesis, James Madison University, 1991).

19. William W. Bennett, *A Narrative of the Great Revival Which Prevailed in the Southern Armies* (Philadelphia: Claxton, Remsen, and Haffelfinger, 1877), 16, 75, 426–27, in Bergen, *Sword of the Lord,* 111.

20. General Order 100, 1863, Article 53, Avalon Project, https://avalon.law.yale.edu/19th_century/lieber.asp#sec3.

21. Fred C. Ainsworth and Joseph W. Kirkley, eds., *The War of the Rebellion: A Compilation of the Official Records of the Union and Confederate Armies,* ser. 2, vol. 6 (Washington, DC: U.S. Government Printing Office, 1899), 249, (cited as OR subsequently) in Charles F. Pitts, *Chaplains in Gray: The Confederate Chaplain's Story* (Nashville: Broadman, 1957), 72.

22. Mark E. Gunn, "The Magnolia Cross: The Role of Mississippi Chaplains during the Civil War" (master's thesis, University of Southern Mississippi, 1991), 81.

23. Smith, "Work of the Civil War Chaplains," 69–70.

24. Bell Irvin Wiley, "'Holy Joe's of the Sixties: A Study of Civil War Chaplains," *Huntington Library Quarterly* 16, no. 3 (1953): 289.

25. Wiley, 290, 297, 298.

26. Armstrong, *For Courageous Fighting and Confident Dying,* 124.

27. Philip Thomas Tucker, *The Confederacy's Fighting Chaplain Father John B. Bannon* (Tuscaloosa: University of Alabama Press, 1992), 176–79.

28. Norton, *Rebel Religion,* 29–30. See also William B. Faherty, S.J., *Exile in Erin: A Confederate Chaplain's Story, the Life of Father John B. Bannon* (St. Louis: Missouri Historical Society Press, 2002), for a detailed study of Fr. Bannon's adventures.

29. Norton, *Rebel Religion,* 31.

30. Norton, 34.

31. Norton, 84. See also Mr. Tom Elmore's entry on the Civil War message board, December 12, 2010, for a list of captured Confederate chaplains after Gettysburg July 3, 1863, http:history-sites.net/cgi-bin/bbs62s/cwpmb/e\webbbs_config.p.

32. Norton, *Rebel Religion,* 85.

33. See Henry T. Thill, "Study of an American Civil War Chaplaincy: Henry Clay Trumbull, 10th Connecticut Volunteers" (master's thesis, Virginia Polytechnic Institute, 1986), 31.

34. Thill, 37. Note that the book of Jeremiah (Chronicles) tells the story of the Babylonian captivity of the Hebrews, and in the subsequent book of Lamentations, the prophet Jeremiah complains to God, blaming him and lamenting for everything that happened to them in captivity. The Israelites returned to Jerusalem in 536 BC and rebuilt the temple and walls (45).

35. Thill, 44, 46.

36. Thill, 55.

37. Edward D. Jervey, ed., *Prison Life among the Rebels: Recollections of a Union Chaplain* (Kent, OH: Kent State University Press, 1990), 24 (emphasis in the original), 52.

38. See Smith, "Work of the Civil War Chaplains," 137–38.
39. See Fort McHenry Prisoner of War Camp, https://www.mycivilwar.com/pow /md-fort-mchenry.html, (accessed May 12, 2020).
40. Rev. Joseph T. Durkin, S.J., ed., *Confederate Chaplain: A War Journal of Rev. James B. Sheeran, C.SS.R., 14th Louisiana, CSA* (Milwaukee: Bruce, 1960), 105, 113.
41. Durkin, 125.
42. Durkin, 128.
43. Dom Aiden Henry Germain, "Catholic Military and Naval Chaplains, 1776–1917" (PhD diss., Catholic University of America, 1929), 133.
44. See U.S. National Park Service, https://www.nps.gov/ande/learn/historyculture /father_whelan.htm (accessed May 12, 2020). See also Donald R. McClarey, "Priest of Andersonville," April 21, 2009, http://www.the-american-catholic.com; Peter J. Meany "The Prison Ministry of Father Peter Whelan, Georgia Priest and Confederate Chaplain," *Georgia Historical Quarterly* 71, no. 1 (1987): 1–24, and "The Valiant Chaplain of the Bloody Tenth," *Tennessee Historical Quarterly* 41, no. 1 (1982): 37–47.
45. Jervey, *Prison Life among the Rebels*, 52.

Chapter Four. 1898 to World War I

1. *United States Statutes at Large* 2 (1789–1848): 359–72, 9th Cong., 1st sess., chap. 20.
2. The Buffalo Soldier Monument at Fort Leavenworth, Kansas, was designed by Eddie Dixon and dedicated in 1991. It celebrates General Colin Powell's desire to memorialize those black soldiers who served so admirably on the American frontier in the nineteenth century.
3. John Langellier, "Soldiers of the Cross: The First Buffalo Soldier Chaplain Lights the Path for Others, Despite a Dishonorable Discharge," *True West Magazine*, July 2015, https://truewestmagazine.com/soldiers-of-the-cross/.
4. Thomas J. Craughwell, *Heroic Catholic Chaplains: Stories of the Brave and Holy Men Who Dodged Bullets While Saving Souls* (Charlotte, NC: Tan Books, 2018), 88, 87. Fr. Chidwick was the only chaplain the USS *Maine* ever had.
5. U.S. Army, *U.S. Army Chaplain Corps*, pamphlet 165-1 (Washington, DC: Headquarters, U.S. Army, 1974), 11.
6. Article 18: Convention (II) with Respect to the Laws and Customs of War on Land and Its Annex: *Regulations Concerning the Laws and Customs of War on Land* (The Hague, July 29, 1899).
7. U.S. Army, *U.S. Army Chaplain Corps*, 13.
8. See Maj. Philip A. Kramer, USA, "The Proximity Principle: Army Chaplains on the Fighting Line in Doctrine and History" (master's thesis, U.S. Command and General Staff School, 2014).

9. Craughwell, *Heroic Catholic Chaplains*, 97.

10. Fr. Duffy's statue sits at Duffy Square on the northern half of New York City's Times Square between Forty-Fifth and Forty-Seventh Streets and is named in his honor.

11. U.S. Army, *U.S. Army Chaplain Corps*, 15.

12. Army Pamphlet 27-1, *Treaties Governing Land Warfare* (Washington, DC: Department of the Army, 1956), 11.

13. Field Manual 27-10, *The Law of Land Warfare* (Washington, DC: Department of the Army, 1956), 28.

14. U.S. Army, *U.S. Army Chaplain Corps*, 15, 17.

Chapter Five. 1942 to 1945: *Via Dolorosa* in the Pacific

1. William F. R. Gilroy and Timothy J. Demy, *A Brief Chronology of the Chaplain Corps of the United States Navy* (Washington, DC: Department of the Navy, 1983), 31.

2. U.S.Army, *The U.S. Army Chaplain Corps*, pamphlet 165-1 (Washington, DC: Headquarters, U.S. Army, 1974), 17.

3. Steven E. O'Brien, "Blackrobe in Blue: The Naval Chaplaincy of John P. Foley, S.J., 1942–1946" (PhD diss., Boston College, 1999), 90. See also Ariane Boltanski, "A Jesuit *Missio Castrensis* in France at the End of the Sixteenth Century: Discipline and Violence at War," *Journal of Jesuit Studies* 4, no. 4 (2017): 581–98. During the Counter-Reformation period of the 1590s, the Jesuits introduced the concept of the *missio castrensis*, in which the Christian soldier's mandate was to reduce the level of violence on the battlefield. The mission failed, and the bloodshed increased rather than decreased.

4. See Leslie F. Zimmerman, John E. Groh, and Carolyn McCormick, eds., *Chaplain Prisoners of War in the Pacific, 1941–1945* (Montgomery, AL: USAF Chaplain Service Institute, Maxwell AFB, 1993), 5–6.

5. Zimmerman, Groh, and McCormick, 5.

6. History.com Editors, "Troops Surrender in Bataan, Philippines, in Largest-Ever U.S. Surrender," November 5, 2009, https://www.history.com/this-day-in-history/u-s-surrenders-in-bataan.

7. History.com Editors, "Troops Surrender in Bataan." Accessed July 23, 2020.

8. Gerard F. Giblin, S.J., *Jesuits as Chaplains in the Armed Forces, 1917–1960* (Woodstock, MD: Woodstock College Press, 1962), 56.

9. Zimmerman, Groh, and McCormick, *Chaplain Prisoners of War*, 5.

10. John K. Borneman, "From Bataan through Cabanatuan," *Army and Navy Chaplain* 16, no. 4 (1946): 23, 27.

11. See Fr. John J. Dugan, S.J., Major, USA, *Life under the Japs: Stories from a Prisoner of War Camp* (Boston: Globe, 1945), 53–58. See also Richard S. Roper, *Brothers of Paul: Activities of Prisoner of War Chaplains in the Philippines during WWII* (Odenton, MD: Revere, 2003), 181, for Fr. O'Keefe's story.

12. Christopher Cross, *Soldiers of God* (New York: E. P. Dutton, 1945), 64.

13. Borneman, "From Bataan through Cabanatuan," 24.

14. Samuel C. Grashio and Bernard Norling, *Return to Freedom: The War Memoirs of Col. Samuel C. Grashio USAF (Ret.)* (Tulsa, OK: MCN Press, 1982), 75.

15. Thomas J. Craughwell, *Heroic Catholic Chaplains: Stories of the Brave and Holy Men Who Dodged Bullets While Saving Souls* (Charlotte, NC: Tan Books), 123–24.

16. Abie Abraham, *Oh God, Where Are You?*, 3rd ed. (Chicora, PA: privately published, 2008), 340–41.

17. Roper, *Brothers of Paul*, 115–16.

18. John E. Duffy to Very Reverend James P. Sweeney, October 15, 1945, in Roper, *Brothers of Paul*, 115.

19. Dan Murr, *But Deliver Us from Evil: Father Duffy and the Men of Bataan* (Jacksonville Beach, FL: self-published, 2008), 152.

20. Roper, *Brothers of Paul*, 222–23.

21. Robert LaForte et al., *With Only the Will to Live* (Wilmington, DE: Scholarly Resources, 1994), 6, in Roper, *Brothers of Paul*, 225.

22. Fr. Talbot was a hospital chaplain but was moved to Cabanatuan POW Camp in 1942, working there with the sick until he was rescued by the 6th Ranger Battalion in January 1945.

23. Billy Keith, *Days of Anguish, Days of Hope* (Garden City, NY: Doubleday, 1972), 115–17.

24. Donald Knox, *Death March: The Survivors of Bataan* (New York: Harcourt, 1981), 217–18.

25. Roper, *Brothers of Paul*, 230–31. See also Calvin E. Chunn, ed., *Of Rice and Men: The Story of Americans under the Rising Sun* (Los Angeles: Veterans, 1946). Written very close to the events, this author still shows a great deal of bitterness.

26. See Gregory F. Michno, *Death on the Hellships: Prisoners at Sea in the Pacific War* (Annapolis, MD: Naval Institute Press, 2001). This book is without a doubt one of the most difficult to read of all the histories of life and death in World War II. See also Lee A. Gladwin, "American POWs on Japanese Ships Take a Voyage into Hell," pts. 1–2, *Prologue* 35, no. 4 (2003); and Preston John Hubbard, *Apocalypse Undone: My Survival of Japanese Imprisonment during World War II* (Nashville: Vanderbilt University Press, 1990).

27. Roper, *Brothers of Paul*, 233–35.

28. Roper, 89–90.

29. Sidney Stewart, *Give Us This Day* (New York: W. W. Norton, 1986), 228. See Roper, *Brothers of Paul*, 93–94. See also Craughwell, *Heroic Catholic Chaplains*, 28–29; and Donald F. Crosby, *Battlefield Chaplains: Catholic Priests in World War II* (Lawrence: University Press of Kansas, 1994), 25–27.

30. Craughwell, *Heroic Catholic Chaplains*, 129; Crosby, *Battlefield Chaplains*, 29.

31. Roper, *Brothers of Paul*, 286.

32. Rev. Joseph Springbot, "The Sallesianum, a Classmate Remembered," *Steubenville (OH) Register*, January 99, 1946, in Roper, *Brothers of Paul*, 287.

33. Roper, 286.

34. Roper, 77–78.

35. For an analysis of the escape ethos and the story of the 1943 Davao escape, see Robert C. Doyle, *A Prisoner's Duty: Great Escapes in U.S. Military History* (Annapolis, MD: Naval Institute Press, 1997), 160, 163–65, and *Voices from Captivity: Interpreting the American POW Narrative* (Lawrence: University Press of Kansas, 1994), 222.

36. Grashio and Norling, *Return to Freedom*, 108, in Roper, *Brothers of Paul*, 81.

37. Roper, 131.

38. See James B. Reuter, S.J., "He Kept Silence in Seven Languages: A Short Sketch of Carl W. J. Hausmann, S.J., Who Died as a Prisoner of War, January 10, 1945," *Woodstock Letters* 74, no. 3 (1945): 443.

39. Grashio and Norling, *Return to Freedom*, 134–35.

40. Grashio and Norling, 188, 187.

41. Grashio and Norling, 251.

42. Grashio and Norling, 255. See also Tiffany File, NARA Record Group 247; Alfred A Weinstein, M.D., *Barbed-Wire Surgeon* (New York: Macmillan, 1948), 149; and Zimmerman, Groh, and McCormick, *Chaplain Prisoners in the Pacific*.

43. Weinstein, *Barbed-Wire Surgeon*, 166.

44. Chaplain James E. Davis, USN, "Religion in a Prisoner of War Camp in Japan," *Army and Navy Chaplain* 16, no. 4 (1946): 6.

45. Davis, 7.

46. J. E. Nardini, CDR, M.C., USN, "Survival Factors in American Prisoners of War of the Japanese," *American Journal of Psychiatry* 109, no. 4 (1952): 241–48.

47. Abraham, *Oh God, Where Are You?*, 460.

48. Peter Eisner, *MacArthur's Spies: The Soldier, the Singer, and the Spymaster Who Defied the Japanese in World War II*, 299.

49. Lyle W. Eads, *Survival Around the Ashes* (Winona, MN: privately published, 1985), 108.

Chapter Six. 1942 to 1945: Resistance in the Philippines

1. There is an extensive bibliography of the Philippine-American War, also known as the Bamboo War to its veterans. For a short history, see Robert C. Doyle, *Prisoners*

in American Hands: Treatment of Enemy Prisoners of War from the Revolution to the War on Terror (Lexington: University Press of Kentucky, 2010).

2. Richard S. Roper, *Holy Smugglers* (Annapolis, MD: n.p., n.d.). See also Cloister Chronicle-Dominicana Journal, https://www.dominicanajournal.org/files/vol30.

3. Roper, *Holy Smugglers*, 9.

4. Roper, 49. See also https://www.tracesofwar.com/persons/81946/Lalor-Fr-John.htm.

5. Roper, 59–60.

6. Hampton Sides, *Ghost Soldiers: The Forgotten Epic Story of Harold War II's Most Dramatic Mission* (New York: Doubleday, 2001), 147–48. Theodore Heinz Buttenbruch was a Catholic priest and member of the Society of the Divine Word. Because he was a German national, the Japanese permitted him to remain in the occupied Philippines. When they discovered his activities on behalf of the Americans and Filipino guerrillas, they executed him by beheading.

7. Leslie F. Zimmerman, John E. Groh, and Carolyn McCormack, eds., *Chaplain Prisoners of War in the Pacific, 1941–1945* (Montgomery, AL: USAF Chaplain Service Institute, Maxwell AFB, 1993), 81–82. Chaplain Tiffany experienced some difficulties and bitterness after he returned from the *Kempeitai*, so he left on the next transport to Japan, the *Arisan Maru*. The unmarked ship was torpedoed on October 24, 1944, and he was lost.

8. Zimmermann, Groh, and McCormack, *Chaplain Prisoners of War*, 67, 92.

9. Zimmermann, Groh, and McCormack, 399.

10. The stories of Claire Phillips, aka High Pockets, and Margaret Utinsky are legendary. See Margaret Utinsky, *Miss U: Angel of the Underground* (San Antonio: Naylor, 1948); Edna Bautista Binkowski, *Code Name High Pockets* (Limay, PI: Valour, 2006); and Claire Phillips and Myron B. Goldsmith, *Manila Espionage* (1947; reprint, Philippines: Bowsprit Books, 2018).

11. Peter Eisner, *MacArthur's Spies: The Soldier, the Singer, and the Spymaster Who Defied the Japanese in World War II* (New York: Viking, 2017), 131–34.

12. See Niall O'Brien, *Columban Martyrs of Manila* (Manila: Kadena Press, 1995).

13. Water treatment consists of inserting a piece of hose put into a victim's mouth, then asking a question. When the victim refuses to tell the truth or to answer at all, one turns the water on to fill up the victim's stomach, forcing the victim to vomit it out. This can be done several times before death comes from drowning. Resisting is difficult in the extreme.

14. See Eisner, *MacArthur's Spies*, xi–xv.

15. Eisner, xiv–xv.

16. See L. Gardner, ed., *Santo Tomas Internment Camp Anniversary Booklet, 1943–1965* (self-published, 1965), 44.

17. Roper, *Holy Smugglers*, 68.
18. Roper, 44.
19. Roper, 45.
20. Eisner, *MacArthur's Spies*, 99. See also Peter Eisner, "Our Man in Manila," *Smithsonian*, September 2017, 42, 44–55.
21. Eisner, *MacArthur's Spies*, 103.
22. Eisner, 159, 163, 192.
23. Eisner, 235.
24. This work addresses military chaplains not civilian clergy who were held as internees by the Japanese in the Philippines during World War II.
25. Eisner, *MacArthur's Spies*, 251.
26. Eisner, 270.

Chapter Seven. 1942 to 1945: Captured Chaplains in World War II Europe

1. 47 Stat., pt. 2, 2021, in Robert R. Wilson, "Status of Chaplains with Armed Forces," *Journal of International Law* (July 1943): 493.
2. Paul McNamara, "Father Gehring" *Catholic Digest* (1945): 47–48.
3. See Lawrence P. Grayson, "Fr. Joseph O'Callahan: The Bravest Man," *TFP*, August 17, 2011. See also https://www.newenglandhistoricalsociety.com/joseph-t-ocallahan -a-claustrophobic-priest-wins-the-medal-of-honor/. "The ship's captain, Les Gehres, went over to his mother and said, 'I'm not a religious man. But I watched your son that day and I thought if faith can do this for man, there must be something to it. Your son is the bravest man I have ever seen.' President Truman awarded Lt. Cmdr. Joseph T. O'Callahan the Medal of Honor on Jan. 23, 1946 at the White House. He returned to Holy Cross in 1948 as head of the mathematics department. Father Joseph T. O'Callahan died March 18, 1964."
4. See http://fourchaplains.org/four-chaplains/ (accessed August 19, 2020) for a complete history of this sad event. See also Sharon Ottoman, "Remembering the Four Chaplains and Their Ultimate Sacrifice," *New York Times*, February 4, 2018, https:nytimes.com/2018/02/04/nyregion/four-chaplains-sacrifice.html.
5. John Way, O.P., "The Soldier-Priest," *Dominicana* 28, no. 2 (1943): 89–93.
6. Robert L. Gushwa, *The Best and Worst of Times: The United States Army Chaplaincy, 1920–1945* (Washington, DC: Department of the Army, Office of the Chief of Chaplains, 1977), 154.
7. Eugene L. Daniel Jr., *In the Presence of Mine Enemies: An American Chaplain in World War II German Prison Camps* (Attleboro, MA: Colonial Lithograph, 1985), 71.
8. Greg Hatton, comp., "American Prisoners of War in Germany," prepared by Military Intelligence Service War Department, July 15, 1944, https://www.b24 .net/powStalag7.htm.

9. Daniel, *In the Presence of Mine Enemies*, 81. The late former Stalag Luft III POW Wayne Beigel told the author all about Father Wilf Coates. A British Roman Catholic chaplain, Fr. Wilf attended American reunions when he could and made lifelong friends with his American POW parishioners.

10. Daniel, 98, 99.

11. Citation in the Military Record of Captain Rev. Wilfrid Coates, Chaplain Corps, British Army, British National Archives, WO 373/148, A-2146, p. 754.

12. *Catholic Courier*, May 3, May 10, 1945; *Catholic Standard and Times*, March 9, 1945, in *Battlefield Chaplains: Catholic Priests in World War II*, by Donald F. Crosby, S.J. (Lawrence: University Press of Kansas, 1994), 85–86.

13. Crosby, *Battlefield Chaplains*, 88.

14. See Arnold Krammer, *Nazi Prisoners of War in America* (1977; reprint, Lanham, MD: Scarborough House, 1996). Dr. Krammer passed away in 2018 but was perhaps the greatest POW scholar of the postwar period.

15. Krammer, 258–59.

16. Krammer, 267. See also Robert C. Doyle, *Prisoners in American Hands: Treatment of Enemy Prisoners of War from the Revolution to the War on Terror* (Lexington: University Press of Kentucky, 2010), for a comprehensive study of enemy POWs in American captivity from the Revolution to the war on terror.

17. Luciano also ordered that the longshoremen of New York, completely controlled by the New York Mafia at that time, not to strike during World War II. See https://www.sunsigns.org/famousbirthdays/d/profile/lucky-luciano/ (accessed August 17, 2020).

18. See Crosby, *Battlefield Chaplains*, 97.

19. Alan Robinson, *Chaplains at War: The Role of Clergymen during World War II* (London: Tauris Academic Studies, 2008), 182. Robinson shows that the bibliography of chaplain issues is at least as extensive in the United Kingdom as it is in the United States, if not more so.

20. Robinson, 197.

21. See Crosby, *Battlefield Chaplains*, 98–121. The chapter "Italy" tells the story of the Italian campaign from a chaplain's point of view and is an outstanding read.

22. Lyle W. Dorsett, *Serving God and Country: U.S. Military Chaplains in World War II* (New York: Berkley Caliber, 2012), 178.

23. Chaplain Mark Moore, excerpt from *Prisoner of the Germans* at www.Indiana Military.orgus. Permission granted for use by Mark R. Moore ©2001. Transcribed by Jon Bosch.

24. Dorsett, *Serving God and Country*, 179. Any "baby boomer" who ever attended Catholic school knows that corporal punishment was well within the scope of Catholic clergy's purview, especially if they were rightly provoked.

25. Crosby, *Battlefield Chaplains*, 149.

26. See also Paul W. Cavanaugh, "Chaplain Prisoner," *Woodstock Letters* 90, no. 1 (1961): 20–49.

27. Paul W. Cavanaugh, S.J., *Pro Deo et Patria: The Personal Narrative an American Catholic Chaplain as a Prisoner of War in Germany*, ed. Robert. E. Skopek (self-published, 2004), 57.

28. Dorsett, *Serving God and Country*, 181.

29. See Dorsett, 182. The author visited this camp in 1994 and found a very old man who witnessed the raid. Today, Hammelburg serves as the Bundeswehr's Infantry School. In 1945 Allied forces were liberating POW and concentration camps throughout Germany and Poland regularly, resulting in an escalating hatred of the enemy. *Oflag* refers to an Officers Camp, whereas *Stalag* is short for *Stammlager*, a POW camp for enlisted personnel.

30. Thomas J. Craughwell, *Heroic Catholic Chaplains: Stories of the Brave and Holy Men Who Dodged Bullets While Saving Souls* (Charlotte, NC: Tan Books, 2018), 114.

31. Chaplain Francis L. Sampson, *Paratrooper Padre* (Washington, DC: Catholic University of America Press, 1948), 45, 47.

32. Craughwell, *Heroic Catholic Chaplains*, 115–16.

33. Many chaplains were killed and wounded during the Normandy landing and subsequent battles in the hedgerows. See Crosby, *Battlefield Chaplains*, 122–45. Fr. Sampson's description of his dealings with wounded German and American soldiers is tough reading. See Sampson, *Paratrooper Padre*, 51–54.

34. Sampson, *Paratrooper Padre*, 77.

35. Crosby, *Battlefield Chaplains*, 167.

36. Crosby, *Battlefield Chaplains*, 167.

37. U.S. Army Command and Staff College, *Chaplain's Duties to Prisoners of War*, "Annex E: Chaplain Sampson's Experience in a World War II POW Camp" (Fort Leavenworth, KS, January 27, 1969), n.p.

38. Crosby, *Battlefield Chaplains*, 173.

39. *Stunde Null* means "Zero Hour," a term the Germans use to designate the end of the Nazi regime. See Crosby, *Battlefield Chaplains*, 174.

Chapter Eight. 1943 to 1946

1. Gerard F. Giblin, S.J., *Jesuits as Chaplains in the Armed Forces, 1917–1960* (Woodstock, MD: Woodstock College Press, 1961), 7.

2. Giblin, 100.

3. Jim Graves, "Father Henry Marusa—World War II Army Chaplain at Invasion of Normandy," National Catholic Register, https://www.ncregister.com/blog/father-henry-marusa-world-war-ii-army-chaplain (accessed September 14, 2020).

4. Chaplains of the 36th Infantry Division, Chaplain (Co.) Herbert E. MacCombie, Division Chaplain, "Interrogating Captured German Chaplains," Texas Military Forces Museum, http://www.texasmilitaryforcesmuseum.org/36division/archives (accessed September 2, 2020).

5. Lyle Dorsett, *Serving God and Country: U.S. Military Chaplains in World War II* (New York: Berkeley Caliber, 2012), 183–84.

6. Paul Link, C.PP.S., *For God and Country*, pt. 2 (Cartegena, OH: Messenger Press, 1993), 241–42. The missionaries came to America in 1844. They had been invited to serve in the United States by Archbishop John Baptist Purcell of the Archdiocese of Cincinnati, who needed priests and brothers to minister to the German-speaking Catholic settlers in central and western Ohio. See "History: Small Beginnings, Big Dreams," https://cpps-preciousblood.org/about/history/.

7. *Woodstock Letters* 74, no. 1 (1945): 7.

8. Alfred Rosenberg, *The Myth of the Twentieth Century* (Munich: Hohenreichen Verlag, 1935), 614, in Doris Bergen, "German Military Chaplains in the Second World War and the Dilemmas of Legitimacy," in *The Sword of the Lord* (Notre Dame, IN: Notre Dame University Press, 2004), 165.

9. Bergen, "German Military Chaplains," 173.

10. Link, *For God and Country*, 49–50.

11. Link, 60–61.

12. Stephen A. Leven, "A Catholic Chaplain Visits Our German Prisoners," *America*, June 24, 1944, 321.

13. Leven, 321. It should be noted that although Leven was not aware of it, the term *Gott-Gläubig* was indicative of what the Waffen SS were taught in school. "Rosenberg" was a true horror, whose book *The Myth of the Twentieth Century* (1935) formed the base of Nazi or mythic belief in an Aryan, non-Christian god. Alfred Rosenberg was tried and executed as an A-Class war criminal after the Nuremberg Trials.

14. "Prisoners of War," in *The Priest Goes to War* (New York: Society for the Propagation of the Faith, 1945), n.p.

15. Mark Hayden, *German Military Chaplains in World War II* (Atglen, PA: Schiffer Military History, 2005), 110–15.

16. Hayden, 31.

17. "The Priests in Dachau," in *The Priest Barracks, Dachau, 1938–1945*, by Guillaume Zeller (San Francisco: Ignatius Press, 2015), 258, 55.

18. Eloi Leclerc in Zeller, *The Priest Barracks*, 55.

19. See *Liberating Dachau*, dir. Mark Felton, www.youtube.com/watch?v=aRksFbsMxw (accessed September 1, 2020).

20. Zeller, *Priest Barracks*, 37.

21. Zeller, 37–38, 40.

22. Fr. Stefan Biskupski quoted in Zeller, *Priest Barracks*, 28.

23. Pauly Fongemie, ed., *Priests: The Persecution of the Catholic Church and the Priests of Dachau*, http://www.catholictradition.org/Priests/daucau.htm (accessed August 31, 2020), 5.

24. Dr. Johannes Neuhaeusler, *What Was It Like in the Concentration Camp at Dachau?*, 17th ed. (Munich: Manz A.G., 1960), 66. The Allies decided to continue using the Dachau camp as a holding facility and trial location after the war for Nazi military war criminals.

25. Bedrich Hoffmann, *And Who Will Kill You: The Chronicle of the Life and Sufferings of Priests in the Concentration Camps*, 2nd ed. (Posnan, Poland: Pallottinum, 1994), 262, in Zeller, *Priest Barracks*, 204ff.

26. John M. Lenz, *Christ in Dachau; or, Christ Victorious* (Vienna: Mission Druckerei St. Gabriel, 1960), 269.

27. Fongemie, *Priests*, 5. There is a growing bibliography of historical work being published now in the twenty-first century about what these people endured.

28. Archbishop Kazimierz Majdanski, *You Shall Be My Witness: Lessons beyond Dachau* (Garden City Park, NY: Square One, 2009), 7.

29. Alexandre Morelli in Zeller, *Priest Barracks*, 210.

30. Link, *For God and Country*, 290, 291.

31. Lenz, *Christ in Dachau*, 275.

32. Fr. Michel Riquet, S.J., to General D.D. Eisenhower, SHAEF, n.d., in Zeller, *Priest Barracks*, 212.

33. Volker Schoendorff, *The Ninth Day/Der neunte Tag* (2004), with Ulrich Matthes.

34. Lenz, *Christ in Dachau*, 285, 286.

Chapter Nine. 1950 to 1953

1. U.S. Army, *United States Army Chaplain Corps*, pamphlet 165-1 (Washington, DC: Headquarters, U.S. Army, 1974), 19.

2. Mark W. Johnson, U.S. Army Chaplain Corps, "Under Fire: Army Chaplains in Korea, 1950," https://www.army.mil/article/100572/Under_Fire_Army_Chaplains_in_Korea_1950/, April 10, 2013.

3. The European Recovery Program was always known as the Marshall Plan in the press, named after Gen. George Marshall (Ret.) who devised it as President Harry Truman's secretary of state. Its real name was the European Recovery Program.

4. Johnson, "Under Fire," n.p.

5. Johnson, n.p.

6. Johnson, n.p.

7. Johnson, n.p.

8. Rev. Philip Crosbie, *Pencilling Prisoner* (Melbourne: Hawthorne, 1955), iii.

9. Crosbie, 26.

10. The American Korean War POW Association has a special group known as the Tiger Survivors Group. At the 1999 reunion that the author attended, they commemorated those Americans murdered by the Tiger on their Long March north in 1950, the same march that the clergy were forced to be on as well.

11. Crosbie, 30. The communists initiated the same procedure against the UN POWs with very few positive results. The communist Vietnamese did the same thing in Hanoi as well.

12. Crosbie, 60.

13. Crosbie, 77, 97.

14. Crosbie, 101, 123, 124.

15. Philip Deane [pseud.], *I Was a Captive in Korea* (New York: W. W. Norton, 1963), 113.

16. Crosbie, *Penciling Prisoners*, 126–27. See also Larry Zellers, *In Enemy Hands: A Prisoner in North Korea* (Lexington: University Press of Kentucky, 1991), 90–91, for a more detailed description of the Tiger's execution of Lieutenant Thornton.

17. U.S. Army, *United States Army Chaplain Corps*, 21.

18. William L. Maher, *A Shepherd in Combat Boots: Chaplain Emil Kapaun of the 1st Cavalry Division* (Shippensburg, PA: Burd Street, 1997), 54–55. See also "Father Emil Kapaun's Acts of Self-Sacrifice," https:billofrightsinstitute.org.father-emil-kapauns-acts-self-sacrifice/ (accessed September 9, 2020).

19. Maher, *Shepherd*, 57.

20. Maher, 64, 73.

21. Maher, 87.

22. Maher, 92. See also Dominic Perotta and Kevin Perotta, "When the Ordinary Becomes Extraordinary: The Life and Death of Army Chaplain Emil Kapaun," *Word among Us* (July–August 2012): 83–88. See also Roy Wenzel and Travis Heying, *The Miracle of Father Kapaun: Priest, Soldier, and Korean War Hero* (Fort Collins, CO: Ignatius Press, 2009).

23. Maher, *Shepherd*, 107.

24. Maher, 118.

25. Thomas J. Craughwell, *Heroic Catholic Chaplains: Stories of the Brave and Holy Men Who Dodged Bullets While Saving Souls* (Charlotte, NC: Tan Books, 2018), 149.

26. Maher, *Shepherd*, 120–21.

27. Harry Spiller, ed., *American POWs in Korea: Sixteen Personal Accounts* (Jefferson, NC: McFarland, 1998), 50.

28. The author encountered Lloyd Pate at the 1999 Korean War POW Association's Reunion. He was forceful in his response concerning Fr. Kapaun, "a wonderful man." No one could ask more of anyone recalling a chaplain not of his faith. Lloyd Pate died in 2013.

29. Lloyd W. Pate, *Reactionary: Revised 2000* (New York: Vantage, 2001), 74–75.

30. Pate, 135.

31. Pate, 139.

32. Robert Jones in Lewis H. Carlson, *Remembered Prisoners of a Forgotten War* (New York: St. Martin's, 2002), 158.

33. Emil J. Kapaun, Medal of Honor Citation, https://www.cmohs.org/recipients /emil-j-kapaun, presented on April 11, 2013, at the White House by President Barack Obama to his nephew. See also U.S. Army, "Bibliography for Chaplain (Capt.) Emil Kapaun," https://www.army.mil/article/98061 /biography_for_chaplain_emil_kapaun.

34. "*The Crux: Taking the Catholic Pulse*," https://cruxnow.com/church-in-the -usa/2020/02/case-for-military-chaplains-sainthood-could-soon-advance/ (accessed September 9, 2020). See also "Medal of Honor Recipient's Remains Identified," *VFW Magazine*, June–July 2021, 6.

35. U.S. Army, *United States Army Chaplain Corps*, 22.

Chapter Ten. 1959 to 1973

1. Commander Herbert L. Bergsma, CHC, USN, *Chaplains with the Marines in Vietnam 1962–1971* (Washington, DC: Headquarters, U.S. Marine Corps, 1985), 145–47.

2. Thomas J. Craughwell, *Heroic Catholic Chaplains: Stories of the Brave and Holy Men Who Dodged Bullets While Saving Souls* (Charlotte, NC: Tan Books, 2018), 170–71.

3. U.S. Army, *United States Army Chaplain Corps*, pamphlet 165-1 (Washington, DC: Headquarters, U.S. Army, 1974), 24.

4. U.S. Army, 24.

5. Maj. James Harvey III, "Catholic Military Chaplains: American's Forgotten Heroes," American Society for the Defense of Tradition, Family, and Property, http://www.tfp.org/catholic-army-chaplains-americas-forgotten-heroes/ (accessed May 16, 2017).

6. Bergsma, *Chaplains with the Marines in Vietnam*, 150–52.

7. Bergsma, 150–52. See also Daniel L. Mode, *The Grunt Padre: Father Vincent Capodanno, Vietnam, 1966–1967* (Oak Lawn, IL: CMJ Marian, 2000); Archdiocese for Military Services, "Father Capodanno Biography," http://www.milarch.org/father -capadanno-bio/.

8. Harvey, "Catholic Military Chaplains," 9.

9. Charlie Plumb and Glen DeWerff, *I'm No Hero* (Mechanicsburg, PA: Executive Books, 1973), 228.

10. The bibliography of Vietnam POWs is enormous. Explaining every detail of captivity in Hanoi and South Vietnam would take hundreds of pages of text. We

must confine remarks only to religious experience and how the POWs chaplain themselves.

11. Plumb and DeWerff, 222.

12. Gerald L. Coffee, *Beyond Survival: A POW's Story* (New York: G. P. Putnam's Sons, 1990), in *Readers Digest,* December 1989, 138.

13. Ibid., 217.

14. Ibid., 234.

15. Jeremiah A. Denton Jr. with Ed Brandt, *When Hell Was in Session* (Washington, DC: Morley Books, 1997), xv.

16. Denton with Brandt, 13, 62.

17. The Code of Conduct was devised in 1954 by President Dwight D. Eisenhower after the POWs returned from Korea in 1953. Prior to the 1954 Code of Conduct, POWs did not know what was expected of them in their relationship to their captors.

18. Denton and Brandt, 70.

19. Modern soldiers, sailors, and airmen receive POW training called SERE, or Survival, Escape, Resistance, and Evasion, part of which is to become hostile to their captors whenever possible.

20. Denton and Brandt, 109, 126, 248. See also *Jeremiah,* dir. Mark Fastoso (Alabama Public Television, 2015), https://www.youtube.com/watch?v=vnPiJJEdVao.

21. Howard Rutledge and Phyllis Rutledge, with Mel White and Lyla White, *In the Presence of Mine Enemies, 1965–1973* (Charlotte, NC: Commission Press, 1977), 93.

22. Rutledge and Rutledge, with White and White, 21.

23. Rutledge and Rutledge, with White and White, 42, 67.

24. Guy D. Gruters, *Locked Up with God* (self-published, n.d.), 94.

25. Gruters, 102.

26. Walter J. Ciszek, S.J., with Daniel L. Flaherty, S.J., *With God in Russia* (New York: Harper, 1964), 14, 103, 134.

27. See *Holy Roman Spies: The Vatican's Secret Agents,* dir. Anedeo Rioucci and Maurizo Carta, DVD (Road Television, EWTN, 2002). See also *With God in Russia: A Grave in Perm; The Story of Fr. Walter Ciszek, SJ,* DVD (Diocese of Allentown, 2002).

28. Ciszek with Flaherty, *With God in Russia,* 381, 386.

Chapter Eleven. War on Terror

1. See Benjamin L. Miller, *In God's Presence: Chaplains, Missionaries, and Religious Space during the American Civil War* (Lawrence: University of Kansas Press, 2019), 7.

2. Miller, 11.

3. Miller, 25.

4. Miller, 137.

5. William N. Tyler, *Memoirs of Andersonville* (Bernalillo, NM: Joel Beer and Gwendy MacMaster, 1992), 19–20, in Steven E. Woodworth, *While God Is Marching On: The Religious World of Civil War Soldiers* (Lawrence: University Press of Kansas, 2001), 75. Although it contains some strong residual taste, the author feels that Providence Spring remains potable at the Andersonville Historic Site in Georgia.

6. Leslie F. Zimmerman, John E. Groh, and Carolyn McCormick, eds., *Chaplain Prisoners of War in the Pacific, 1941–1945* (Montgomery, AL: USAF Chaplain Service Institute, Maxwell AFB, 1993), 4.

7. Mark R. Moore, *Prisoner of the Germans* (Kansas City, MO: Beacon Hill, 1945), 35.

8. Moore, 35–36.

9. Moore, 64.

10. U.S.Army, *U.S. Army Chaplain Corps*, pamphlet 165-1 (Washington, DC: Headquarters, U.S. Army, 1974), 25. Vietnam was odd in that about 16 percent of the Vietnamese people in South Vietnam were Catholics, converts to Catholicism by the French during their colonial influence; thus, the American chaplains often included the local Catholic Vietnamese in their everyday activities. There were practically no Protestant Vietnamese.

11. "The Global War on Terrorism" (Washington, DC: Coalition Information Center), 3.

12. U.S. Department of Defense, "Casualty," www.defense.gov/casualtyu.pdf, in *Chaplain Combat Ministry during the Global War on Terror in Afghanistan and Iraq: Twenty Narrative Stories; Instructor's Guide* (Provo, UT: Brigham Young University, 2017), 4.

13. See Douglas Carver, foreword to *Military Chaplains in Afghanistan, Iraq, and Beyond*, ed. Eric Patterson (Lanham, MD: Rowman & Littlefield, 2014), 20–21, in *Chaplain Combat Ministry*, 6.

14. Thomas J. Craughwell, *Heroic Catholic Chaplains: Stories of the Brave and Holy Men Who Dodged Bullets While Saving Souls* (Charlotte, NC: Tan Books, 2018), 175.

15. Joan Desmond, "As U.S. Withdraws from Iraq, a Chaplain Completes 2nd Tour," *National Catholic Register*, December 5, 2011, in U.S. Department of Defense, "Casualty," in *Chaplain Combat Ministry*, 24–25.

16. Chad S. Hawkins, *Faith in the Service: Inspirational Stories from LDS Servicemen and Servicewomen* (Salt Lake City: Deseret Books, 2008), 170–71, in U.S. Department of Defense, "Casualty," in *Chaplain Combat Ministry*, 37.

17. U.S. Department of Defense, 37.

18. Sgt. Victoria Willoughby, "Chief of Chaplains Brings Encouragement and Support," www.army.mil/artile12599/chief-of-chaplains (accessed October 12, 2020), 2.

❧ BIBLIOGRAPHY ❧

Books

Abraham, Abie. *Oh God, Where Are You?* 3rd ed. Cahicora, PA: privately published, 2008.

Ainsworth, Fred C., and Joseph W. Kirkley eds. *The War of the Rebellion: A Compilation of the Official Records of the Union and Confederate Armies.* Ser. 2, vol. 6. Washington, DC: U.S. Government Printing Office, 1899.

Armstrong, Warren B. *For Courageous Fighting and Confident Dying: Union Chaplains in the Civil War.* Lawrence: University Press of Kansas, 1998.

Bennett, William W. *A Narrative of the Great Revival Which Prevailed in the Southern Armies.* Philadelphia: Claxton, Remsen, and Haffelfinger, 1877.

Bergen, Doris L. *The Sword of the Lord: Military Chaplains from the First to the Twenty-First Century.* Notre Dame, IN: University of Notre Dame Press, 2004.

Bergsma, Commander Herbert L., CHC, USN. *Chaplains with the Marines in Vietnam, 1962–1971.* Washington, DC: Headquarters, U.S. Marine Corps, 1985.

Binkowski, Edna Bautista. *Code Name High Pockets.* Limay, PI: Valour, 2006.

Brinsfield, John Wesley, Jr. *The Spirit Divided: Memoirs of Civil War Chaplains, the Confederacy.* Macon, GA: Mercer University Press, 2006.

Carlson, Lewis H. *Remembered Prisoners of a Forgotten War.* New York: St. Martin's, 2002.

Carver, Douglas. Foreword to *Military Chaplains in Afghanistan, Iraq, and Beyond,* edited by Eric Patterson. Lanham, MD: Rowman & Littlefield, 2014.

Cavanaugh, Paul W., S.J. *Pro Deo et Patria: The Personal Narrative an American Catholic Chaplain as a Prisoner of War in Germany.* Edited by Robert. E. Skopek. Self-published, 2004.

Chaplain Combat Ministry during the Global War on Terror in Afghanistan and Iraq: Twenty Narrative Stories; Instructor's Guide. Provo, UT: Brigham Young University, 2017.

Chunn, Calvin E., ed. *Of Rice and Men: The Story of Americans under the Rising Sun.* Los Angeles: Veterans, 1946.

Ciszek, Walter J., S.J., with Daniel L. Flaherty, S.J. *With God in Russia.* New York: Harper, 1964.

Coffee, Gerald L. *Beyond Survival: A POW's Story.* New York: G. P. Putnam's Sons, 1990. In *Readers Digest,* December 1989, 137–44, 203–5, 208, 212–14, 216–18, 220–21, 224–27, 229–32.

Craughwell, Thomas J. *Heroic Catholic Chaplains: Stories of the Brave and Holy Men Who Dodged Bullets While Saving Souls.* Charlotte, NC: Tan Books, 2018.

Crosbie, Rev. Philip. *Pencilling Prisoner.* Melbourne: Hawthorne, 1955.

Crosby, Donald F., S.J. *Battlefield Chaplains: Catholic Priests in World War II.* Lawrence: University Press of Kansas, 1994.

Cross, Christopher. *Soldiers of God.* New York: E. P. Dutton, 1945.

Daniel, Eugene L., Jr. *In the Presence of Mine Enemies: An American Chaplain in World War II German Prison Camps.* Attleboro, MA: Colonial Lithograph, 1985.

Deane, Philip [pseud.]. *I Was a Captive in Korea.* New York: W. W. Norton, 1963.

Delaware, Edith. *Saint Martin.* New York: Macmillan, 1962.

Denton, Jeremiah A., Jr., with Ed Brandt. *When Hell Was in Session.* Washington, DC: Morley Books, 1997.

Dorsett, Lyle W. *Serving God and Country: U.S. Military Chaplains in World War II.* New York: Berkeley Caliber, 2012.

Doyle, Robert C. *A Prisoner's Duty: Great Escapes in U.S. Military History.* Annapolis, MD: Naval Institute Press, 1997.

———. *Prisoners in American Hands: Treatment of Enemy Prisoners of War from the Revolution to the War on Terror.* Lexington: University Press of Kentucky, 2010.

———. *Voices from Captivity: Interpreting the American POW Narrative.* Lawrence: University Press of Kansas, 1994.

Drape, Joe. *The Saint Makers.* New York: Hachette Books, 2020.

Drury, Clifford Merrill. *The History of the Chaplain Corps, United States Navy, 1939–1949.* Vol 2. Washington, DC: U.S. Government Printing Office, 195.

Dugan, John J., S.J., Major, USA. *Life under the Japs: Stories from a Prisoner of War Camp.* Boston: Globe, 1945.

Durkin, Rev. Joseph T., S.J., ed. *Confederate Chaplain: A War Journal of Rev. James B. Sheeran, C.SS.R., 14th Louisiana, CSA.* Milwaukee: Bruce, 1960.

Eads, Lyle W. *Survival around the Ashes.* Winona, MN: privately published, 1985.

Eisner, Peter. *MacArthur's Spies: The Soldier, the Singer, and the Spymaster Who Defied the Japanese in World War II.* New York: Viking, 2017.

Faherty, William B., S.J. *Exile in Erin: A Confederate Chaplain's Story, the Life of Father John B. Bannon.* St. Louis: Missouri Historical Society Press, 2002.

Gardner, L., et al., ed. *Santo Tomas Internment Camp Anniversary Booklet, 1943–1965.* Self-published, 1965.

Giblin, Gerard F., S.J. *Jesuits as Chaplains in the Armed Forces, 1917–1960.* Woodstock, MD: Woodstock College Press, 1962.

Gilroy, William F. R., and Timothy J. Demy. *A Brief Chronology of the Chaplain Corps of the United States Navy.* Washington, DC: Department of the Navy, 1983.

Grashio, Samuel C., and Bernard Norling. *Return to Freedom: The War Memoirs of Col. Samuel C. Grashio UASAF (Ret.).* Tulsa: MCN Press, 1982.

Gruters, Guy D. *Locked Up with God.* Self-published, n.d.

Gushwa, Robert L. *The Best and Worst of Times: The United States Army Chaplaincy, 1920–1945.* Washington, DC: Department of the Army, Office of the Chief of Chaplains, 1977.

Hayden, Mark. *German Military Chains in World War II.* Atglen, PA: Schiffer Military History, 2005.

Headley, Joel Tyler. *Chaplains and Clergy of the Revolution.* New York: Charles Schribner, 1864.

Heidler, David. *Encyclopedia of the War of 1812.* Annapolis, MD: Naval Institute Press, 2004.

Herman Norton, *Rebel Religion: The Story of Confederate Chaplains.* St. Louis: Bethany Press, 1961.

Hoffmann, Bedrich. *And Who Will Kill You: The Chronicle of the Life and Sufferings of Priests in the Concentration Camps.* 2nd ed. Posnan, Poland: Pallottinum, 1994.

Hubbard, Preston John. *Apocalypse Undone: My Survival of Japanese Imprisonment during World War II.* Nashville: Vanderbilt University Press, 1990.

Jervey, Edward D., ed. *Prison Life among the Rebels: Recollections of a Union Chaplain.* Kent, OH: Kent State University Press, 1990.

Jones, Cole. *Captives of Liberty.* Philadelphia: University of Pennsylvania Press, 2020.

Jorgenson, Daniel P. *Air Force Chaplains.* Vol. 1. New York: U.S. Government Printing Office, 1962.

Keith, Billy. *Days of Anguish, Days of Hope.* Garden City, NY: Doubleday, 1972.

Knox, Donald. *Death March: The Survivors of Bataan.* New York: Harcourt, 1981.

Krammer, Arnold. *Nazi Prisoners of War in America.* 1977. Reprint. Lanham, MD: Scarborough House, 1996.

Kurtz, William B. *Excommunicated from the Union: How the Civil War Created a Separate Catholic America.* New York: Fordham University Press, 2016.

LaForte, Robert, et al. *With Only the Will to Live.* Wilmington, DE: Scholarly Resources, 1994.

Lawson, Kenneth E. *Reliable and Religious: U.S. Army Chaplains in the War of 1812.* Washington, DC: Department of the Army, Office of the Chief of Chaplains, 2012.

Lenz, John M. *Christ in Dachau; or, Christ Victorious.* Vienna: Mission Druckerei St. Gabriel, 1960.

Link, Paul, C.PP.S. *For God and Country.* Pt. 2. Cartegena, OH: Messenger Press, 1993.

Maher, William L. *A Shepherd in Combat Boots: Chaplain Emil Kapaun of the 1st Cavalry Division.* Shippensburg, PA: Burd Street, 1997.

Majdanski, Archbishop Kazimierz. *You Shall Be My Witness: Lessons beyond Dachau.* Garden City Park, NY: Square One, 2009.

McLane, Rogers, ed. *American Chaplains of the Revolution.* Louisville, KY: National Society Sons of the American Revolution, 1991.

Michno, Gregory F. *Death on the Hellships: Prisoners at Sea in the Pacific War.* Annapolis, MD: Naval Institute Press, 2001.

Miller, Benjamin L. *In God's Presence: Chaplains, Missionaries, and Religious Space during the Civil War.* Lawrence: University Press of Kansas, 2019.

Miller, Robert Ryal. *Shamrock and Sword: The St. Patrick's Battalion in the U.S.-Mexican War.* Norman: University of Oklahoma Press, 1989.

Mode, Daniel L. *The Grunt Padre: Father Vincent Capodanno, Vietnam, 1966–1967.* Oak Lawn, IL: CMJ Marian, 2000.

Moore, Mark R. *Prisoner of the Germans.* Kansas City, MO: Beacon Hill, 1945.

Murr, Dan. *But Deliver Us from Evil: Father Duffy and the Men of Bataan.* Jacksonville Beach, FL: self-published, 2008.

Neuhaeusler, Dr. Johannes. *What Was It Like in the Concentration Camp at Dachau?* 17th ed. Munich: Manz A.G., 1960.

Norton, Rev. Mr. John. *The Redeemed Captive: Narrative of the Capture and Burning of Fort Captivity of All Those Stationed There to the Number of Thirty Persons.* Albany, NY: S. G. Drake of Boston, 1870.

O'Brien, Niall. *Columban Martyrs of Manila.* Manila: Kadena Press, 1995.

Office of the Chief of Chaplains. *American Army Chaplaincy: A Brief History.* Washington, DC: Chaplains Association, 1946.

Pate, Lloyd W. *Reactionary: Revised 2000.* New York: Vantage, 2001.

Phillips, Claire, and Myron B. Goldsmith. *Manila Espionage.* 1947. Reprint, Philippines: Bowsprit Books, 2018.

Pinheido, John C. *Missionaries of Republicanism: A Religious History of the Mexican-American War.* New York: Oxford University Press, 2014.

Pitts, Charles F. *Chaplains in Gray: The Confederate Chaplain's Story.* Nashville: Broadman, 1957.

Plumb, Charlie, and Glen DeWerff. *I'm No Hero.* Mechanicsburg, PA: Executive Books, 1973.

Polk, James K. *The Diary of James K. Polk.* Vol. 1. Chicago: A. C. McClurg, 1910.

Robinson, Alan. *Chaplains at War: The Role of Clergymen during World War II.* London: Tauris Academic Studies, 2008.

Roper, Richard S. *Brothers of Paul: Activities of Prisoner of War Chaplains in the Philippines during WWII.* Odenton, MD: Revere, 2003.

————. *Holy Smugglers.* Annapolis, MD: n.p., nd.

Rosenberg, Alfred. *The Myth of the Twentieth Century.* Munich: Hohenreichen Verlag, 1935.

Rutledge, Howard, and Phyllis Rutledge, with Mel White and Lyla White. *In the Presence of Mine Enemies, 1965–1973.* Charlotte, NC: Commission Press, 1977.

Sampson, Chaplain Francis L. *Look Out Below! A Story of the Airborne by a Paratrooper Padre.* Washington, DC: Catholic University of America Press, 1958.

Sampson, Chaplain Francis L. *Paratrooper Padre.* Washington, DC: Catholic University of America Press, 1948.

Sides, Hampton. *Ghost Soldiers: The Forgotten Epic Story of Harold War II's Most Dramatic Mission.* New York: Doubleday, 2001.

Spiller, Harry, ed. *American POWs in Korea: Sixteen Personal Accounts.* Jefferson, NC: McFarland, 1998.

Stewart, Sidney. *Give Us This Day.* New York: W. W. Norton, 1986.

Tucker, Philip Thomas. *The Confederacy's Fighting Chaplain Father John B. Bannon.* Tuscaloosa: University of Alabama Press, 1992.

Tyler, William N. *Memoirs of Andersonville.* Bernalillo, NM: Joel Beer and Gwendy MacMaster, 1992.

U.S. Army. *United States Army Chaplain Corps.* Pamphlet 165-1. Washington, DC: Headquarters, U.S. Army, 1974.

Utinsky, Margaret. *Miss U: Angel of the Underground.* San Antonio: Naylor, 1948.

Weinstein, Alfred A. *Barbed Wire Surgeon.* New York: Macmillan, 1948.

Wenzel, Roy, and Travis Heying. *The Miracle of Father Kapaun: Priest, Soldier, and Korean War Hero.* Fort Collins, CO: Ignatius Press, 2009.

Williams, Eugene Franklin. *Soldiers of God: The Chaplains of the Revolutionary War.* New York: Carlton, 1950.

Woodworth, Steven E. *While God Is Marching On: The Religious World of Civil War Soldiers.* Lawrence: University Press of Kansas, 2001.

Zeller, Guillaume. *The Priest Barracks, Dachau, 1938–1945.* San Francisco: Ignatius Press, 2015.

Zellers, Larry. *In Enemy Hands: A Prisoner in North Korea.* Lexington: University Press of Kentucky, 1991.

Zimmerman, Leslie F., John E. Groh, and Carolyn McCormick, eds. *Chaplain Prisoners of War in the Pacific, 1941–1945.* Montgomery, AL: USAF Chaplain Service Institute, Maxwell AFB, 1993.

Dissertations and Theses

Burke, Robby Wray, Jr. "Confederate Chaplains, the Great Revival, and the Prolongation of the Civil War." Master's thesis, James Madison University, 1991.

Germain, Dom Aidan Henry. "Catholic Military and Naval Chaplains, 1776–1917." PhD diss., Catholic University of America, 1929.

Kramer, Maj. Philip A., USA. "The Proximity Principle: Army Chaplains on the Fighting Line in Doctrine and History." Master's thesis, U.S. Command and General Staff School, 2014.

O'Brien, Steven E. "Blackrobe in Blue: The Naval Chaplaincy of John P. Foley, S.J., 1942–1946." PhD diss., Boston College, 1999.

Smith, Charles Edward. "The Work of the Civil War Chaplains." Master's thesis, University of Arizona, 1965.

Thill, Henry T. "Study of an American Civil War Chaplaincy: Henry Clay Trumbull, 10th Connecticut Volunteers." Master's thesis, Virginia Polytechnic Institute, 1986.

Articles

Applegate, Howard Lewis. "Duties and Activities of Chaplains." *Picket Post,* July 1958, 10.

Bergen, Doris. "German Military Chaplains in the Second World War and the Dilemmas of Legitimacy." In *The Sword of the Lord,* 165–85. Notre Dame, IN: Notre Dame University Press, 2004.

Borneman, John K. "From Bataan through Cabanatuan." *Army and Navy Chaplain* 16, no. 4 (1946): 23–26.

Boltanski, Ariane. "A Jesuit *Missio Castrensis* in France at the End of the Sixteenth Century: Discipline and Violence at War." *Journal of Jesuit Studies* 4, no. 4 (2017): 581–98.

Cavanaugh, Paul W. "Chaplain Prisoner." *Woodstock Letters* 90, no. 1 (1961): 20–49.

Davis, Chaplain James E., USN. "Religion in a Prisoner of War Camp in Japan." *Army and Navy Chaplain* 16, no. 4 (1946): 6–7.

Desmond, Joan. "As U.S. Withdraws from Iraq, a Chaplain Completes 2nd Tour." *National Catholic Register,* December 5, 2011.

Eisner, Peter. "Our Man in Manila." *Smithsonian,* September 2017, 42, 44–55.

Faust, Drew Gilpin. "Christian Solders: The Meaning of Revivalism in the Confederate Army." *Journal of Southern History* 53 (1987): 63–73.

Gladwin, Lee A. "American POWs on Japanese Ships Take a Voyage into Hell." Pts. 1–2. *Prologue* 35, no. 4 (2003).

Grayson, Lawrence P. "Fr. Joseph O'Callahan: The Bravest Man." *TFP,* August 17, 2011.

"History: Small Beginnings, Big Dreams." https://cpps-preciousblood.org/about/history/.

Knight, Chaplain J. A., USNR. "Prisoner of War Evacuation from Japan." *Army and Navy Chaplain* 16, no. 4 (1946): 8–10.

Leven, Stephen A. "A Catholic Chaplain Visits Our German Prisoners." *America,* June 24, 1944, 320–21.

McNamara, Paul. "Father Gehring." *Catholic Digest* (1945): 42–48.

Meany, Peter J. "The Prison Ministry of Father Peter Whelan, Georgia Priest and Confederate Chaplain." *Georgia Historical Quarterly* 71, no. 1 (1987): 1–24.

———. "The Valiant Chaplain of the Bloody Tenth." *Tennessee Historical Quarterly* 41, no. 1 (1982): 37–47.

"Medal of Honor Recipient's Remains Identified." *VFW Magazine*, June–July, 2021, 6.

Metzger, Charles H. "Chaplains in the American Revolution." *Catholic Historical Review* 31, no. 1 (1945): 31–79.

Nardini, J. E., CDR, M.C., USN. "Survival Factors in American Prisoners of War of the Japanese." *American Journal of Psychiatry* 109, no. 4 (1952): 241–48.

Perotta, Dominic, and Kevin Perotta. "When the Ordinary Becomes Extraordinary: The Life and Death of Army Chaplain Emil Kapaun." *Word among Us* (July–August 2012): 83–88.

"Prisoners of War." In *The Priest Goes to War*. New York: Society for the Propagation of the Faith, 1945.

Reuter, James B., S.J. "He Kept Silence in Seven Languages: A Short Sketch of Carl W. J. Hausmann, S.J., Who Died as a Prisoner of War, January 10, 1945." *Woodstock Letters* 74, no. 3 (1945): 326–55.

Stoffer, Jeff. "Lore of the Legion." *American Legion Magazine*, February 2019, 40.

U.S. Army Command and Staff College. *Chaplain's Duties to Prisoners of War*. "Annex E, Chaplain Sampson's Experience in a World War II Prisoner of War Camp," (Fort Leavenworth, Kansas, 27 January 1969), np.

Way, John, O.P. "The Soldier-Priest." *Dominicana* 28, no. 2 (1943): 89–94.

Wiley, Bell Irvin. "'Holy Joes' of the Sixties: A Study of Civil War Chaplains." *Huntington Library Quarterly* 16, no. 3 (1953): 287–304.

Wilson, Robert R. "Status of Chaplains with Armed Forces." *Journal of International Law* (July 1943): 490–94.

Films

Holy Roman Spies: The Vatican's Secret Agents. Directed by Anedeo Rioucci and Maurizo Carta. Road Television, EWTN, 2002. DVD.

I Was an American Spy. Directed by Lesley Selander, 1951. DVD.

With God in Russia: A Grave in Perm; The Story of Fr. Walter Ciszek, SJ. Diocese of Allentown, PA, 2002. DVD.

Web

Archdiocese for Military Services. "Father Capodanno Biography." http://www.milarch.org/father-capadanno-bio/.

The Chaplain Kit. https://thechaplainkit.com/history/army-chaplaincy/first-army-catholic-chaplains/.

Chaplains of the 36th Infantry Division, Chaplain (Col.) Herbert E. MacCombie, Division Chaplain. "Interrogating Captured German Chaplains." Texas Military Forces Museum. http://www.texasmilitaryforcesmuseum.org/36division/archives (accessed September 2, 2020).

Citation in the Military Record of Captain Rev. Wilfrid Coates, Chaplain Corps, British Army, British National Archives, WO 373/148, A-2146, 754.

Cloister Chronicles. https://www.dominicanajournal.org›files›vol30.

Conway, Christopher. "The U.S. Mexican War." *Oxford Bibliographies*, last modified September 25, 2018, https://doi.org/10.1093/obo/9780199913701–0132.

The Crux: Taking the Catholic Pulse. "The Case for Military Chaplains' Sainthood Could Soon Advance." https://cruxnow.com/church-in-the-usa/2020/02/case-for-military-chaplains-sainthood-could-soon-advance/ (accessed September 9, 2020).

Elmore, Tom. Entry on the Civil War Message Board, December 12, 2010. For a list of captured Confederate chaplains after Gettysburg July 3, 1863. http:history-sites.net/cgi-bin/bbs62s/cwpmb/e\webbbs_config.p.

"Father Emil Kapaun's Acts of Self-Sacrifice." https:billofrightsinstitute.org .father-emil-kapauns-acts-self-sacrifice/.

Fongemie, Pauly, ed. *Priests: The Persecution of the Catholic Church and the Priests of Dachau.* http://www.catholictradition.org/Priests/daucau.htm.

"General Antonio. Lopez de Santa Anna." https://www.biography.com/military-figure /antonio-lopez-de-santaanna#:~:text=Antonio%20L%C3%B3pez%20de%20 Santa%20Anna%2C%20born%20on%20February,staving%20off%20 Spain%E2%80%99s%20attempt%20to%20recapture%20the%20country.

Graves, Jim. "Father Henry Marusa—World War II Army Chaplain at Invasion of Normandy." National Catholic Register. https://www.ncregister.com/blog /father-henry-marusa-world-war-ii-army-chaplain (accessed September 14, 2020).

Hatton, Greg, comp. "American Prisoners of War in Germany." Prepared by Military Intelligence Service, War Department, July 15, 1944. https://www.b24.net /powStalag7.htm.

Harvey, Maj. James, III. "Catholic Military Chaplains: American's Forgotten Heroes." American Society for the Defense of Tradition, Family, and Property. http://www .tfp.org/catholic-army-chaplains-americas-forgotten-heroes/ (accessed May 16, 2017).

History.com Editors. "Troops Surrender in Bataan, Philippines, in Largest-Ever U.S. Surrender," November 5, 2009. https://www.history.com/this-day-in-history /u-s-surrenders-in-bataan.

Jeremiah. Directed by Mark Fastoso. Alabama Public Television, 2015. https://www .youtube.com/watch?v=vnPiJJEdVao.

Johnson, Mark W., U.S. Army Chaplain Corps. "Under Fire: Army Chaplains in Korea, 1950." April 10, 2013. https://www.army.mil/article/100572/Under_Fire _Army_Chaplains_in_Korea_1950/.

Kapaun, Emil J. Medal of Honor Citation. https://www.cmohs.org/recipients/emil-j
-kapaun (accessed September 9, 2020).

Lalor, Father John. https://www.tracesofwar.com/persons/81946/Lalor-Fr-John.htm/.

Langellier, John. "Soldiers of the Cross: The First Buffalo Soldier Chaplain Lights the
Path for Others, Despite a Dishonorable Discharge." *True West Magazine*, July 2015.
https://truewestmagazine.com/soldiers-of-the-cross/.

Liberating Dachau. Directed by Mark Felton, www.youtube.com/watch?v=aRksFbsMxw
(accessed September 1, 2020).

https://www.sunsigns.org/famousbirthdays/d/profile/lucky-luciano/

National Park Service. https://www.nps.gov/people/alexander-cochrane.htm.

O'Callahan, Joseph T., S.J. "Joseph T. O'Callahan, a Claustrophobic Priest, Wins
the Medal of Honor in WWII." New England Historical Society (last updated
2022). https://www.newenglandhistoricalsociety.com/joseph-t-ocallahan-a
-claustrophobic-priest-wins-the-medal-of-honor/.

Ottoman, Sharon. "Remembering the Four Chaplains and Their Ultimate Sacrifice."
New York Times, February 4, 2018. https:nytimes.com/2018/02/04/nyregion/four
-chaplains-sacrifice.html.

"St. Martin of Tours." Catholic Online. https://www.catholic.org/saints/saint
.php?saint_id=81.

U.S. Army. "Bibliography for Chaplain (Capt.) Emil Kapaun." https://www.army.mil
/article/98061/biographyforchaplainemilkapaun.

U.S. Department of Defense. "Casualty." www.defense.gov/casualtyu.pdf.

Willoughby, Sgt. Victoria. "Chief of Chaplains Brings Encouragement and Support."
www.army.mil/artile12599/chief-of-chaplains (accessed October 12, 2020).

❧ INDEX ❧

Suver, Charles, 92
The Sword of the Lord: Chaplains from the First to the Twenty-First Century (Bergen), 107
Syngman Rhee, 119, 122

Table of Moses, as insignia for Jewish chaplains, 56
Taiwan, 68, 69, 119
Takao Bay, Formosa, 70
Talbot, Albert D., 66, 88
Task Force Baum, 101, 154
Task Force Smith, 120
Taylor, Robert Preston, 64, 65–68, 69, 73, 81
Taylor, Zachary, American Army of, 30
Tecumseh, 23.
Tet holiday, 141
Texas, acquisition of, 26
Thaxter, Joseph, 10
This Is Your Life (radio show), 89
Thomas, Joshua, 24–25
Thompson, General, 17
Thornton, Lt., 125
Three Rivers (Pittsbugh), 17
Tiffany, Frank L., 67, 73, 81
Tiger, 124–25, 127
Tinian, 79
Tories, 15
Trenton, battle at, 16
Trumbull, Henry Clay, 46–48; prison journal of, 46–47
Tucker, Samuel, 19
Turner, Fr., 75
Turner, William, 101
Tydings-McDuffie Act, 79
Tyler, William N., 150–51
Tyrol, 107

Uniform Code of Military Justice, 53
Union POWS at Andersonville, 55
United Confederate Veterans, 40
United States, purchase of the Philippines from Spain, 78
University of Libby Prison, 35
UN POWs, 129
Unsan, North Korea, battle at, 126
U.S. Army: Chaplain School (Fort Jackson, SC), 22; expansion and contraction of, 52
U.S. Army Chaplain Corps, 118–19
U.S. Army Chaplain School, 56, 118
U.S. Christian Commission, 35–36
U.S. Colored Troops, demobilization of, 53–54
USAT *Dorchester*, chaplains on, 6, 92–93
USCGC *Comanche*, 92
USCGC *Escanaba*, 92
USCGC *Tampa*, 92
USS *America*, x
USS *Arizona*, explosion of, 62
USS *Bonhomme Richard*, 141
USS *Cumberland*, ramming of, by CSS *Virginia*, 36
USS *Franklin*, 92, 131
USS *Maine*, 151
USS *Oklahoma*, 62
USS *Steinaker*, x, xi
Utah, acquisition of, 26
Utah Beach, 102
Utinsky, John, 81
Utinsky, Margaret, 80, 88; claim for restitution of funds, 89

Vakoc, Timothy, 156
valley, 127
Van Courtlandt, Stephen, 17

❧ ABOUT THE AUTHOR ❧

ROBERT C. DOYLE, a professor of U.S. history at the Franciscan University of Steubenville, Ohio, speaks from many years of study as well as his experiences as an officer in the U.S. Navy, 1967–71. He is an expert on the American fascination with prisoner of war stories that have echoed through the ages and is a prevailing refrain no matter the war being fought.